Essays On
'The Welfare State'

by the same author

Poverty and Population
(Macmillan)

Parents Revolt (with K. C. Titmuss)
(Secker & Warburg)

Birth, Poverty and Wealth
(Hamish Hamilton)

Problems of Social Policy
(History of the Second World War, H.M.S.O.)

The Cost of the National Health Service
(with B. Abel-Smith)
(Cambridge University Press)

and other works

RICHARD M. TITMUSS
Professor of Social Administration
in the University of London

Essays on 'The Welfare State'

Ruskin House
GEORGE ALLEN & UNWIN LTD
MUSEUM STREET LONDON

First Published in Great Britain in 1958

Second Impression 1958
Third Impression 1960

Printed in Great Britain
in 11-12 *point Bell Type*
by Simson Shand Ltd
London, Hertford and Harlow

PREFACE

SIX of these ten lectures have already been printed, the first in 1951, the last in 1957. At intervals during these years I was reminded by some of my friends responsible for the teaching of social administration that students of the subject had difficulty in obtaining the relevant journals and reports. It is true that these lectures reached the sometimes unwelcome finality of print in a variety of published forms, and that certain journals are not easily available to students, particularly those less fortunately placed than students at a university. In publishing them now in book form I must, however, make one or two personal comments.

All these lectures except one were written with two kinds of audience in mind; those who come to listen and those who prefer to read. In revising them in the interests of the latter I have tried to remove some of the more obvious adornments that go to the making of a public lecture. Nothing of any consequence can have been lost in the process. I have added footnotes and references here and there, and corrected the most noticeable lapses in visual style.

What I have not been able to do much about without injury to the flow of the essays is a certain repetitiveness of content and ideas; a tendency, in several of them, for the same point to be taken up, treated in one more lightly, in another in more detail, yet never worked out as satisfactorily as if one were writing a book. For these faults I apologize.

In reprinting these six lectures I have taken the opportunity to include four that have not been published. One is a Fawcett Memorial Lecture on 'The Position of Women', given at Bedford College, London, in 1952. Here I have included some new material and added more up-to-date references.

The remaining three lectures, all on the National Health Service, were given under the auspices of the Sherrill Foundation in the Law Faculty at Yale University in the United States in April 1957. Though addressed to an American audience they contain material which may be of interest to students of the subject in Britain and other countries. They were subsequently submitted, with other evidence, to the Royal Commission on Doctors' and Dentists' Remuneration.

The Appendix to these Health Service lectures is perhaps a curiosity and needs a word of explanation. In reflecting on the many misconceptions about the Service that are current in the United States as well as in Britain I felt that something more than general statements would be appreciated. Yet one has to deal heavily in generalities in the delivery of public lectures. In respect to certain problems I wished to discuss I therefore assembled the relevant facts and Professor Eugene Rostow, Dean of the Law Faculty, was good enough to arrange for this appendix to be mimeographed and circulated to the audience.

Since these lectures were given at Yale some new evidence of value to students of the Health Service has appeared. I refer particularly to the *Report of the Committee on Administrative Tribunals and Enquiries* (the Franks Committee). I have therefore included some of the material from this report in my discussion of the question of the professional freedom of the doctor under the Health Service.

Apart from these additions I have made no effort to bring up to date either the content or the documentation of these ten essays. To have undertaken such a task would have meant a complete recasting of the subjects discussed. Yet there were times when I was tempted to do so. Some of the themes I have pursued here have been overtaken by events; some by books. Our understanding of certain fundamental problems of social life in contemporary Britain has been deepened by a number of important books published in the last few years. They underline, for students of social administration in particular, one conclusion that, I hope, reviewers will draw from these essays. The social services (however we define them) can no longer be considered as 'things apart'; as phenomena of marginal interest, like looking out of the window on a train journey. They are part of the journey itself. They are an integral part of industrialization.

The recent works I have in mind include the contribution to the study of social mobility by Professor Glass, Mrs Floud and their colleagues; the research undertaken by Professor Simey and his colleagues at Liverpool on industrial and social change; Mr Peter Townsend's book *The Family Life of Old People*; Mr John Vaizey's study of *The Costs of Education*; and Mr C. A. R. Crosland's book *The Future of Socialism*. These I would have singled out as the most important sources of new material and new thinking in relation to the topics discussed in these essays had I embarked on the task of rewriting. If the role of the social services is to be re-interpreted in the light of the social structure of Britain in the second half of the twentieth century then it is to sources such as these that we must turn, both for the facts and for a clearer vision of reality.

I have had much advice and thoughtful criticism from friends who read particular drafts of these essays. I am grateful to Mr B. Abel-Smith, Mr N. H. Carrier, Mrs C. Cockburn, Mrs M. M. Gowing, Miss P. Jephcott, Dr J. N. Morris, Professor K. de Schweinitz, Mr J. Smith, Mr P. Townsend and Mr P. Willmott. I am also grateful to Mr Paulding Phelps for the considerable assistance he gave me in compiling the Appendix. In thanking them for their kindness I wish to absolve them all from any attachment to the often controversial views expressed in these essays. To Miss Judith Mason, my secretary, I owe an exceptional debt of gratitude for her patience and help in many ways. And to my students at the London School of Economics I am grateful for their continuing spirit of questioning. Finally, I wish to thank Mr Donald MacRae, Managing Editor of *The British Journal of Sociology*; the Liverpool University Press; the Editors of *The Political Quarterly*; the Editor of *The Listener*; the Editor of the *Proceedings of the Eighth International Conference of Social Work*; and the Editor of *The Hospital* for permission to reprint the essays published in their journals.

London RICHARD M. TITMUSS

January 1958

of the journey itself. They are an integral part of industrialization.

The recent works I have in mind include the continuation of the study of social mobility by Professor Glass, Mrs Floud and their colleagues; the research undertaken by Professor [illegible] and his colleagues [illegible]; Mr Peter Townsend's [illegible] *Family Life of Old People*; Mr John Vaizey's study of *The Costs of Education*; and Mr C. A. R. Crosland's book *The Future of Socialism*. These I would have singled out as the most significant sources of new material and new thinking in relation to the [illegible] of these essays had I embarked on the task of rewriting. If the role of the social services is to be reinterpreted in the light of the social structure of Britain in the second half of the twentieth century then it is to sources such as these that we must look for the facts and for a clear revision of our [illegible].

I have had much advice and helpful criticism from friends who read particular drafts of these essays. I am grateful to Mr B. Abel-Smith, Mr [illegible], Mrs [illegible], Mrs M. M. Gowing, Miss P. Jephcott, Dr J. [illegible], Professor [illegible], Mr [illegible] Smith, Miss [illegible] Townsend and Mr P. Willmott. I am also grateful to Mr [illegible] for the considerable assistance he gave me in compiling the Appendix. In thanking them for their help I wish to absolve them all from any attachment to the often controversial views expressed in these essays. To Miss [illegible], my secretary, I owe an exceptional debt of gratitude for her patience and help in many ways. And to my students at the London School of Economics I am grateful for their continuing spirit of questioning. Finally, I wish to thank Mr Donald MacRae, Managing Editor of *The British Journal of Sociology*, the [illegible] University Press; the Editors of *The Political Quarterly*, the Editor of *The Lancet*, the Editor of the *Proceedings of the English Association of* [illegible] *Society* and the Editor of *The* [illegible] for permission to reprint the essays published in their journals.

London
January 1958

RICHARD M. TITMUSS

CONTENTS

CHAPTER 1

Social Administration in a Changing Society[1]

THE decision of the University of London to create a new chair in Social Administration was an expression, I suppose, of the importance of the social services today in the life of the community. It was also perhaps a sign that, in the eyes of the University authorities, the subject had advanced to a respectable age and had acquired some academically respectable disciples; that it had grown out of its former preoccupation with good works for the deserving poor; and that the subject now justified an academic chair, and someone to invade, on the one side, a modest corner of the territory of public administration and, on the other, some part of the broad acres of sociology.

It might be said, then, that the days when social administration, with its interest in the education of future social workers, was regarded in University circles as a poor but virtuous relation, are now coming to an end. It is an interesting speculation, but hardly justified, I think, by the arrival of a new professor. 'Promise,' as George Eliot remarked in *Middlemarch*, 'was a pretty maid, but being poor she died unwed.'

The future of social administration depends, to some extent, on the future of the great experiments in social service which have been launched in Britain in recent years. Their future is uncertain. To this uncertainty must be added, in the teaching of

[1] An Inaugural Lecture delivered on May 10, 1951, at the London School of Economics and Political Science (University of London), and published in *British Journal of Sociology*, Vol. II, No. 3, September 1951.

social administration, the awareness of intellectual uncertainty which attends on those concerned with the study of human relations, for only now are we beginning to grope our way towards some scientific understanding of society. Uncertainty, then, is part of the price that has to be paid for being interested in the many-sidedness of human needs and behaviour. However, we draw some comfort from Karl Mannheim's thought[1] that it is precisely our uncertainty which brings us closer to reality than is possible for those who have faith in the absolute or faith, I would add, in the pursuit of specialization.

It is customary on these occasions to begin with a broad definition of one's subject. After these preliminaries, I propose to say something about the origins of the Social Science Department. Next, I shall briefly discuss certain aspects of the historical development of the social services since the beginning of the century, and I shall attempt to explain how these developments have contributed to some of our present difficulties. Then I shall try to formulate certain problems of social, economic and administrative importance which seem to me to require more study. Finally, I shall attempt a few generalizations about the nature of some elements of social change which, by their effect on the individual and the family, affect also the structure and roles of the social services.

Social administration may broadly be defined as the study of the social services whose object, to adapt Simey's phrase, is the improvement of the conditions of life of the individual in the setting of family and group relations.[2] It is concerned with the historical development of these services, both statutory and voluntary, with the moral values implicit in social action, with the roles and functions of the services, with their economic aspects, and with the part they play in meeting certain needs in the social process. On the one hand, then, we are interested in the machinery of administration, which organizes and dispenses various forms of social assistance; on the other, in the lives, the needs, and the mutual relations of those members of the com-

[1] Mannheim, K., *Ideology and Utopia*, 1936, p. 75.
[2] Simey, T. S., *Principles of Social Administration*, 1937, p. 9.

munity for whom the services are provided by reason of their belonging to that community. To take part in the study and teaching of these subjects in the spiritual home of Sidney and Beatrice Webb is a privilege. For this and other reasons I am deeply conscious of the honour of being the first occupant of this chair, not only because it is a new one, but because it carries with it the headship of the Department of Social Science and Administration. The department has for long been associated with many distinguished men and women. Nearly forty years ago, Professor Tawney was in at the start of the department. Academically speaking, it was not perhaps a very respectable affair in those days. That it is more acceptable now is due to Professor Tawney and to many men and women who, like him, never ceased to demonstrate their belief in the possibility of social progress. Thus, it is not chance that brings me here tonight but faith, the substance of things hoped for by my predecessors, 'the evidence of things not seen'.

In December 1912, on a proposition by Mr Martin White, seconded by Mr Sidney Webb, it was decided to establish a Department of Social Science as part of the School of Economics to continue, according to the minutes, 'the work so admirably carried on since 1903 under Mr C. S. Loch of the Charity Organization Society'.[1] The new department was helped by financial aid from Mr Ratan Tata, an Indian millionaire, who promoted the Ratan Tata Foundation, whose main function, under the directorship of Professor Tawney, was to inquire into the causes of poverty. The Foundation was linked to the new department, which was then known as the Ratan Tata Department of Social Science. It was not until 1919 that the School assumed complete responsibility.

At the start, in 1913, there was a straightforward bluntness about the teaching purposes of the department. 'It is intended,' states the Calendar for that year, 'for those who wish to prepare themselves to engage in the many forms of social and charitable effort.' A one-year course of theory and practical work was pro-

[1] London School of Economics: minutes of meeting of Court of Governors December 31, 1912.

vided, and the students were examined for the award of a certificate. Some of the questions set in the first examination bear a strong resemblance to those which *The Economist* asks of its readers from time to time. 'How far,' ran one question, 'is the danger of demoralizing the handworking classes by over-legislation a real one?' And just as pertinent was the question—'To what extent are we justified in regarding the theories of the earlier economists as the outcome of the social needs of their day?' A value-judgment, as we should call it now, seems to have slipped into this question which suggests that later economists were more objective in the formulation of their theories.

It may seem to some of us today, conscious of the need for a better understanding of motive in human behaviour, of the dynamic relationship between man and society, that the educational problems facing the new department were relatively simple. It was still possible to accept the surface view of reality in behaviour, for awareness of the new layers of the human mind opened up by Freud's study of the unconscious had not as yet penetrated very far. The anthropologists had not yet begun to stress the importance of the configuration of culture, economics could still be unashamedly taught to social work students without much reference to theory, while statistics in the hands of Mr Bowley (as he then was) were, by all accounts, a pleasurable experience. The staff of the department, like the syllabus, was more manageable than it is today. Professor Urwick, who was in charge, was assisted by Mrs Bosanquet and by visiting lecturers. Under the heading of 'Economics' a course of lectures was given by one practical-minded visitor on 'The Household Economics of the Handworking Poor'. For the sum of 10*s*. 6*d*. the students were told in six lectures how the poor bought their food, stored it and cooked it. Karl Pearson came and discussed the merits and demerits of breast-feeding and the relationship of alcoholism to infant mortality. Early in 1913 a new staff appointment was made, and judging by the book on social work which the new assistant subsequently wrote,[1] he seems to have

[1] Attlee, C. R., *The Social Worker*, 1920.

been a good choice. There were only two applicants for the post and, according to the minutes, the selection committee, 'after very careful consideration', appointed Mr C. R. Attlee. Unfortunately, the minutes are silent about the committee's opinion of the rejected candidate. He was Mr Hugh Dalton.

Throughout the years of change and expansion that followed, the department established a reputation for flexibility in teaching, for friendliness in relations, and for the interest it took in the welfare of its students that was largely due to the influence of five people: to Urwick, for his pioneering work as head of the London School of Sociology from 1903 to 1912 and from then until 1921 as head of the Social Science Department; to Hobhouse, for his faith in social progress based on his concept of the 'liberation of the individual'[1] and for his personal interest in the studies of each student to whom he was known, I am told, as 'Father Christmas'; to the stimulating personality of C. M. Lloyd who succeeded Hobhouse in 1922; to my predecessor, Professor Marshall, who took over the department during a difficult period of reconstruction at the end of the Second World War and, lastly, to the wisdom and devotion of Miss Eckhard who has played such a large part in steering the fortunes of the department and its many students since she first joined the School in 1919.

This department for the study of social administration was founded at a time when fundamental moral and social issues were being debated with vigour and a new sense of purpose. It was a product of the ferment of inquiry to which the Webbs, Charles Booth and many others contributed so much. Poverty, on the one hand, and moral condemnation of the poor on the other, were being questioned. Inquiry was moving from the question 'who are the poor?' to the question 'why are they poor?' Professor Tawney, aware, as he has repeatedly taught us, that the most important thing about a man is what he takes for granted, was in his element when he gave his inaugural lecture as Director of the Ratan Tata Foundation before the new social science stu-

[1] Hobson, J. A., and Ginsberg, M., *L. T. Hobhouse: His Life and Work*, 1931.

dents. The problem of poverty, he said, is not a problem of individual character and its waywardness, but a problem of economic and industrial organization. It had to be studied first at its sources, and only secondly in its manifestations.[1]

This warning was timely, because it was a period when social policies were being shaped by diagnoses which took account of the presenting symptoms rather than of the causes of contemporary social ills. The great collectivist advances at the beginning of the century, with their positive achievements in social legislation, were aimed at the gradual overthrow of the poor law. But because there were no alternative ideas to work with, no new insights into the social phenomena of human needs and behaviour, the ideas and methods of the poor law were transplanted to the new social services. Many of the services which were born in this period—perhaps the most formative period in the evolution of the British social services—had their character moulded by the moral assumptions of the nineteenth century. This antithesis of social purpose and administrative policy had, as I shall attempt to describe, far-reaching effects on the structure and functions of the new services.

The poor law, with its quasi-disciplinary functions, rested on assumptions about how people ought to behave. It only went into action if people behaved in a certain way and the services it provided were based on conditions that people should thereafter behave in a certain way. Such principles of retribution, when applied to problems of poverty and ill-health, played an important role in settling the structure and the methods of administration of the new services. If poverty was a mark of waywardness then the poor needed moral condemnation or rewarding; as the Old Age Pensions Act of 1908 set out to apply in separating the worthy from the unworthy poor by withholding pensions from those 'who had habitually failed to work according to ability and need and those who had failed to save money regularly'. If poverty was a matter of ignorance then it was the moral duty of one class in society to teach another class how to

[1] Tawney, R. H., *Memoranda on Problems of Poverty*, No. 11. The Ratan Tata Foundation, 1913.

live, and to lead them, through sanitation, soap and thrift to a better station in life, described by Stephen Reynolds as 'the spiritual squalor of the lower-middle classes'.[1] If ill-health was a matter of individual error then, as the Webbs put it, there could not be free choice of doctor among the poor for such freedom would encourage the prevailing passion for bottles of medicine, and would not lead (I quote from the Webbs' book *The State and the Doctor*) 'to stern advice from the doctor about habits of life on which recovery really depends—to look to him to speak plainly about the excessive drinking or the unwise eating which cause two-thirds of the ill-health of the poor'.[2]

These valuations about the nature of man were written into the social legislation of the day. They informed the means of policy. Derived, as they commonly were, from the norms of behaviour expected by one class from another, and founded on outer rather than inner observation—on abstract 'knowledge about' rather than concrete 'acquaintance with' (to use William James's words)—their application to social questions led the new services to treat manifestations of disorder in the individual rather than the underlying causes in the family or social group. Thus, there was no attempt to look closely at the mainsprings of behaviour; to ask why great quantities of medicine were consumed at the time; why one-third of the national population of old people aged seventy and over were on poor relief;[3] why family life had so changed that families would not, it was said, accept responsibility for aged parents and why there was, according to Masterman, so much talk of a weakening in the willingness to work.[4] These valuations of Edwardian days have a curiously topical ring about them.

The inner realities of behaviour were largely ignored in this formative period of the social services and many started their careers dressed with assumptions about how people ought to behave. Insight was lacking, partly because the means of acquir-

[1] Reynolds, S., *A Poor Man's House*, 1908, p. 264.
[2] Webb, S. and B., *The State and the Doctor*, 1910, p.149.
[3] *Report of the Royal Commission on the Poor Laws*, Vol. I, 1909, p. 59.
[4] Masterman, C. F. G., *The Condition of England*, 1911.

ing it were not yet to hand, and partly because the structure of society then did not encourage those who influenced social policy to understand the lives of those for whom the services were intended. Need and behaviour were still conceived of in terms of the individual rather than the family or the work-group. The abstractions of economic thought lingering on from the nineteenth century were wrapped round the concept of individual man acting outside the matrix of his particular society. Some philosophers continued to affirm that man alone was responsible for his sins and his suffering. Administrators and industrialists still tried to ignore, against the rapidly advancing ideas of mutual aid, the social relationships of the worker. Metaphysical individualism of the nineteenth century still exerted some effect, as Dewey has observed, by keeping the system of values in subjection to unexamined traditions, conventions and institutionalized customs.[1]

The social services of the early years of the twentieth century cannot be understood apart from the particular culture in which they grew up. Many have survived to this day with few modifications in structure. The extent to which poor law ideas were carried into the new legislation which sought to destroy the poor law, and the tensions that result from the clash between social changes and institutional rigidities have presented, and continue to present, some difficult problems. One or two examples may add concreteness to these generalizations.

When, in 1911, National Health Insurance provided a cash payment for periods of sickness a single man received the same as a man with a wife and several children to support. Nearly forty years passed before the State gave partial recognition to the existence of the wives and children of sick workers. The concept of insurance, in which individual premiums relate to individual risks, may have been more applicable under the 1911 Act which covered only a section of the population and excluded dependency with its greater variation in risk. Today, the insurance element in health insurance benefits is practically a

[1] Dewey, J., *Theory of Valuation*, International Encyclopaedia of Unified Science, Vol. II, No. 4, University of Chicago, 1939.

myth. Nevertheless, we still retain an expensive administrative machine, part of whose functions is to check the premium record before millions of benefit payments are made.[1]

When medical care by general practitioners was introduced in 1913 for insured workers, a service which Sir James Barr, the President of the British Medical Association, prophesied would produce 'a race of gently-reared hot-house plants',[2] the wives and children of these workers were excluded—excluded for thirty-five years. Throughout this period, the profession continued to talk of 'the family doctor'. Whether this situation of family doctoring has ever had any reality for the mass of the people has not been investigated. For all we know about general practice, the family doctor may be a projection of middle-class norms of behaviour.

The way in which these and other institutions took structure and form, and the extent to which they detached the needs of the individual from the needs of the family, partly explain the *ad hoc* and fragmentary growth of the British social services. From these beginnings the new services were developed, in no coherent order, to cater for certain categories of individual need; for certain categories of disease and incapacity, and for certain special needs of special groups. Classes of persons in need and categories of disease were treated; not families and social groups in distress.

During the ensuing thirty years we went on breaking off more fragments of need from the poor law, from the general body of medicine and from the scattered activities of voluntary organizations. As the accepted area of social obligation widened, as injustice became less tolerable, new services were separately organized around an individual need. Through all these complications of social service imposed on an unreformed local government structure there was drawn a tangle of administra-

[1] The 'Insurance' element in National Insurance Schemes is discussed in *The Problems of Budgetary Reform*, Hicks, J. R., 1948, and 'The Finance of British National Insurance', Peacock, A. T., in *Public Finance*, 3, 1950.

[2] Presidential address to the Eighteenth Annual Meeting of the British Medical Association, *British Medical Journal*, July 27, 1912.

tive rule and regulation; a frightening complexity of eligibility and benefit according to individual circumstances, local boundaries, degrees of need and so forth. The complications of social provisions and administrative structure—the fixed person for the fixed duty in a fixed situation—helped to call into being a variety of social workers and professional groups part of whose functions, narrowly conceived, was to translate the complications for the ordinary man and to match a variety of individual aids to a family in need.

How all this came to pass, untidily human and perversely shaped as it was, can be learnt only by understanding the history of the social services since the great surge forward in legislation for collective help during the decade before the First World War. The benefits and stimulus of combination—of mutual aid—among the workers joined with the passionate effort of social reformers drawn from all classes in society to achieve, first an advance here and then there. The advances that were made represented an accumulation of political and social compromise; each perhaps constituting, in the circumstances of the day, the limit of reform which could be put into effect without upsetting the existing social order. The second great revolution of this century in social care, beginning after Dunkirk and quickening into effect after 1945, continued the process.

The fact of all these achievements, representing in terms of cost about 30 per cent of the national budget, and affecting, in the services provided, nearly everyone in the community, has brought to the surface certain fundamental problems which were less obvious when the services were fewer and far less comprehensive. It is, indeed, the absolute scale on which advances in social welfare have been made that has contributed to the importance of these problems; problems which are partly historical in origin, partly institutional and administrative in character, partly caused by changes in society, and which now raise new questions of priority of need and quality of service.

Many forces have been at work to produce these problems. A half-century of unprecedented social and technical change has altered the nature and order of social needs. Rising standards of living and of education have shifted the emphasis in social service from quantity to quality. The growth of the services has stimulated the expansion of certain institutions and professional associations each with their own self-regarding interests. The social gains from developing specialization have, in their turn, produced other problems. Yet, while these forces have been growing within a widening area of social provision, many of the services themselves have remained unchanged in structure, arrangement and administration both centrally and locally.

The lack of flexibility and change in these institutions suggests a danger of excessive economic costs and of increased rigidity in administration. The dangers are enhanced by the greater difficulty today of measuring the standard or quality of service provided. Such dangers were smaller and less likely in the past when, as I have said, a limited range of services were provided only for the poor; when needs were assumed and the quality of treatment was often disregarded. The enemies of the social good were more easily seen forty years ago than they are today. There was work to be done among 'a shabby scuffle of tired people' (in Masterman's words) whose conditions of life were such as to settle the major priorities of social policy.

The priorities, like the needs, are harder to define today. In a situation of limited resources, quality of service comes into conflict with quantity of service; if the standard is set for (what Defoe called) 'the middling classes'[1] then the quantitative needs of other groups may not be met. Too high an investment in services in kind may cause hardships among those needing services in cash. The problem of priorities is not, therefore, just a matter of the respective claims of different branches of the social services but of the claims of different types of service catering for different categories of need. Moreover, within and between each service there arises the most difficult question of all: the question of quality or standard of service. The answers, insofar as answers can be found, depend to some extent on our knowledge of contemporary social needs. By what means, then,

[1] Defoe, D., *A Journal of the Plague Year*, 1722.

can we identify and measure the more subtle and complex needs of today and their distribution among different sections of the population? And in attempting to meet these needs what criteria can be used to assess the quality and value of the service provided; in schools, in hospitals, in doctors' surgeries, in children's institutions and so on? How, in this situation of qualitative demand and supply, do we know when needs are not satisfactorily met? To what extent, if at all, are they being artificially developed by the professional, administrative and technical interests upon whose skills the services depend? What, to put it crudely, are we getting for our money? Is an increasing proportion of the cost going, first, to those who do the welfare rather than to those who need the welfare and, second, for treating at a higher standard the symptoms of need rather than in curing or preventing the causes of need?

These questions are raised by a situation in which a far larger slice of the social service budget is now devoted to services in kind. On the other hand, while the principle of allowances for the family has made a big difference, advances in cash benefits have not been nearly as great as is sometimes supposed. The individual payments to adult workers for sickness and unemployment are worth less today in purchasing power than before the Second World War. Indeed, the amount of the weekly sickness benefit for an individual worker in 1911 represented a much higher proportion of the average wage; it was worth more in purchasing power and, taken by itself, was altogether more generous than the amount paid today.[1]

This example suggests that, willy-nilly, questions of priority are being settled by the cumulative play of many forces. The pressure of these forces, and the policies of those who would disarm the social services, may lead to the services in kind claiming a disproportionate share of resources. Several factors may contribute to this situation. One is the difficulty of measuring and controlling standards and quality of service. A second lies in the acceptance by the State of responsibility for the salaries and

[1] The basic payment for an adult man was 10*s*. a week in 1911. It is now 26*s*. a week.

pensions of large numbers of administrative, professional and technical workers whose skills are needed to run the services. For example: roughly 60 per cent of the £450,000,000 or so for the National Health Service comes under this head. But that is only a part of the bill. The great expansion of the social services in recent years has been accompanied by the introduction and extension of some of the most generous public superannuation schemes in the world.[1] These schemes suggest the possibility of new rigidities arising within the social services and, simultaneously, may make more difficult the problems of employment in an ageing population. At a time when men and women are urged to continue in work up to the age of seventy the State is committed to the payment of superannuation at a lower age to some 1,500,000 professional and technical workers and administrators.[2] Retirement at age sixty to sixty-five is sanctioned in the National Health Service and other superannuation schemes. Many people—like doctors and nurses—who formerly would have been forced to go on working will now retire earlier. The greater part of the huge total of future expenditure—to come chiefly out of the social service budget as the State finds most of the money through contributions and deductions from income tax—is unfunded as the schemes are financed on an emerging cost basis.[3]

The main principles of these schemes stem from the Act of 1834, except that civil servants were then subject to a means test and there was no absolute right to a pension.[4] The com-

[1] See, for example, the National Health Service (Superannuation) Regulations, 1950, S.I. 1950, No. 497.

[2] Approximately 1,000,000 persons are covered by the National Health Service, Civil Service and other Central Government Schemes and 500,000 by some 480 Local Government Schemes. In addition, a large number of other non-manual workers are covered by schemes for employees of the nationalized boards (Lloyd, F. J., *J. Inst. Actuaries*, 76, Part I, No. 342, June 1950).

[3] It has been estimated that the public cost of these benefits, including substantial lump sum payments, will rise ultimately to about 30 per cent of the pay-roll—apart from the rate of interest and further reductions in mortality (Robb, A. C., *J. Inst. Actuaries*, 76, Part I, No. 342, June 1950).

[4] 'And whereas the Principle of the Regulations for granting Allowances of this Nature is and ought to be founded on a Consideration, not only of the Services performed by the Individual to the State, but of the Inadequacy of his private Fortune to maintain his Station in Life' (Superannuation Act, 1834, 4 & 5, W4, C24).

mitments accepted under this historic Act were not very onerous because many of those entitled to pension died before reaching the stipulated age of sixty-five—the equivalent, perhaps, in physiological terms of seventy-five today. The expectation of life then was much lower than it is now.[1] Perhaps for the reason that many died in harness the normal retirement age for the civil service was reduced to sixty by the Act of 1859, at which it has since remained.[2] The expectation of life for men at sixty is now seventeen years and for women nearly twenty years. The State has thus accepted the responsibility of making generous provision for a period of years amounting to nearly half the working life of these professional, technical and administrative workers.

Differences in public policy on the needs of this age span among one group of workers in contrast to the needs of the generality of workers may be, in the future, a possible source off social tension. But that, for the moment, is a digression. The relevant point here, apart from the rising burden of cost, is that the development of salary and fixed pension arrangements on this scale is unlikely to make for greater flexibility in the structure of the social services. Indeed, such schemes may mean more rigidity and, therefore, may represent a force resistant to social change. These dangers may be reinforced, rather than lessened, by the continuing growth of specialization and professionalism in the social services. This trend affects, not only the professions in the generally accepted sense, but a large and increasing number of administrative and technical groups claiming professional status and rewards on the grounds of some specialized technique for which examinations and tests of competence multiply at an alarming rate.

The social services, which have helped to nourish them, de-

[1] From forty years at birth for men it is now sixty-five (Royal Commission on Population, *Reports and Selected Papers of the Statistics Committee*, Vol. II, pp. 54–8).

[2] During the committee stage of the superannuation bill in March 1859, it was stated that 'a very large portion of the public servants died or disappeared before the time for superannuation arrived'. At this date, members of the House of Commons were exempt from serving on committees at the age of sixty (*Hansard*, Vol. Ser. 3, CLIII, 1859).

pend to an increasing extent on the valuable skills and specialized knowledge of these occupational groups. Because of the contribution they can make, there is a tendency to give these groups more representation upon policy-making and advisory bodies which form part of the services employing them.[1] The continuing growth of scientific and technical knowledge adds to their prestige and influence in matters of policy. Criticism from without of professional conduct and standards of work tends to be increasingly resented the more highly these groups are organized. 'Just at the very point where there is the greatest need of criticism,' says Ruth Benedict in discussing the difficulty of scrutinizing dominant traits in our culture, 'we are bound to be least critical'.[2] It is, perhaps, symptomatic that there has been no criticism of the decision to withhold information about the recipients of public money now distributed annually, as distinction awards and as pensionable additions to income, by certain highly placed members of several professions to other members of the same professions.

As the social services become more complex, more specialized and subject to a finer division of labour they become less intelligible to the lay councillor or public representative. A possible consequence is that, collectively, more power may come to reside in the hands of these interests. The question that needs to be asked of professional associations is whether they are prepared to assume greater social responsibilities to match their added knowledge and the power that accompanies it. Professional associations are not the only repositories of knowledge, but they are the repositories of a very special kind of knowledge; and the establishment of proper relations between them and the democratic State is, today, one of the urgent problems affecting the future of the social services. These groups represent, by the nature of the interests which unite them, forces resistant to

[1] 'In Great Britain only the less obvious forms of corruption in public life persist. Among these perhaps the commonest is the giving of representation on an administrative or investigating body to the "interests concerned".' This tendency has increased since Sir Arthur Newsholme wrote in 1925 (Newsholme, A., *The Ministry of Health*, 1925, p. 83).

[2] Benedict, R., *Patterns of Culture*, 1935, p. 179.

social change, and sometimes resistant, therefore, to needed changes in the social services. 'Each profession makes progress, but it is progress in its own groove,' said A. N. Whitehead.[1] Serious thought is confined to a narrow range of facts and experiences; 'the remainder of life is treated superficially. The fixed person for the fixed duties, who in older societies was such a godsend, in the future will be a public menace. The dangers arising from this aspect of professionalism are particularly great in democratic societies,' added Whitehead.

We have long since reached the stage in the development of the social services when we need to consider, not only embarking on new services, but the reform of existing ones. Social services, like other institutions, need to change in sensitive association with the changing needs of society. But the forces which resist change tend to become stronger. In part, their strength derives from 'the intensified division of labour' which, as Merton observed, 'has become a splendid device for escaping social responsibilities'.[2] One result is that more attention may be paid to modifying human behaviour than to changing the environment. This aspect of the shifting power-structure in administration deserves careful and methodical inquiry. All I am attempting here is to put forward some hypothetical points of view which I conceive to be important in the study of social administration.

These questions that I have asked concerning the structure and functions of the social services, the role of professionalism, and the relations of economic resources to social priorities require systematic study and research. If they are proper questions then it follows, I think, that we cannot expect to achieve a better relationship between the services provided and the needs of a changing society without more knowledge of both; of the nature of social needs and of how the services actually work as distinct from how we suppose they work. Or, as Professor Ginsberg has said in the context of ethical judgment, 'of the ends actually attained in relation to the ends the institutions

[1] Whitehead, A. N., *Science in the Modern World*, 1926, pp. 275–6.
[2] Merton, R. K., *Social Theory and Social Structure*, Chicago, 1949, p. 323.

are intended to attain'.[1] In the past, knowledge in both these fields has been inadequate. There has been too little research into the operational working of the services; too little recognition of the rapid and all-pervasive character of social change. Indeed, it has often been assumed that a social service had arrived at some sort of finality. In much the same way, Macaulay saw, in the political history of man, a culmination in the English constitutional system of his day. This notion of finality, with its presupposition that statutory promise and administrative performance are highly correlated, prevented us from understanding that all legislation is experimental and that a social service is a dynamic process—not a finished article. To accept this concept implies a need to know constantly what is happening. Flexibility in the structure of the social services is as important as flexibility in the structure of economic institutions. Even now, after the achievements of the last five years, the responsibility of providing social services carries with it the further responsibility of keeping them in a good state of repair; of preventing them from getting out of order and out of balance with social needs. For they will get out of balance, if only because of the often contrary pulls made on the human organism by biological and social forces.

The fact that many more people now survive to experience old age and retirement confronts the modern State with a series of new problems. For millions of people an extra span of life has come into being with its own economic and social needs. Provision for this span now comes into conflict with the needs of other age spans. The growth of the social services in recent years has, it seems, operated in part as an instrument which promises a future redistribution of income in favour of certain professional, technical and administrative groups during their passage through this span of around fifteen years. Members of these schemes, drawing pensions based on final salaries, thus already hold a large claim on the goods and services likely to be available for old people. These welfare commitments appear to

[1] Ginsberg, M., 'Social Science and Social Philosophy in the Universities', *Sociological Review*, 29, No. 4, 1937, p. 328.

have been accepted partly because we took over what was appropriate to one age and applied it to the circumstances of another age without thought to the social and biological changes which have transformed the problems in less than one hundred years.

Among the odd survivals from the past is the custom of paying large sums of money at the milestone of sixty. This custom, now embedded in many public superannuation schemes, seems to have little relevance to the present distribution of economic needs over life. It is an instance of social change outpacing the capacity of institutions to change. It is only a single instance, however, of the manner in which changes in the rates of birth, marriage and death, with all their accompanying and consequential effects during the past century on living and working and getting and spending, have fundamentally changed the character and distribution of needs over the lives of individuals and their families.

The dwindling in the size of the family with the contribution that smaller families have made towards the social emancipation of women, the lengthening of life, and the narrowing of the life-span during which children are dependent upon adults; all these changes in the structure and composition of the working and dependent population raise new problems in economic behaviour, in social organization and in human relationships. The whole pattern of roles and responsibilities over an individual's life has been shifting in time and changing in intensity during the past seventy years. Most married couples have finished with child dependency at an earlier age than in the past. The responsibilities of parenthood are now more concentrated in a shorter span of years. The rise in the esteem of the child and the revolution in standards of child care since the nineteenth century has meant, however, that parents are more conscious of the social and economic costs of children. The institution of the small family together with the lengthening of life results in more old people being dependent, in psychological and economic terms, on fewer grown-up children. New periods in the life cycle have appeared in which economic responsibilities are slight—in the late teens and early twenties and, again, in the fifties and sixties. The decline in the birth rate in the past is now resulting in an inflationary economic scramble for a smaller number of young workers whose earnings bear less relationship to responsibilities than formerly.

The present distribution of social and economic rewards is tending to get out of balance with the changed pattern of needs and dependencies. Among many workers at most income levels, the relatively privileged groups are young men and women, young married couples without children and parents in late middle life whose children have grown up. These groups are greatly favoured by their freedom to work outside the home, by taxation reliefs, by fewer ties and dependencies. Some groups, whose earnings reach their peak early in life, enjoy a brief period of prosperity when social appetites are being formed; others ascend on a rising scale of rewards till they arrive at a plateau of prosperity in late middle life when their responsibilities have diminished. Those groups where responsibilities and needs are greatest—married couples with two or more children and only one wage-earner and old people living on retirement pensions—are less favoured by social policy.

Despite all the social benefits of recent years, the general effect in most economic groups is that a higher proportion of the national income is being received by those without dependent children. In other words, the distribution of the national product is out of sympathy with the contemporary distribution of social need arising from the dependencies of childhood, widowhood, sickness and old age. Disharmonies of this kind over the life-span, observed and experienced differences in standards, rises and falls in the net balance of effort and reward at different age spans in different social groups, sometimes the contradictions between, on the one hand, the code of behaviour in which out-working one's fellows is unethical and, on the other, the needs of the family for more prestige and approval; all these subtle psychological preoccupations can lead to situations of conflict and stress. Concepts and standards of living cultivated by relatively high earnings before marriage may be shattered by the lower standards resulting from marriage and parenthood. The prosperities of late middle life may make the hardships of living on old age pensions seem harder than they really are. The margin of comfort allowed by two wage-earners in a family may disappear when there is but one wage-earner. The higher the cost of living the more it may benefit—in relative terms—the single traveller through life and the more it may undermine the family. The greater the rise in the desired standard of life, stimulated by cultural pressures on parents in relation to child upbringing, by habits and attitudes formed before parenthood, and by the spending patterns of those without dependent children, the greater may be the consciousness of injustice among those with children. The outlook on life of those groups with no incremental ladder in front of them, no middle-class ethos of economic ascent, no provision of lump sum payments at sixty and more worth-while pensions in old age, must be difficult for other groups, differently placed, to comprehend. Comparisons are inevitable in a society which has promised and tried hard to practise social justice, fair shares and equal educational opportunities. To the extent that social benefits get out of harmony and are felt to be out of harmony with the cycle of actual and desired needs, the greater the likelihood of social and psychological stress.

In these situations, the family seeks a new equilibrium. Somehow or other it has to conform to the contrary pulls of a changing society. We know little, however, of the forces that are shaping the norms of family life. We do not understand the fundamental reasons for the falling birth rate; for the greater popularity of marriage, for the rising esteem of children in our society, or the significance of the large increase in the number of married women who now leave their homes to work in factory and office. On the surface, there are contradictions here; just as there are when the problem of incentives, perhaps the crucial problem in economic inquiry today, is considered alongside these trends. May be there is in process a new division of labour in the family, a rearrangement of role, of function; a new calculus of effort and reward in which the frontier between workplace and home is becoming blurred. Such processes, which may upset current theories about industrial productivity, may also lead to situations of stress in the home and the factory; new situations of dishonesty in which men find their inherited system of norms no longer rewarding. But while families may be hurt by these stresses, people rarely die from them. The maladjustments in society do not now kill as they did in the nineteenth century. Medical science at least keeps people alive. Our old indices of social disorder are now less useful. We cannot so easily measure the complex sicknesses of a complex society; the prevalence of the stress diseases of modern civilization, the instabilities of family relationships or the extent of mental ill-health in the community. Difficulties of accurate measurement should not prevent us, however, from seeking to extend our knowledge of the causes at work.

These are some of the important problems at present challenging the social sciences. They are of practical concern to social administration, which, as a humble partner in this broad field of study, cannot hope to understand the working of social institutions and services without understanding the needs which arise from changing ways of living.

The forces of the past in terms of how we live together in society create new situations; if the structure and functions of the social services cling too closely to the needs of the age when they originated, and if the interests which resist change become too powerful, these services will not meet the needs of the new situations. We shall not achieve a better balance between the needs of today and the resources of today by living-out the destinies of tradition; by simply attending to the business of the State. Without knowledge of wind and current, without some sense of purpose, men and societies do not keep afloat for long, morally or economically, by baling out the water.

CHAPTER 2

The Social Division of Welfare: Some Reflections on the Search for Equity[1]

I

SOME students of social policy see the development of 'The Welfare State' in historical perspective as part of a broad, ascending road of social betterment provided for the working classes since the nineteenth century and achieving its goal in our time. This interpretation of change as a process of unilinear progression in collective benevolence for these classes led to the belief that in the year 1948 'The Welfare State' was established. Since then, successive Governments, Conservative and Labour, have busied themselves with the more effective operation of the various services, with extensions here and adjustments there and both parties, in and out of office, have claimed the maintenance of 'The Welfare State' as an article of faith.

On this view it could be supposed that speaking generally, Britain is approaching the end of the road of social reform; the road down which Eleanor Rathbone and other reformers and rebels laboured with vision and effect. This would seem to be the principal implication of much public comment on the social services during the past few years, and one which has received

[1] The Sixth Eleanor Rathbone Memorial Lecture, given at the University of Birmingham on December 1, 1955, and published by Liverpool University Press in 1956.

endorsement in policy statements of the Conservative and Labour parties.[1] An analysis of the more important writings on the subject since 1948 lends support, for the dominant note, far from suggesting that social needs have been neglected, has been that 'The Welfare State' was 'established' too quickly and on too broad a scale. The consequences, it is argued, have been harmful to the economic health of the nation and its 'moral fibre'.

Against this background, compounded of uneasiness and complacency, criticism has mainly focused on the supposedly equalitarian aims or effects of the social services. It is said that the relief of poverty or the maintenance of a national minimum as an objective of social policy should not mean the pursuit of equality; 'a fascinating and modern development' for the social services according to Hagenbuch.[2] The Beveridge 'revolution' did not, it is argued, imply an equalitarian approach to the solution of social problems. The error of welfare state policies since 1948 has been, according to this diagnosis, to confuse ends and means, and to pursue equalitarian aims with the result that the 'burden' of redistribution from rich to poor has been pushed too far and is now excessive. Thus, the upper and middle classes have been impoverished, in part a consequence of providing benefits for those workers who do not really need them. 'Why,' asks Macleod and Powell, 'should any social service be provided *without* [their italics] test of need?'[3] Their conclusion, like that of Hagenbuch in his analysis of 'The Rationale of the Social Services'[4] and other writers, is that there should be a closer relationship between what people pay in and what they take out. Social security should be based on 'more genuine' actuarial principles, while the ultimate objective for other social services should be 'self-liquidation' as more and more people are raised above a minimum standard of living to a position of freedom in

[1] See, for example, *One Nation*, Conservative Political Centre, 1950, and *The Welfare State*, Labour Party Political Discussion Pamphlet, 1952.
[2] Hagenbuch, W., *Lloyds Bank Review*, July 1953, p. 5.
[3] Macleod, I. and Powell, J. E., *The Social Services—Needs and Means*, 1949.
[4] Hagenbuch, W., *op. cit.*

which they may purchase whatever medical care, education, training and other services they require. The mass of the people would thus, in time, come to behave like, if they do not resemble, the middle classes (who at present are presumed to derive little benefit from the social services). Pursued to its logical conclusion then, 'The Welfare State' would eventually be transformed into 'The Middle Class State'. Meanwhile, social legislation and its application should recognize much more clearly than it does at present that (as Macleod and Powell put it) 'the social services only exist for a portion of the population',[1] namely, that portion which takes out more than it puts in.

These views were tersely summed up by *The Economist* in June 1954, when it affirmed, as a guiding principle for social policy, that 'no one should live on the taxpayer unless he needs to'.[2] Already, 'the social well-being of the nation had been endangered by the redistribution of wealth'[3] a phrase which, according to a variety of social theorists, embraced more deeply-felt anxieties than a simple material concern about economic and fiscal trends. De Jouvenel, for example, drew attention to the 'sordid utilitarianism' of redistributionist social services; to a 'precipitous decline' in voluntary, unrewarded services upon which culture and civilization depends, and to a 'tremendous growth' in the power of the State as a consequence of the rising cost of the social services.[4] At the same time, two popular books by Lewis and Maude rounded out the picture of a decaying, overworked and anxious middle class.[5] Finally, we may note the

[1] Macleod, I. and Powell, J. E., *op. cit.*, p. 4.

[2] *The Economist*, June 5, 1954, p. 783.

[3] This statement, expressing a widely-held view of the effects of social policy, appeared in *One Nation*, published by the Conservative Political Centre in 1950.

[4] De Jouvenel, B., *The Ethics of Redistribution*, 1951.

[5] The authors illustrate their theme by describing how middle-class leisure has been drastically reduced while that enjoyed by the working-class has increased (*The English Middle Classes*, 1949, p. 214 and *Professional People*, 1952, Lewis, R. and Maude, A.). This apparently undesirable happening (if it has happened) is not peculiar to this country. In the United States 'there is a tendency among social scientists today, not mitigated by Kinsey, to think that the lower classes have all the fun, the middle classes all the miseries and inhibitions' (Denney, R. and Riesman, D. in *Creating an Industrial Civilization*, Ed. Staley, E., 1952).

specific counter-proposals of two other critics. Ffrangcon Roberts has entered a vigorous plea for State medicine to return a business profit, and for the benefits of the National Health Service to be reserved for economically productive workers.[1] Colin Clark, foreseeing a totalitarian threat in the continued existence of the social services, would 'denationalize' them and entrust some remnant of their functions to the Churches, local friendly societies and voluntary organizations.[2]

II

Whatever their validity in fact or theory, these views have had an important influence in shaping opinion since 1948 about the future of the social services. They have helped, no doubt unwittingly, to produce in the public eye something akin to a stereotype or image of an all-pervasive Welfare State for the Working Classes. Such is the tyranny of stereotypes today that this idea of a welfare society, born as a reaction against the social discrimination of the poor law may, paradoxically, widen rather than narrow class relationships. As Gerth and Mills have pointed out '. . . if the upper classes monopolize the means of communication and fill the several mass media with the idea that all those at the bottom are there because they are lazy, unintelligent, and in general inferior, then these appraisals may be taken over by the poor and used in the building of an image of their selves'.[3] That is one danger in the spread of the 'Welfare State' stereotype. A second emanates from the vague but often powerful fears that calamity will follow the relaxation of discipline and the mitigation of hardship which, in the eyes of the beholders, seems implicit in this notion of collective benevolence. Such fears inevitably conjure up a demand for punishment and reprisal; the history of public opinion in recent years on the subject of juvenile delinquency (to take one example) is sug-

[1] Roberts, F., *The Cost of Health*, 1952, pp. 134–7.

[2] Clark, C., *Welfare and Taxation*, 1954.

[3] Gerth, H. and Mills, C. W., *Character and Social Structure*, 1953, pp. 88–9.

gestive of the operation of what Flugel called the 'Polycrates complex'.[1]

These brief observations on contemporary thinking about social policy are essential to the argument that follows; they constitute the political frame of reference. Nevertheless, they are a poor substitute for a close and detailed analysis of the critical views so summarily mentioned. Such an analysis would require many more words than one essay allows and must, therefore, be deferred. However, having set the stage in this general way, it is now proper to state the main purposes of this paper: first, to examine certain assumptions underlying these views; second, to outline the development of three major categories of social welfare and, third, to relate these developments to trends in the division of labour and the search for social equity. At the end, in drawing together these different threads, it emerges that much of the criticism and all the complacency about 'The Welfare State' is either irrelevant or unbalanced and that we need to re-examine, by returning to first principles, current notions of what constitutes a social service.

First, however, it is necessary to bring into view certain assumptions, seldom made explicit, which run through practically all the recent critical writings on social policy. It is assumed:

Firstly, that the intended or declared aims of social policy since the Beveridge Report of 1942 have been wholly or largely achieved in the translation of legislation into action. In other words, that the performance of welfare has more or less fulfilled the promise of welfare.

Secondly, that the aggregate redistributive effects of social service activity since 1948 have wholly or largely represented a transfer of resources from rich to poor.

Thirdly, that in the present inadequate state of knowledge about the working of social institutions it is possible to define what is a 'social service' and to identify, in each sector of State intervention, who has benefited and who has paid.

Fourthly, that it is practicable, desirable and has any meaning

[1] Flugel, J. C., *Man, Morals and Society*, especially chapters 11 and 18, 1945.

in a complex society undergoing rapid and widespread change to abstract a 'social service world' from the Greater Society, and to consider the functions and effects of the part without reference to the life of the whole.

The first and second assumptions call, I would suggest, for a detailed study of the 'unintended consequences' of social policy over the past decade. This cannot be attempted here.[1] I must content myself with making explicit the nature of these assumptions. In the following section, however, I examine certain facts relevant to the third and fourth assumptions.

III

All collectively-provided services are deliberately designed to meet certain socially recognized 'needs'; they are manifestations, first, of society's will to survive as an organic whole and, secondly, of the expressed wish of all the people to assist the survival of some people. 'Needs' may therefore be thought of as 'social' and 'individual'; as inter-dependent, mutually related essentials for the continued existence of the parts and the whole. No complete division between the two is conceptually possible; the shading of one into the other changes with time over the life of all societies; it changes with time over the cycle of needs of the individual and the family; and it depends on prevailing notions of what constitutes a 'need' and in what circumstances; and to what extent, if at all, such needs, when recognized, should be met in the interests of the individual and/or of society.

When we apply these formulations to modern society we note the importance of definition. What is a 'need'? What is a 'service'? What was yesterday's conception of 'need' and 'service'?

[1] A critical examination of the primary data used by A. M. Cartter (to quote only one recent attempt to measure the redistributionist effects of the social services) would serve to show how tenuous are the conclusions, commonly drawn, about the fiscal consequences of 'The Welfare State' (Cartter, A. M., *The Redistribution of Income in Post-war Britain*, 1955). Much the same could be said when individual social schemes are considered (see, for example, Ch. 3 on pensions and superannuation).

Of one thing at least we can be certain when all else is uncertain; the situation in which different kinds of need arise and are recognized as 'needs' has changed and will continue to do so. The Britain of the 1950's is a very different society from the Britain of the 1900's. Not only are the 'needs' and 'situations' different but they are differently seen. The social-individual equation of need is a different equation and, again, it is differently seen. Freud for one, in undermining our psychological innocence, and Marx for another, in opening our eyes to economic realities, contributed to changing our perception of the equation. So have the infinite and cumulative processes of social and technological change since the end of the nineteenth century.

It is this period I want to consider particularly, for it is this period of roughly fifty years—the era of rising expectations—that has witnessed the emergence and growth of those forms of state intervention which, by custom and common approval, have come to be called 'the social services'. The development of these services from the welfare revolution of 1905–14 under a reformist Liberal Government, through the experience of two world wars and mass unemployment, to the Beveridge 'insurance revolution' and its aftermath has been amply documented in legislative detail. At the same time as the services themselves developed in scope and range, the term 'social service' has come to be applied to more and more areas of collective provision for certain 'needs'. It has indeed acquired a most elastic quality; its expanding frontiers, formerly enclosing little besides poor relief, sanitation and public nuisances, now embrace a multitude of heterogeneous activities. For example, Boer War pensions and disablement benefits were officially classified as social services in 1920; the Universities and public museums were added after the Second World War. And so on. No consistent principle seems to obtain in the definition of what is a 'social service'.

The following simple examples, taken from the present Treasury classification,[1] give some indication of the area of confusion concealed by the assumptions of the critics of social

[1] This classification relates to 'social service' expenditure. (*Monthly Digest of Statistics*, Central Statistical Office, May 1955).

policy,[1] and warn us of the dangers in any conception of a self-contained social service system expressly designed for the transmission of benefits from one income group of the population to another.

1. Approved Schools and remand homes are social services. The probation service is not.

2. Further Education and Training for ex-members of the Defence Forces is a social service. The Youth Employment Service is not.

3. The training of doctors is a social service. Marriage guidance services are not.

4. Pensions and allowances attributable to the Boer War and First World War are social services. Industrial health services are not.

5. The family allowance is a social service. The child allowance as remission of tax is not.

6. The investigation of legal aid applications is a social service. Legal aid grants are not.

7. Village halls and playing fields are social services. Cheap tobacco for old age pensioners is not.

8. Technological training and further education is a social service. Subsidized housing for miners is not.

9. Compensation to doctors for loss of right to sell medical practices is a social service. Non-contributory pensions and superannuation under occupational pension schemes are not.

10. University education is a social service. The training of domestic workers is not.

When so much confusion exists (and these examples are but a selection from a large body of data) it is difficult to know precisely what it is that the critics are criticizing. The assumptions concealed behind such vague generalities as 'the social services' and 'The Welfare State' thus seem to be largely irrelevant. This becomes clearer when it is understood that those acts of state intervention which have somehow or other acquired the

[1] It should also be noted that all the definitions employed by the various authorities mentioned in this essay differ very substantially, namely, those used by *The Economist*, Macleod and Powell, Hagenbuch, Cartter, De Jouvenel and Clark.

connotation of 'social' have developed alongside a much broader area of intervention not thought of in such terms but having in common similar objectives. It is this differential development I want to emphasize: the growth in the social division of welfare in response to changing situations and conceptions of 'need'.

Considered as a whole, all collective interventions to meet certain needs of the individual and/or to serve the wider interests of society may now be broadly grouped into three major categories of welfare: social welfare, fiscal welfare, and occupational welfare. When we examine them in turn, it emerges that this division is not based on any fundamental difference in the functions of the three systems (if they may be so described) or their declared aims. It arises from an organizational division of method, which, in the main, is related to the division of labour in complex, individuated societies. So far as the ultimate aims of these systems are concerned, it is argued that their similarities are more important than their dissimilarities. The definition, for most purposes, of what is a 'social service' should take its stand on aims; not on the administrative methods and institutional devices employed to achieve them.

The development in this century of our first category of welfare—that which commonly goes by the term 'social service'—has already been mentioned. A major factor in this development should now be noted, for it has played a similarly important role in the growth of our two other categories of welfare.

With the gradual break-up of the old poor law, more 'states of dependency' have been defined and recognized as collective responsibilities, and more differential provision has been made in respect of them. These 'states of dependency' arise for the vast majority of the population whenever they are not in a position to 'earn life' for themselves and their families; they are then dependent people. In industrialized societies there are many causes of dependency; they may be 'natural' dependencies as in childhood, extreme old age and child-bearing. They may be caused by physical and psychological ill-health and incapacity; in part, these are culturally determined dependencies. Or they may be wholly or predominantly determined by social and cultural factors. These, it may be said, are the 'man-made' dependencies. Apart from injury, disease and innate incapacity, they now constitute the major source of instability in the satisfaction of basic needs. They include unemployment and under-employment, protective and preventive legislation, compulsory retirement from work, the delayed entry of young people into the labour market, and an infinite variety of subtle cultural factors ranging from the 'right' trade union ticket to the possession of an assortment of status symbols. All may involve to some degree the destruction, curtailment, interruption or frustration of earning power in the individual, and more pronounced secondary dependencies when they further involve the wives, children and other relatives.

In general, many of these culturally determined dependencies have grown in range and significance over the past century, partly as a result of a process of cumulative survivorship, for those who experience such states of dependency do not now die as others did before the twentieth century. The total of current needs may be higher because of a proportionately higher representation of survivors of past dependency-creating experiences —wars, unemployments, injuries, enforced family separations and so forth. Apart, however, from the effects of this process, the dominating operative factor has been the increasing division of labour in society and, simultaneously, a great increase in labour specificity. This is perhaps one of the outstanding social characteristics of the twentieth century; the fact that more and more people consciously experience at one or more stages in their lives the process of selection and rejection; for education, for work, for vocational training, for professional status, for promotion, for opportunities of access to pension schemes, for collective social benefits, for symbols of prestige and success, and in undergoing tests of mental and physical fitness, personality, skill and functional performance.[1] In some senses at least, the

[1] The assessment of specific labour skills now includes, in addition to the standard intelligence tests which attempt to measure verbal ability, visualization and numerical skill, such concepts as tone discrimination, accident proneness, taste sensitivity, colour blindness, digital dexterity, analogizing power, mechanical and clerical aptitude, and mental maturity. (See Caplow, T., *The Sociology of Work*, 1954).

arbiters of opportunity and of dependency have become, in their effects, more directly personal, more culturally demanding, more psychologically threatening. There are more roles for the super-ego to play as one's appreciation of reality becomes more accurate.

We cannot, however, pursue here the deeper psychological implications of this trend, implied but not described in detail by Durkheim when he observed that as man becomes more individual and more specialized he becomes more socially dependent.[1] This is of primary importance in understanding the development of systems of welfare; this and the fact that, simultaneously, man becomes more aware of what has caused his dependency, and thus more exposed to uncertainty and conflict about the purposes and roles he himself is expected to fulfil. More self-knowledge of the 'man-made' causes of dependency has been reflected in social policies through the greater recognition accorded to individual dependencies and their social origins and effects. It has also influenced the growth of our other categories of welfare.

I now turn, therefore, to consider these notions in relation to the development of fiscal welfare and occupational welfare.

IV

Under separately administered social security systems, like family allowances and retirement pensions, direct cash payments are made in discharging collective responsibilities for particular dependencies. In the relevant accounts, these are treated as 'social service' expenditure since they represent flows of payments through the central government account. Allowances and reliefs from income tax, though providing similar benefits and expressing a similar social purpose in the recognition of dependent needs, are not, however, treated as social service expenditure. The first is a cash transaction; the second an accounting convenience. Despite this difference in administrative method, the

[1] Durkheim, E., *The Division of Labour in Society*, trans. G. Simpson, 1933, p. 131.

tax saving that accrues to the individual is, in effect, a transfer payment.[1] In their primary objectives and their effects on individual purchasing power there are no differences in these two ways by which collective provision is made for dependencies.[2] Both are manifestations of social policies in favour of identified groups in the population and both reflect changes in public opinion in regard to the relationship between the State, the individual and the family.

Since the introduction of progressive taxation in 1907 there has been a remarkable development of social policy operating through the medium of the fiscal system. This has chiefly taken the form of increasing support for the family through the recognition of more types of dependencies and substantial additions to the value of the benefits provided. Another important aspect of this development is that, originally, these dependants' benefits were deliberately restricted to the lowest paid sections of the income tax population; in the course of time these restrictions have disappeared. The Royal Commission on Taxation now propose that such benefits should be allowed in the calculation

[1] As Cartter observed: 'By reducing the tax liability of a person with dependants the State is sharing in the responsibility of caring for each taxpayer's family just as certainly as if it were paying cash allowances in each case.' (Cartter, A. M., 'Income-Tax Allowances and the Family in Great Britain', *Population Studies*, Vol. VI, No. 3, 1953, p. 219). Other authorities also take the view that no distinction can be made between implicit and explicit transfer payments; see, for example, United Nations, *Economic Bulletin for Europe*, Vol. 4, No. 2, 1952; Haynes, A. T. and Kirton, R. J., 'Income Tax in Relation to Social Security', *Journal of the Institute of Actuaries*, Vol. LXXII, Pt. 1, No. 333, 1944, pp. 83–5; and *Samordning Af De Nordiske Landes Statistik Vedrorende Den Sociale Lovgivning*, Copenhagen, 1955, reporting the agreement of the five Northern Countries that 'tax deductions are quite analogous to . . . allowances in cash'). Though the Royal Commission on the Taxation of Profits and Income did not address itself directly to this question there are innumerable references in the 612 pages of its Second and Final Reports which support this approach. Thus, in discussing relief for charities costing around £35m. a year, the Commission observes that this 'does amount in effect to a grant of public moneys'. (*Final Report*, Cmd 9474, 1955, p. 55; also *Second Report*, Cmd 9105, 1954).

[2] Pigou recognized this in his *The Economics of Welfare* (4th ed. 1932, p. 98) when he wrote of tax relief for children as 'deliberate and overt bounties' for large families. Curiously, however, the similarity of these reliefs to family allowances seems to have escaped Eleanor Rathbone.

of liability to surtax.[1]

A brief historical sketch of the main features of fiscal welfare shows the growth in public concern and responsibility for 'states of dependency', family and kinship relationships, individual 'self-improvement' and standards of 'minimum subsistence' among income taxpayers. It shows too, as W. Friedmann has pointed out, the extent to which Taxation Acts are now regarded as social purpose Acts;[2] that taxation has more or less ceased to be regarded as an impertinent intrusion into the sacred rights of private property and that, for the purposes of social policy, it can no longer be thought of simply as a means of benefiting the poor at the expense of the rich.[3]

A child allowance of £10 for all children aged under 16 for those—as a 'special consideration'[4] —whose incomes were under £500 was introduced in 1909; thus ante-dating by thirty-seven years family allowances for second and subsequent children.[5] This has gradually risen (through thirteen changes) to £100 in 1955.[6] The income qualification was raised in 1916, 1918 and 1919 and finally extended to all taxpayers in 1920. The allowance has been further developed to include children receiving full-time education at a university or other educational establishment for the reason that, in the words of the Royal Commission, 'the child's immediate earning capacity has been foregone in order that he should qualify himself for work on a higher level in the future'.[7] Social policy has thus been extended

[1] *Second Report*, Cmd 9105, 1954, p. 56.

[2] Friedmann, W., *Law and Social Change in Contemporary Britain*, 1954, p. 262.

[3] This would seem to be the implication of Professor Lewis' article 'A Socialist Economic Policy', in *Socialist Commentary* (June, 1955, p. 171), and of Professor Robbins' criticisms of progressive taxation ('Notes on Public Finance', *Lloyds Bank Review*, October 1955).

[4] The Chancellor of the Exchequer in his Budget Speech, 1909, *Hansard*, Vol. IV, cols. 507–8.

[5] Thus, fiscal policy supports the first child in all circumstances; social welfare policy only does so when the parents are sick or unemployed.

[6] The 1909 benefit represented, at the maximum, an annual tax saving of 7*s*. 6*d*. per child. The corresponding figure for 1955 (earned income £2,000) is approximately £48.

[7] *Second Report*, p. 55. Or as Talcott Parsons puts it: 'The development of adaptive socialized anxiety in middle-status life is all the more essential because the

beyond the confines of support for childhood dependency to the support of individual 'self-improvement'. These allowances are given regardless of education and scholarship awards.[1] The Royal Commission now propose a further major development, namely, that the allowance should vary with the size of the taxpayer's income up to a limit of £160 for all income and surtax payers, and that such allowance should continue to the age of twenty-one for all 'incapacitated' children.[2] The estimated cost of the existing allowances in 1955–6 was £200 m.,[3] covering broadly about half the child population. We may illustrate these differences in social policy by considering the respective awards to two married men, one earning £2,000 a year and one earning £400 a year. Both have two children aged under fifteen. The first father now receives an annual net bounty of £97; the second one of £28.[4] Over the lives of the two families the former will receive a total of £1,455 and the latter a total of £422.[5] If the Royal Commission's proposal is adopted the bounty for the first father will rise to over £2,200. The fact that already the child bounty rises steeply with increasing income appears to have been overlooked by Professor Robbins in his plea that, to 'eliminate some of the injustices of progression', these allowances should be provided 'in some measure propor-

social and prestige rewards of this status must necessarily be postponed during the prolonged training of the child and adolescent for high skills and complex responsibilities.' (Parsons, Talcott, cited in *The Sociology of Work*, Caplow, T., 1954).

[1] The scale of assessing parents' contributions for state scholarships laid down by the Ministry of Education further increases the total benefit for taxpayers. It does so by allowing as deductions from income, superannuation contributions and life assurance payments up to a specified proportion of income. National insurance contributions are not allowable (see *Report of Working Party on Grants to Training College Students*, 1955, p. 21).

[2] Pp. 56–61.

[3] Information supplied by the Treasury (letter November 9, 1955).

[4] The basis of this calculation is a comparison, in both cases, with a married man without children. It assumes earned income, and takes account of family allowances, national insurance contributions (including tax treatment), earned income allowance and personal allowances. The rates used are for 1955–6.

[5] If the first father happens to be a University don or eligible for an employer's child allowance scheme of £50 per child per year his total bounty is further increased.

tionate to the expenses of the income group into which they are born'.[1]

Equally fascinating to the sociologist is the story of when and why wives were recognized in this system of social welfare (significantly enough in 1918); aged, incapacitated and infirm kinship dependants; housekeepers according to particular situations of family need; widowed mothers; incapacitated wives; unmarried daughters assisting infirm taxpayers; 'unmarried wives' and children of deceased members of the Forces; mourning costs (under Estate Duty); old age; professional 'self-improvement';[2] divorced wives,[3] unemployed taxpayers (loss of office compensation); married women at work (first introduced in 1920 in recognition of 'extra household expenses');[4] housekeepers for professional women on full-time work, and as a 'special indulgence' for poorer taxpayers and those with precarious incomes finding it difficult to save for their dependents and for old age,[5] life assurance and superannuation allowances.[6]

[1] Robbins, L., 'Notes on Public Finance', *Lloyds Bank Review*, October 1955, p. 12.

[2] Partly through benefits up to age 21; partly through relief for professional training expenses, and partly through the provision of 'added years' in increased superannuation benefits. These 'added years' are intended to cover years of professional training during which superannuation contributions were not paid (see, for example, *Local Government Superannuation (Benefits) Regulations*, 1954, Reg. 12).

[3] 'A super-tax payer may and quite frequently nowadays does have a number of wives living at the same time since after divorce his ex-wives are not treated as one with him for tax purposes he can manage quite nicely since he is permitted to deduct all his wives' maintenance allowances from his gross income for tax purposes leaving his net income comparatively slightly affected.' (Memorandum by Lord Justice Hodson to the Royal Commission on Marriage and Divorce, MDP/1952/-337).

[4] *Second Report*, pp. 39–40. The allowance rose from a maximum of £45 in 1920 to, in effect, £172 in 1954. On grounds of social policy apparently the Royal Commission thought the present figure excessive.

[5] *Report of the Royal Commission on the Income Tax*, Cmd 615, 1920, para. 296.

[6] The conditions laid down for the right to these various fiscal benefits are mostly far more generous and pay more regard to the social realities of kinship relationships than those specified in the National Insurance Scheme. They merit an anthropological analysis. Under the former, for instance, widows can claim a housekeeper's benefit while, under the latter, elderly widows found by the Ministry to be 'cohabiting' with elderly men have their pensions withdrawn. The fiscal benefit for adult dependants does not stipulate residence with the claimant; the corresponding

The latter benefit, though partly attributable to developments in fiscal policy, would seem to be more logically classified under 'occupational welfare'. It is, therefore, discussed under this head.

Underlying all these individual stories of the growth in fiscal welfare policies is a continuous search for a reasonable 'subsistence minimum' for income tax payers.[1] It was needed as a basis for the various benefits, for fixing exemption limits and for determining the extent to which a taxpayer's kinship relationships and particular states of need should be recognized. This problem is, however, part of a much more fundamental one which has plagued the Royal Commissions after both world wars of reconciling, on the one hand, the imperious demands of preferential social policies with, on the other, 'a general equitable principle' of fairness and progression in assessing individual taxable capacity.[2] This duality of roles is the major source of conflict and confusion. The more that the uniqueness of individual needs and dependencies is recognized and relieved in an occupational society based on individual rewards the more may principles of individual equity fall into disrepute. Since 1920, the concept of individualism in direct taxation has increasingly become more tenuous. For both Royal Commissions, the claims of

National Insurance benefit does. Dependent relatives by marriage are covered for fiscal benefits; they are not prescribed under the Unemployment and Sickness Regulations (see also Section 24 of the National Insurance Act, 1946). There is no limit to the number of dependent relatives for whom fiscal benefits can be claimed; under the National Insurance scheme claimants are allowed only one dependent relative. If, however, payment is made for a dependant wife even one dependant relative is not admissible. The definition of a dependant relative for whom fiscal benefits can be claimed is wide enough to include almost any relative; for National Insurance purposes there is a narrowly prescribed list of kinship relationships. Moreover, male relatives must prove incapacity. This means that benefits can be claimed for a daughter at a University (though she must not earn more than 20*s.* a week in the vacations or at any other time) but not for a son.

[1] Not the least remarkable aspect of this search is the complete absence of any reference in all the relevant reports to the simultaneous search for a 'subsistence minimum' as a basis for social welfare policies from 1920 to the Beveridge Report and subsequently .(See, for example *Second Report*, p. 50 and Shehab, F., *Progressive Taxation*, 1953, especially pp. 260–6).

[2] Cmd 9474, p. 21.

social policy have overruled the claims of individual equity.[1] As a result, the cost of dependant's benefits has risen from a negligible figure in the early 1920's to over £425 m. today.[2] This compares with a total net cost to the Exchequer in 1954–5 of £770 m. for all direct cash payments under national insurance, industrial injuries, family allowances, national assistance and non-contributory pensions.[3]

V

During the period that has witnessed these far-reaching developments in social and fiscal welfare benefits there has also occurred a great expansion in occupational welfare benefits in cash and in kind. They have now reached formidable and widespread proportions as the Final Report of the Royal Commission recognized.[4] Their ultimate cost falls in large measure on the Exchequer. They include pensions for employees, wives and dependants; child allowances; death benefits; health and welfare services; personal expenses for travel, entertainment, dress and

[1] The 1920 Commission concluded 'that in all ranges of income some regard should be had to the taxpayer's marital and family responsibilities.' (Pt II, p. 29). The 1954 Commission went further in their recommendations: '. . . their general tendency is to advocate that the tax scheme should recognize variations of individual circumstance more fully than it does at present.' (*Second Report*, p. 25). It therefore proposed, *inter alia*, a substantial disability benefit without test of means; an automatic infirmity benefit for all taxpayers at age seventy-five again without any test; a dependant relatives' allowance for deserted wives and mothers without proof of incapacity; an extension of the housekeeper allowance to cover non-resident child care services; universal superannuation benefits and so forth (p. 70).

[2] Including only child allowance, dependant relative allowance, age relief, housekeeper allowance, life assurance relief and wife's earned income relief. (Letter from Treasury, November 9, 1955).

[3] Central Statistical Office, *National Income and Expenditure*, 1955, table 37.

[4] Pp. 67–75 and 410–2. In the 1955 Chance Memorial Lecture on 'Welfare in Industry' Mr H. V. Potter gave estimates of the total cost to industry in Britain of what he called 'the social indirect services'. These estimates, for twenty-two million employees, ranged from £550 m. to £880 m. a year (excluding national insurance contributions and statutory holiday payments). They also appear to exclude many of the items listed below involving individual benefits such as personal expenses, car allowances and so forth. (Potter, H. V., *Chemistry and Industry*, September, 1955, pp. 5–7).

equipment; meal vouchers; motor cars and season tickets; residential accommodation; holiday expenses; children's school fees; sickness benefits; medical expenses; education and training grants; cheap meals; unemployment benefit; medical bills[1] and an incalculable variety of benefits in kind ranging from 'obvious forms of realizable goods to the most intangible forms of amenity'.[2] The implications of this trend are cautiously noted by the Royal Commission: 'Modern improvements in the conditions of employment and the recognition by employers of a wide range of obligations towards the health, comfort and amenities of their staff may well lead to a greater proportion of an employee's true remuneration being expressed in a form that is neither money nor convertible into money'.[3]

A substantial part of all these multifarious benefits can be interpreted as the recognition of dependencies; the dependencies of old age, of sickness and incapacity, of childhood, widowhood and so forth. They are in effect, if not in administrative method, 'social services', duplicating and overlapping social and fiscal welfare benefits. The rapidity of their growth in recent years has increasingly diminished the value and relevance of salary, wage and income statistics. Occupational pension schemes, to give one example of the present order of provision, may now cover one-half of the total male labour force (excluding agriculture).[4] Their cost to the Exchequer (including tax-free deferred salaries) already runs to £100 m. a year,[5] a figure substantially in excess of the present Exchequer cost of national insurance pensions.[6] Contrary to the apparent intentions of the 1920 Royal Commission, which considered tax relief for such

[1] To give evidence on one point: according to a statement in the *British Medical Journal*, 25 per cent of all medical bills at one 'leading nursing-home' are paid for their employees by firms. (*Journal Supplement*, October 8, 1955, p. 81).

[2] P. 68.

[3] P. 72.

[4] For more details see Ch. 3. See also *Report of the Committee on the Economic and Financial Problems of the Provision for Old Age* (Cmd 9333, 1954) and Abel-Smith, B., and Townsend P., *New Pensions for the Old*, 1955.

[5] In addition, life assurance relief was costing the Exchequer £35 m. in 1955–6. (Letter from Treasury, November 9, 1955).

[6] See Ch. 3, p. 69.

schemes appropriate for poorer taxpayers, the benefits have increasingly favoured wealthier taxpayers, through the medium of tax-free lump sums and other devices.[1] In this sense, they function as concealed multipliers of occupational success. Sick pay and other 'social service' benefits have followed a similar upward trend. A recent official sample inquiry tentatively suggested that about half the claimants for national insurance sickness benefit were also covered by employer's sick pay schemes, the proportion ranging from one-third among manual workers to 90 per cent for administrators.[2] Adding these benefits together, sickness is now a better financial proposition for many people than health.

No doubt many of these forms of occupational social services express the desire for 'good human relations' in industry. Their provision is part of the model of the 'good' employer.[3] But as they grow and multiply they come into conflict with the aims and unity of social policy; for in effect (whatever their aims may be) their whole tendency at present is to divide loyalties, to nourish privilege, and to narrow the social conscience as they have already done in the United States, in France and in Western Germany.[4] One fundamental question of equity that they raise (which is analogous to that raised by the dual roles of fiscal policy) is whether and to what extent social service dependency

[1] If the far-reaching proposalsf or extended benefits of the Millard Tucker Report are accepted—a State Paper which ranks in importance with the Beveridge Report —the cost of these benefits might well double in a few years, particularly as the Report insists that they 'should not depend on a "means test"'. (*Report of the Committee on the Taxation Treatment of Provisions for Retirement*, Cmd 9063, 1954, p. 101).

[2] The great majority of these schemes were non-contributory. The inquiry was made by the Ministry of Pensions and National Insurance into a 5 per cent sample of new claims for benefit in September, 1953. The results are probably subject to a substantial margin of error. (*Report of the National Insurance Advisory Committee on the Question of Benefit for Short Spells of Unemployment or Sickness*, 1955, paras. 73–5).

[3] The Conservative Party advocates a wide extension in these schemes. (*The Industrial Charter. A Statement of Conservative Industrial Policy*, 1947, p. 30).

[4] See United States Chamber of Commerce, *Fringe Benefits 1953*, and United Nations, *Economic Bulletin for Europe*, 1952, Vol. 4, No. 2.

benefits should be proportionately related to occupational and income achievement. That is a question which, along with others, must be left unexamined in this paper.

VI

Three different systems of 'social services' have been briefly surveyed in this paper. Considered as a whole, their development shows how narrowly conceived and unbalanced are the criticisms so frequently levelled at the one system traditionally known as 'the social services' or, more recently and more ambiguously, as 'The Welfare State'. The latent assumptions which commonly underlie these criticisms can, therefore, have little relevance while they remain attached to a stereotype of social welfare which represents only the more visible part of the real world of welfare. The social history of our times inevitably becomes, in the process, sadly distorted.

At present, these three systems are seen to operate as virtually distinct stratified systems. What goes on within and as a result of one system is ignored by the others. They are appraised, criticized or applauded as abstracted, independent, entities.[1] Yet, despite this division, they all in varying degrees signify that man can no longer be regarded simply as a 'unit of labour power'; they all reflect contemporary opinion that man is not wholly responsible for his dependency, and they all accept obligations for meeting certain dependent needs of the individual and the family. Nevertheless, despite these common social purposes, the search for equity between taxpayers—that like cases should be treated in like manner—proceeds regardless of the need for equity between citizens. The drive to 'buy' good human relations in industry widens class and vocational divisions

[1] The Beveridge Report paid no particular regard to fiscal welfare benefits; the Reports of the Royal Commission on Taxation in discussing social policies virtually ignore the commonly termed 'social services', and the Phillips Committee disregard fiscal benefits even to the extent of suggesting that the development of occupational pension schemes might reduce pension costs falling on the Exchequer (Cmd 9333, p. 64).

through the provision of differential welfare benefits based on occupational achievement. The lack of any precise thinking about what is and what is not a 'social service' confuses and constrains the social conscience, and allows the development of distinctive social policies based on different principles for arbitrarily differentiated groups in the population.

Behind the facts of this development we can see the play of powerful economic and political forces; the strength and tenacity of privilege; the continuing search for equity in a rapidly changing society. Conceptions of 'need' and 'dependency' have simultaneously been profoundly affected by technological, industrial and social change—'the gales of creative destruction' to use Schumpeter's striking phrase.[1] The problems of equity in social policy have thus become more complex as a result of the accumulation of long-lived 'disservices';[2] the increasing division of labour; higher standards of labour specificity; the lengthening of the 'natural' dependencies of childhood and old age; the diversification, creation and decay of functional skills and roles; and the growth of sectional solidarities which, in turn, have tended to enlarge the area and significance of social differentiation. More social differentiation—whether by age, class, education, personality, physical standards, intelligence quotient or professional qualification—may result, as G. Friedmann has observed, in more social inequalities.[3] Failure, ineffectiveness and social inferiority thus acquire a deeper significance. External inequalities—those which do not express natural inequalities—become 'more insupportable as labour becomes more divided'.[4] More insight into the complexities of human stress allied to the tendency of special groups to become more self-conscious leads to the search for sectional equalities. Insofar as

[1] Schumpeter, J. A., *Capitalism, Socialism and Democracy*, p. 84.

[2] Pigou developed systematically the notion of 'uncharged disservices' and 'uncompensated services' in his *The Economics of Welfare* (4th ed., 1932). For a discussion on trends and a more detailed treatment generally see Kapp, K. W., *The Social Costs of Private Enterprise*, 1950.

[3] Friedmann, G., 'The Social Consequences of Technical Progress,' *International Social Science Bulletin*, Vol. IV, No. 2, 1952, p. 254.

[4] Durkheim, *op. cit.* pp. 384–5.

they are achieved, the interests of society as a whole at one extreme, and of the 'unattached' and dependent individual at the other, are subordinated to the interests of the group or class. The aims of equity, ostensibly set for society as a whole, become sectional aims, invariably rewarding the most favoured in proportion to the distribution of power and occupational success.

At the centre of this process of division based on the specialized content of individual occupational performance man becomes more dependent; he also becomes, in the pursuit of individual life goals, more aware of his dependency, more viable to failure, more exposed to pain.[1] The corollary for any society which invests more of its values and virtues in the promotion of the individual is individual failure and individual consciousness of failure.

Within this theoretical framework it becomes possible to interpret the development of these three systems of social service as separate and distinctive attempts to counter and to compensate for the growth of dependency in modern society. Yet, as at present organized, they are simultaneously enlarging and consolidating the area of social inequality. That is the paradox: the new division of equity which is arising from these separate responses to social change. And that, today, is the real challenge to social policy and to those who, mistakingly, still look to the past for a solution.

[1] For extended theoretical treatment see Durkheim, E., *op. cit.*

CHAPTER 3

Pension Systems and Population Change[1]

I

VIEWED historically, it is difficult to understand why the gradual emergence in Britain of a more balanced age structure should be regarded as a 'problem of ageing'. What we have to our credit as humanists and good husbanders is a great reduction in premature death since the nineteenth century; as a result, we have derived many benefits from our growing ability to survive through the working span of life. Much of the inefficiency and waste of early death has been eliminated by an increase in the expectation of life at birth of the working classes to a point that now approaches closer to that achieved by more prosperous classes.

This should be a matter for satisfaction. Paradoxically, however, we are alarmed by our success. Perversely, we speak about the 'crippling' burden of old age, forgetting that the extraordinarily youthful structure of Victorian society entailed a phenomenal rate of growth in numbers and was accompanied by great losses from morbidity and mortality among children and young people.

I believe that the present alarm is unjustified; that the demographic changes which are under way and are foreseeable have been exaggerated, and that unless saner views prevail harm may be done to the public welfare.

The purpose of this essay is to discuss certain aspects of social

[1] Published in *Political Quarterly*, XXVI, No. 2, 1955.

provision for old age and, in particular, some of the issues raised by the report of the Phillips Committee.[1] This involves consideration of five other important state documents which, in one way or another, bear on the question of standards of living for old people.[2] All these reports exhibit in common a deep concern about future population trends.

No attempt is made in this essay to offer alternatives to present policies and practices. What is presented here is a broad analysis of contrasting pension systems in the context of population change.

II

Much of the present anxiety about the effects of an 'ageing' population on the social services can be traced back to the Beveridge Report and the measures that followed from that report. Among a number of factors which heavily influenced the Beveridge recommendations perhaps the most important were the estimates of future population which the report employed. These suggested that the population of pensionable ages[3] in Britain would rise from 5,571,000 or 12 per cent in 1941 to 9,576,000 or 21 per cent in 1971.[4] This projection assumed an unprecedented fall in mortality at the older ages, the significance of which was not made explicit although the assumption of *de-*

[1] *Report of the Committee on the Economic and Financial Problems of the Provision for Old Age*, Cmd 9333, 1954.

[2] *Social Insurance and Allied Services* (Beveridge Report), Cmd 6404, 1942; *Taxation Treatment of Provisions for Retirement* (Millard Tucker Report), Cmd 9063, 1954; *Report by the Government Actuary on the First Quinquennial Review of the National Insurance Scheme*. HCI, 1954–5; *Ministry of Pensions and National Insurance Report on Reasons for Retiring or continuing at Work*, 1954; *First Report of National Advisory Committee on the Employment of Older Men and Women*, Cmd 8963, 1954.

[3] Men sixty-five and over; women sixty and over.

[4] These estimates were taken from the Government's White Paper *Current Trend of Population in Great Britain* (Cmd 6358, 1942). This paper adopted the fundamental assumption of 'generation' improvements in mortality; namely, that past improvements in mortality among younger age groups would, in time, be reflected in lowered mortality at ages over sixty. This is an interesting but speculative hypothesis which can hardly be verified until after 1960 at the earliest.

clining mortality constituted a complete break with practice during the past thirty years of insurance.[1] In striking contrast to this optimism about a substantial lengthening in man's *span of life*—of which there had been little sign in the previous century[2] —was the pessimism of the Government Actuary. In the bases he used in calculating rates of contribution for the Beveridge Report he assumed an increase of 12½ per cent in sickness claims.[3] Within four years he had become more pessimistic; when the contribution rates were settled in 1946 it was assumed that sickness claims would rise by about 20 per cent for men and 25 per cent for women.[4] Simultaneously, the assumptions were also made that there would be a trend towards earlier retirement, that proportionately fewer widows would work, and that unemployment would be as high as 10 per cent for the occupations covered by the existing unemployment scheme.

On the one hand, then, the policy recommendations of the Beveridge Report were influenced by the assumption of a strikingly large increase in the population of pensionable ages thus presupposing some remarkable achievements in arresting the rate of organic decline; on the other hand and contrariwise, contribution rates were fixed in the expectation of more sickness claims, earlier retirement and widespread unemployment. Experience has been very different. Sickness claims (despite or because of a 'free' health service) have been substantially lighter than expected since 1948 (to the extent of about £80 m. or 15 to 20 per cent),[5] unemployment has averaged about 1½ per cent for the insured population, more widows have worked, fewer employed men and women have retired from work,[6] while

[1] Previous insurance projections had been based on constant mortality (see, for example, HC 82 of 1935).

[2] The expectation of life of a man at the age of sixty-five has risen by only about one year since 1838–54. Among women the gain is about three years. (England and Wales: 'The Ageing Population,' Benjamin, B., *Monthly Bulletin of the Ministry of Health*, Vol. 13, December 1954).

[3] Over the experience shown by the National Health Insurance Scheme for the less well-paid sections of the working population.

[4] Cmd 6730, 1946.

[5] For the period July 1948 to March 1954 (HCI, 1954–5, p. 10).

[6] Cmd 9333, p. 24.

death rates among elderly men have risen slightly and those for elderly women have varied little since 1942 from the average for 1950–2.[1]

The revised estimates of future population employed by the Phillips Committee envisage a pensionable population of 9,500,000 in 1979 or 18·2 per cent compared with the more formidable figure for 1971 which influenced the Beveridge Report. Even these lower estimates, however, still make generous assumptions about declining mortality in the future and, once again, the Government Actuary in his report assumes an increase in sickness claims.[2] If we discount the mortality assumption and suggest, instead, that death rates among elderly people will remain at the current level then we have to reduce the elderly population of 1979 to 8,800,000 or 17·2 per cent.[3] By extrapolating the Beveridge estimates to 1979 we obtain, for comparison, a round figure of 10,500,000. It thus appears that the figures used by Beveridge envisaged 1,700,000 more elderly people in 1979 than are indicated by a 1954 estimate assuming constant mortality. Nor is this all. A revised estimate in 1954 by the Ministry of Labour of the expected *working* population in 1979 gives a figure of over 1,000,000 more producers than had previously been forecast.[4]

Swings of such magnitude in favour of production and away from 'dependency' cannot but lift much of the gloom that settled on the pages of Beveridge and which has brooded over social policy ever since. According to the figures in the Phillips Report the ratio of the working population of all ages to total population was 47·0 per cent in 1954. On the assumptions put forward in the report about mortality and fertility, and if the proportion of persons gainfully occupied in each age group bears the same relationship as at present to the total population in each age

[1] Cmd 9333, p. 18.

[2] HCI, 1954–5, p. 45.

[3] A figure of 8,723,000 for 1977 is given by Projection No. 1 of the Royal Commission on Population. This was based on a continuation of the relatively low mortality of 1942–4 (*Royal Commission, Selected Papers*, Vol. II, 1950).

[4] Compare Table VII of the Phillips Report with p. 11 of the Report of the National Advisory Committee (Cmd 8963), 1953.

group, this ratio will fall to 46·7 per cent in 1979 or by only 0·3 per cent. If, however, it is assumed that mortality will remain constant among the pensionable population the ratio of 'producers' will actually rise to 47·3 per cent.[1] By a small margin, this would give Britain the highest proportion of producers to non-producers than at any other time since, at least, the beginning of this century.[2] There will, of course, be a decided shift in 'dependency' to the elderly as the number of pensionable people rises by about 2 to 2½ million but, on the assumptions made, the total burden of dependency in terms of numbers is not likely to be greater than it is now.

We may sum up here by saying that we are half-way—or perhaps more than half-way—in a long-term shift from an 'abnormally' youthful population in the nineteenth century to a more 'normal' age structure in a relatively 'stable' population in the 1970's. Given the expected increase in the working population, this shift does not appear to raise acute economic problems. But it does involve far-reaching adjustments in the distribution of goods and services. Inevitably, this is a painful process. No modern industrial society has yet faced squarely the redistributive implications of adjusting to a more 'normal', relatively stable population. And because, in a sense, some part of the adjustment process has to be planned and experienced in advance of the expected changes the expected effects may, for various reasons, be exaggerated. This arises inevitably from the nature of pension systems which decide to a substantial extent the future pattern of distribution both vertical and horizontal. Once founded—or thought to be founded—on actuarial concepts these systems become highly resistant to change. Contributory 'rights' and privileges, spanning perhaps fifty years, become sacrosanct. It follows that decisions taken yesterday and today about the 'build-up' of rights to income in old age will substantially determine the allocation of

[1] Assuming 700,000 fewer pensionable people (6 per cent working).

[2] See also Table 2 'The Growth of Pension Rights and their Impact on the National Economy', Bacon, F. W., and others, *Journal of the Institute of Actuaries*, Vol. 50, Pt 2, No. 355, 1954.

claims on resources among different sections of the elderly population in the future.

All the adjustments involved in changing over to a different population structure can only be made with the minimum of social friction if the redistributive effects are equitably shouldered. They are as much a national affair as war or mass unemployment. It thus behoves us to take account of the total complex apparatus of social policy in relation to old age—direct taxation as well as compulsory contributions representing the two main strands. As yet, we are, it is suggested, making explicit decisions today about only one sector of provision for old age—the national insurance scheme—and we are making them under the influence of exaggerated notions concerning the future 'burden of ageing'. In essence, this article constitutes a plea for a wider view; for social change to be accompanied and eased by social justice.

The need for such a view may now be demonstrated; first, by considering the development of national insurance; second, by examining the growth of private pension rights.

III

To understand the apprehensions in the recent past about the 'burden of ageing' explains in part the relative harshness of the Beveridge pension proposals. One example will suffice. The report insisted that contributions should be paid over the whole of working life instead of the 'generous'[1] five-year contributory period in the then existing system. This was part of the price of providing retirement pensions 'at above subsistence needs'.[2] Another part of the price was that such pensions could be given only to persons who retired from work. Hence the introduction of the retirement condition. This established a basic difference in the treatment of persons with national insurance

[1] So described by the International Labour Office in a review of social security systems (*Beveridge Report*, Appendix F).

[2] P. 90.

pensions and those in receipt of pensions from their employers.

In the future, a considerable proportion (perhaps one-third to one-half) of the male working population will be receiving pensions from their employers to which the Exchequer will have contributed a substantial proportion. In taking their pensions and 'retiring' from their employers they will not, however, have to 'retire' from work. Those without such pensions will have, as the Beveridge Report proposed,[1] to retire from work as a 'logical consequence of receiving a full subsistence income' through a national insurance pension.[2] If they continue in work so as to earn an increment to these pensions they will not be accorded 'exact actuarial equity'. The Beveridge Report recommended (endorsed by the Phillips Report)[3] that actuarial principles should be dropped and that such people should receive only part of the saving resulting from postponed retirement. It might thus be argued that the saving to the Fund, chiefly contributed by manual workers, helps to subsidize those who retire earlier.[4]

IV

The Phillips Report, while taking a less serious view of future population trends, was alarmed at the 'mounting burden' on the Exchequer as a result of the growth in expenditure on national insurance pensions. The figures are given in that report and in the reports from the Government Actuary[5] and will be only summarily stated here. On the basis of the higher benefits and contributions under the 1954 Act it is estimated that in 1955–6

[1] Pp. 59 and 95.

[2] Apart from the rule under which casual or part-time earnings up to £2 a week are disregarded. No attempt is made here to assess the 'full subsistence' value of the present pension.

[3] P. 53.

[4] The substantial differences in the length of working life between manual and non-manual workers, particularly after age 60, are shown in the report on *Reasons for Retiring or continuing at Work*.

[5] HCI, 1954–5 and Cmd 9332, 1954.

total expenditure under the National Insurance Scheme will amount to £652 m. (retirement pensions £436 m.) and that total income will be £651 m. The cost to the Exchequer for all benefits will be £91 m., or about £50 m. less than was estimated by the Beveridge Report and when the 1946 Act was passed.[1] Thus, the scheme is now costing the Exchequer substantially less than was expected when it was introduced; when it was formulated by Beveridge and, for pensions alone, when the pensionable age for women was reduced to 60 in 1940.[2] This relief to the Exchequer is partly attributable to favourable claims and contributions experience and partly to the fact that contributors are now carrying a higher proportion of the costs of all insurance benefits. The point is further discussed later.

Despite, however, the favourable Exchequer outcome during the past five years the Phillips Committee, looking to the growth of the unfunded deficit, proposes that a still higher proportion should be borne by contributors. Estimates of future income and outgo by the Government Actuary (under the 1954 Act) suggest that the cost of pensions will rise from £436 m. in 1955–6 to £798 m. in 1979–80. This assumes, as pointed out above, a decline in mortality rates and may be, therefore, an over-estimate. The emerging deficiency or unfunded deficit (estimated at £424 m.) arises, as was expected, from in part the method of finance and in part from the terms which, at the outset, were accorded both to persons already contributing or drawing benefit under earlier schemes and to the new classes coming into insurance for the first time. Unless a society is prepared to wait fifty years before a pension scheme is fully operative all this is inevitable. But it does raise the question: how should the costs be distributed of the 'uncovered' capital liability of the past and of additional 'uncovered' costs arising from inflation and higher benefits?

It was a fundamental principle of the scheme when it was enacted that, in addition to a statutory Exchequer supplement to

[1] The total cost to the Exchequer in 1955 was put at £141 m. in the *Beveridge Report* (pp. 199 and 206) and £143 m. in the 1946 White Paper (Cmd 6730, p. 17).
[2] Cmd 6169, 1940, p. 9.

tripartite insurance, all capital liabilities and excess expenditure should be met, as the deficiencies emerged, out of general taxation. Provision was, however, made for a small or 'token' payment in the future by contributors towards the emerging deficiency. The 1951 Act gave expression to this requirement by raising contributions. The 1954 Act continues and extends this policy for, as the Government Actuary points out, the new contributions 'are materially greater than the amounts of the actuarial contributions'.[1] The Phillips Committee now proposes a further extension of this policy.

Yet there is nothing particularly new or surprising about the future picture emerging deficiencies as drawn by the Phillips Report; it was expected by both the Beveridge Report and by the 1946 Act. It was, indeed, expected in 1925 when Mr Winston Churchill and the Government of the day, foreseeing the coming increase in the number of old people, began a thirty-year process of transferring more of the cost of all pensions to insurance contributors.[2] The estimates framed at that time of the number of persons of pensionable ages expected in 1954 were within 7 per cent of the actual number in 1954.[3] To make this contributory Act of 1925 more attractive and because, in effect, it reversed the decision in 1911 that pensions were too heavy a burden to be laid on a contributory insurance scheme,[4] the pensionable age for men was reduced to sixty-five—an historical fact which makes it more difficult for the present Government to now raise the age as recommended by the Phillips Committee. Even so, the estimates made in 1925 of the cost of all pensions to the Exchequer in the 1950's were, in fact, substantially higher than they actually are today despite the changes in the value of money which have occurred.[5]

[1] Cmd 9332, pp. 5–6.

[2] Widows' Orphans' and Old Age Contributory Pensions Act 1925. Also *Hansard*, 1924–5, Vol. 183, col. 71 *et seq*.

[3] Cmd 2406, 1925.

[4] Cmd 5995, 1911. This Explanatory Memorandum to the Bill emphasized the disadvantages of the German contributory scheme which had to carry the 'burden' of pensions.

[5] The cost to the Exchequer of all pensions in 1955 was estimated in 1925 at

What is different in 1955 is that pensions are now costing the Exchequer considerably less than they were expected to do in 1925, in 1940, in 1942 and in 1946, and that the future looks much less 'burdensome' than it did when the Beveridge Report was written. What is also different is that a higher proportion of the total costs of all benefits is now being borne by contributors. This situation has come about as a result of two main factors. First, the effects of a policy pursued since 1925 of transferring to contributors an increased proportion of the pension costs of adjusting to a more 'normal' age structure; second, as a consequence of a gradual reduction in the Exchequer's contribution to the costs of other insurance benefits. Under the 1954 Act, the Exchequer supplement as a proportion of the employee-employer weekly contribution for the main body of employed persons is 17 per cent. In respect to all benefits, therefore, the combined weekly contribution from employees and employers at present (1954–5) covers 83 per cent of the cost including expenditure on administration, subsidies to Northern Ireland,[1] training costs[2] and other items.[3] This proportion is much greater than that which obtained before 1948 and, indeed, in any period in the history of national insurance since 1911. Before 1948, the Exchequer's contribution to unemployment insurance had been 50 per cent of the combined contribution thus upholding, for the 'risk' of unemployment, the sacred principle of tripartite contributions. The 'continuance of the tripartite scheme for financing social security'[4] was stressed by the Beveridge Report, particularly on the ground that at least one-third of the cost of unemployment benefit should be borne, according to the accepted values in income tax of 'fairness and progression', by the whole community. The Exchequer's contribution to sickness benefit

£78 m. (Cmd 2406, 1925). In 1955 prices this is equivalent to £162 m. (London and Cambridge Economic Service Retail Price Index). Excluding remitted tax, the current cost to the Exchequer of all contributory and non-contributory pensions is approximately £65 m.

[1] Amounting to over £13 m. up to March 1954 (HCI, 1954–5, p. 22).

[2] Under the Employment and Training Act, 1948 (S. 3(6)).

[3] Excluding interest and contributions to the National Health Service.

[4] P. 109.

during 1912–48 was about 15 per cent for men and 20 per cent for women,[1] a higher proportion than under the 1954 Act when allowance is made for the imposition on the insurance fund since 1948 of a flat rate charge of £40 m. a year towards the cost of the National Health Service.[2] For all old age pensions, the Exchequer's share of the total contributions or expenditure during 1925–48 was greater than it is now.[3] A similar shift towards the contributory system has taken place in respect to the costs of industrial injuries. With the changeover from workmen's compensation to a funded National Insurance (Industrial Injuries) Scheme a large part of the costs—in effect a subsidy to industry—is now borne by the employee.[4] The Exchequer's share of total contributions is now 17 per cent. Expenditure under this scheme is expected to rise from £30 m. to £65 m. in 1979–80. Over half this rise is accounted for by the pension element in disablement benefits which will be carried, in the main, by contributors.

Taking a long view, the direction of all these changes over the whole field of national insurance is to place a larger proportion of the costs of unemployment, sickness, injuries, old age, maternity and widowhood on to a flat-rate compulsory contribution. If the proposals of the Phillips Committee are implemented little will remain in practice of the concept of tripartite social insurance. In retrospect, the financial recommendations of the Beveridge Report can now be seen as playing a critical role in influencing this long-term trend partly because of the fears, so prominent in its financial calculations, concerning the future 'burden of ageing'. If we desire more and not less equity in the social processes of adjusting to a 'normal' age structure then it would seem that there can be no 'return to Beveridge'. In a sentence,

[1] At the start, in 1912, the proportions were: men 22 per cent, women 25 per cent (Cmd 5995, 1911). The Exchequer contribution was reduced in 1926 as a result of the 'Geddes Axe' and was not, subsequently, reinstated (Economy (Miscellaneous) Provisions Act, 1926).

[2] As Lafitte pointed out in 1945 this regressive poll-tax was unprecedented and indefensible (Lafitte, F., *Britain's Way to Social Security*, pp. 100–1).

[3] Wilson, A., and Mackay, G. S., *Old Age Pensions*, Ch. XII, 1941; and HC 82, 1935.

[4] HC 22, 1954–5, pp. 2, 18 and 26.

the obvious answer is that these costs—the long-term and foreseeable dependencies of old age—should be shouldered by progressive taxation just as the long-term dependencies of childhood are. Such short-term and unforeseeable contingencies as unemployment, sickness and injuries may still be considered appropriate 'risks' for tripartite social insurance.

As things are at present, the heaviest weight of transferring more of the costs of pensions to contributors falls upon the less well-paid sections of the working population. There are at least two reasons for this. First, those persons brought into the scheme in 1948 and who will first receive pensions in 1958 along with their wives will, in effect, be subsidized by the classes who were paying contributions before 1948 and, in some cases, back to 1925. The former are mainly composed of persons earning more than £420 a year in 1948, bank and insurance officials previously outside the national system in special non-contributory schemes, civil servants and local government officials. Many of this group (totalling about one-third of a million) who were accorded generous ten-year terms under the 1946 Act[1] will also receive in and after 1958 superannuation from their employers.

The second and principal reason is the effect of a flat-rate contributory system which, unlike direct taxation with its elaborate search for equity between two taxpayers with different dependencies, pays no regard to individual circumstances.[2] It has, indeed, been one of the outstanding features of income-tax policy during recent decades that it has increasingly sought for a greater adjustment of tax to individual circumstances. Many of the recommendations of the Second Report of the Royal Commission on Taxation and the Millard Tucker Report heavily underline this

[1] An entrant at age 55 in 1948 will receive in July, 1958 a pension of which less than 10 per cent will have been covered by contributions paid.

[2] Professor Hicks, in his Reservation concerning a higher income tax exemption limit, argued that the effects of taxation and compulsory contributions should be considered together. He preferred to see more weight being placed on direct taxation because it attempted to adjust capacity to pay to individual circumstances, and less weight being laid on the less equitable taxes (*Second Report of the Royal Commission on the Taxation of Profits and Income*, Cmd 9105, 1954, p. 90).

policy.[1] Yet, on the whole, the national insurance scheme is working in precisely the opposite direction. Not only does this lead to less 'fairness and progression'; to a steady retreat from the principle of progressive taxation adopted, before the first world war, in place of a proportional tax, but it often contradicts accepted social policies in other spheres. One illustration must suffice. At a time when the demands of the economic situation require that all who can—and especially older workers, married women, the partially disabled and other actuarial 'bad risks'—should make as large a contribution as possible to production the effect of the 'insurance principle' is to tax heavily some forms of part-time work. Thus, while social policy sets out to encourage part-time employment the national insurance scheme demands that—to take an extreme example—women working only for one employer and earning, say, 12*s.* 6*d.* a week must pay a contribution of 5*s.* 6*d.* a week.[2] The employer is taxed to the extent of 4*s.* 11*d.* a week.[3]

The higher the contributions are pushed because of the real or supposed 'burden of ageing' the more regressive in its effects will this poll-tax system become and the more may conflicts arise between the requirements of this system and the objectives of social policy. In contrast to this method of financing a 'social service' for income needs in old age we now turn to consider a second 'social service' with a similar purpose but quite dissimilar principles and methods.

V

It would not seem inappropriate to apply the term 'social service' to private pension schemes for two particular reasons. First, because these schemes, in pursuing a similar objective to

[1] Cmd 9105 and Cmd 9063, 1954.

[2] Working for more than four hours a week in any employment other than domestic work.

[3] Professor Robson, in a dissenting note in 1948 to a report of the National Insurance Advisory Committee, commented on the possible effects of the regulations in preventing and penalizing part-time work (Report of the Committee on National Insurance (Classification) Regulations, 1948).

national insurance of providing for the dependent needs of old age and widowhood, are supported in various ways by state policy. Secondly, because for many individuals covered by these schemes the percentage Exchequer contribution to the 'build up' and taxation treatment of pension rights may be at present two to three times higher than the percentage Exchequer contributions today to *all* benefits under the national insurance scheme.[1] For retirement benefits alone, the total Exchequer payment under this scheme is at present about £45 m.[2] (plus about £34 m. in remitted tax)[3] whereas the cost to the Exchequer of private pension schemes (though covering a substantially smaller proportion of the population) is already £100 m. a year.[4] This figure may well be an under-estimate. It was officially made several years ago, since when the numbers covered by these schemes have probably been growing by 500,000 a year, and it takes no account of the loss of revenue resulting from the payment of lump sums, other *ex gratia* pension benefits and various unestimated factors. When such sums are paid the employee is taxed neither on his benefit nor on the notional contributions the employee would have had to make to provide it. The last ten years have witnessed a phenomenal growth in private schemes. The essence of most of these schemes is to spread the employee's remuneration (and generally a higher total remuneration) over a longer period than the period of actual service, so that he becomes chargeable at a lower rate of tax during that service and, in addition, obtains a right or option under which all or part of the remuneration so deferred can be received in non-taxable lump sum form (up to £40,000) plus superannuation carrying a lower rate of tax. The effect, of course, is to sharply reduce the gradient of progressive taxation.

[1] Compare the Exchequer's contribution of 17 per cent with the figures given on pp. 20–3 'The Growth of Pension Rights', Bacon, F. W., and others, 1954.

[2] Estimated at half the total supplement (see 'The Growth of Pension Rights', p. 10).

[3] On that part of the weekly contribution relating to pensions. This remission has, of course, the effect of accentuating the regressive nature of the contribution. (*Hansard*, December 13, 1954, Vol. 535, col. 1441).

[4] Cmd 9333, p. 62.

Apart from 1,000 or so separate public service pension schemes (covering about 2½ million persons) which are excluded from the scope of this article, there are two main types of private schemes. These may be distinguished from a bewildering variety of methods all of which, by private arrangement, are determining the future allocation among retired persons of claims on the available supply of goods and services.

Either a pension fund is administered by an employer himself under trust, or a pension scheme is administered by an insurance company in return for premiums. Beginning with executive and salaried classes in commerce and industry, schemes of both types have in recent years been extended to include manual workers. The two classes are treated differently. Pensions and lump sum benefits for the executive and salaried classes are often related to the last year's salary before pension or to the average salary over the last three or five years' service. For manual workers, what counts is the number of years of service. No distinction is drawn between the unskilled worker and the chargehand; earnings do not usually effect the size of the pension which, in the most generous schemes, averages about 50*s.* a week after 50 years' service. These schemes may be contributory or non-contributory, but the general trend appears to be in the direction of non-contributory arrangements. The present tax law governing these voluntary and contractual schemes is complicated, inconsistent, and arbitrary. On the principle that income should be taxed only once, employers' and employees' pension contributions are not taxed, while tax is, in general, levied on all pensions and annuities (beneficially treated as earned income). This principle is violated, however, by the payment of lump sums which, so long as there is no contractual right to such sums, are free of tax subject to certain conditions laid down by the Inland Revenue Commissioners. Employees covered by approved superannuation trust funds enjoy the further advantage that all investment and deposit interest on such funds is completely exempt from tax.

A large and growing number of private schemes are established for individual employees and approved for tax exemption.

In a frequent case in the salary range £4,000–£5,000, for which the employer pays the whole contribution of £1,600 a year (allowed for tax) for sixteen years, the benefits are life cover until retirement of £28,000, a tax-free lump sum of £7,000, and a taxable pension for life of £1,900 a year. To achieve this himself through ordinary life assurance would have cost the employee £3,200 a year. Over the sixteen years, therefore, the taxpayer will have contributed the balance of £25,600.

It is a matter of great difficulty to estimate the extent of private retirement schemes, let alone the size of future commitments. The Phillips Committee made no serious attempt to investigate these matters, nor did it suggest that the thousands of unscanned files in the Board of Inland Revenue might repay study. In its report it devotes only about ten of its 120 pages to considering this category of social service provision and offers but a few out-of-date, inadequate and undefined statistics. The various 'guessed' estimates that have been made of the number of persons now covered by private schemes range from three to five-and-a-half million apart from one-and-a-half million in schemes run by the nationalized industries. The total may be in excess of seven million, the vast majority of whom are men. Including the public service schemes, it may be that about 50 per cent of the total male labour force in civil employment in Britain (excluding agriculture) have now been granted certain rights or claims on the future production of the community. In terms of individual rights, the most costly Exchequer element is represented by individual and 'top hat' pension schemes. The Phillips Report gives a minimum figure for 1953 of 400,000 'lives' and a total sum assured of about £350 m.[1] The present and future cost to the Exchequer—particularly for tax-free lump sum benefits—is not known. It may be that something like 25 per cent of 'top-hat' pension rights will be taken in tax-free lump sums.[2]

Although these private schemes are at present more 'costly' to the Exchequer than national insurance pensions, the Phillips

[1] P. 115.
[2] Estimated in 'The Growth of Pension Rights', p. 54.

Committee made no attempt to estimate their future role in the economy. So far as Exchequer costs are concerned, however, it does not look as though the future position will be very different from that which obtains today. The number of employees covered by private schemes has been growing at the rate of 10 per cent a year;[1] the cost of benefits actually payable (those already contracted for) is expected to increase about six times in the next thirty years whereas the cost of national insurance pensions will rise by only about one to one-and-a-half times;[2] and as a substantial element in private schemes is based on final salaries any increases in salary are heavily reflected in increased pensions and, thus, in a greater loss of revenue resulting from higher tax-free lump sums and lower rates of taxation. Unless continual adjustments are made, the effect of inflation falls almost wholly on those whose pensions are based on average wages over most of working life (as in private schemes for manual workers) or average contributions (as in national insurance pensions). By contrast, many non-manual workers are, relatively speaking, strongly shielded against inflation in the future—but at the expense of higher Exchequer costs.

For these and other reasons it would seem that, considered solely from the Exchequer's viewpoint, private pensions in the future may outweigh in importance national insurance pensions. If the recommendations of the Millard Tucker Report are accepted by the Government they are likely to become even more important.[3] This report, perhaps the most significant social document published in Britain since the Beveridge Report, proposes that the 'special indulgences' accorded to a privileged group[4] in the form of tax-free lump sums, special contribution reliefs, 'back-service' allowances, tax-free investment income and other pension concessions should be extended, as a matter of justice, to the self-employed, controlling directors, part-time directors

[1] Schemes effected through Life Offices ('The Growth of Pension Rights', p. 12).
[2] 'The Growth of Pension Rights', pp. 10–11.
[3] Cmd 9063, 1954.
[4] So described by the Royal Commission on the Income Tax, 1920, Cmd 615, para. 296.

and employees not at present covered by any scheme arranged by their employers. The total cost of all recommendations for this element of 'retirement justice' is guessed to be over £70 m. This would raise the total Exchequer cost of private pensions to over £170 m. in comparison with the present Exchequer cost of national insurance pensions of approximately £80 m.[1] What the ultimate costs will be it is impossible to say; that the structure of British society is likely to be profoundly changed can hardly be disputed.

The Phillips Committee looked with favour on private schemes; they regarded their continued development as desirable. They did so by advancing the curious argument that such development 'might, in the long run, give substantial relief to the Exchequer'.[2] The expansion of private schemes is also supported in the Conservative Party's *The Workers' Charter* and by *The Economist*, the latter maintaining that the Millard Tucker Report should be viewed as a non-political document.[3] These and other advocates all appear to dismiss lightly the danger of a gradual hardening in the economic arteries of the nation which may result from the growth of restrictions on industrial and commercial mobility, and from the extension of employers' control over pension rights. Yet these new laws of settlement may, in time, constitute impediments to change as formidable in their own way as the laws which Adam Smith indicted in 1776.

VI

This essay has not attempted more than a broad statement of the facts and estimates about pensions and superannuation now and in the future. Its main purpose has been to rescue from the obscurity of a mass of technical detail the essential elements in present policies and practices. The outlines of a dangerous social schism are clear, and they are enlarging. The direction in which

[1] Including remitted tax (£34 m.).
[2] P. 62.
[3] February 20, 1954, p. 555.

the forces of social and fiscal policy are moving raises fundamental issues of justice and equality; not simply issues of justice between taxpayers as a separate class, or between contributors as a separate class, but between all citizens. Already it is possible to see two nations in old age; greater inequalities in living standards after work than in work; two contrasting social services for distinct groups based on different principles, and operating in isolation of each other as separate, autonomous, social instruments of change.

CHAPTER 4

War and Social Policy[1]

PROFESSOR GIBBS, in reappraising the contribution made by Clausewitz to military studies,[2] has politely but firmly criticized past historians for bringing their histories to a stop when the guns started firing, and in opening a new chapter only with the return of peace—of normal diplomatic and institutional relationships between sovereign States. Following Clausewitz—a much misunderstood thinker—Professor Gibbs deplored this historical interregnum. He was faced with a lack of balance in the material available to him in reflecting about the nature of war and society. He could hardly complain, however, about the *quantity* of historical studies at his disposal. Military and naval documents, regimental histories, the lives of captains and kings, political, diplomatic and even philosophical works jostle each other for a place in the crowded 'war' index and bear witness to the energy and interests of past students of war, and to the endemic character of war in the history of man.

By contrast, I am doubly handicapped in discussing the relationship of war and social policy. So far as the story of modern war before 1939 is concerned, little has been recorded in any systematic way about the social and economic effects of war on the population as a whole. Only long and patient research in out-of-the-way documentary places can reveal something of the

[1] Delivered at King's College, London, on March 3, 1955, in a series of public lectures on 'War and Society'. A shortened version was published in *The Listener*, November 3, 1955.

[2] Printed in *The Listener*, October 6, 1955.

characteristics and flavour of social life during the experience of wars in the past. And these records are often undisciplined and unreliable. There are, for example, somewhat highly-coloured accounts of popular reactions on the south coasts of England to the threat of invasion when Napoleon Bonaparte was master of all Western Europe; of the effects of the Crimean and Boer Wars on poor law policy in those days; of a remarkable decline in criminal behaviour among civilians in Britain during the First World War and an equally remarkable outbreak of panic among the civilians of London when the first Zeppelins arrived with their primitive bombs, most of which failed to explode.[1] But even such accounts, unreliable as they may be, are hard to come by. And, strangely enough, one often turns away from the novelists in disappointment; it is difficult to believe, for instance, that some of Jane Austen's novels were written during one of the great wars in history; a war which signified for this country, if the late Professor Greenwood got his sums right, a proportionately greater loss of life among soldiers and sailors than during the First World War and, consequently, more widespread effects among the families of those who served in the Armed Forces.[2]

These are some of the reflections which I have recalled—though in a more tranquil mood—from the days when I was engaged on the Social Policy History of the Second World War. In studying the effects of the evacuation of civilians from London and other cities, I was led to wonder whether there were any recorded accounts of the movement of civilian populations in past wars as a calculated element in war strategy. I had to go back to the Greeks—to the great Hellenic wars—before I was rewarded. Here is Plutarch's description of the evacuation of the civilian population of Athens as a military necessity during the Persian invasion in 480 BC. The Peloponnesian city of Troezen,

[1] See Titmuss, Richard M., *Problems of Social Policy*, 1950, and Trotter, W. *Instincts of the Herd in Peace and War*, 1916, and *British Medical Journal* (1940) i, 270.

[2] Greenwood, M., 'British Loss of Life in the Wars of 1794–1815 and 1914–8', *Journal of the Royal Statistical Society*, Vol. CV, Pt 1, 1942.

on the far side of the Saronic Gulf, became (what we now call) a 'reception area'. According to Plutarch, 'The most part of them [the Athenians] did convey their aged fathers and mothers, their wives and little children, into the city of Troezen, where the Troezenians received them very lovingly and gently. For they gave order that they should be entertained of the common charge, allowing them apiece, two oboloes of their money a day, and suffered the young children to gather fruit wheresoever they found it, and furthermore, did hire schoolmasters at the charge of the commonwealth, to bring them up at school.'[1]

From this account it would seem that conscious thought was given by the responsible authorities to the social and psychological needs of the evacuated population. There was, in fact, a plan; a concerted social policy; a deliberate public attempt to foresee events; to estimate behaviour; to minimize hardships and to control a social situation in the interests of a community at war.

It was this fragment of history, illuminating the way in which war and social policy influence each other, that helped to shape the ideas for this essay. In discussing social policy, I mean those acts of Governments deliberately designed and taken to improve the welfare of the civil population in time of war. I am not, therefore, simply concerned with the social and biological consequences of war; my main interest, then, is with the organized attempts of Governments to control these consequences. Much of what I have to say will be confined to the experiences of this country since the middle of the nineteenth century. For a definition of 'social', I take, for convenience, the scope of the two published volumes on social policy during the Second World War. There is, however, a difficulty here which cannot be so lightly resolved. In essence, it is the problem of distinguishing between policies related to peace-time needs and policies concerned only with the immediate war-time situation. It is bound up with the assumption that war is an abnormal situation; that peace is—or ought to be—the normal lot of mankind.

In considering, however, the results of deliberate attempts to

[1] *Vita Themistoclis*, 10, 5 (North's translation).

organize a society for war—either in the military, economic or social spheres—we are confronted with one of the major characteristics of large-scale, modern war; the fact that modern war casts its shadow long before it happens and that its social effects are felt for longer and longer periods after armed conflict has ceased. In the time-scale of these effects, modern war stretches over a greater span of men's lives, unlike the wars of religion and those wars which Toynbee called in his studies of *War and Civilization*, 'The sport of Kings'.[1] Many of them started abruptly, without planning; without any preparatory action to provide for the needs of the civilian population; without any consideration of how war might affect the social and economic life of the country. They were, in fact, organized military wars; otherwise, and apart from the particular territories over which battles were fought, normal life proceeded—and was assumed to proceed—normally. By contrast, however, as the plans and policies of twentieth-century Governments for war and peace have become more inter-related it is, in consequence, increasingly difficult to detach the 'abnormal' from the 'normal', and to attribute precisely the acts of Government to one or other of these situations.

I turn now to consider how developments in modern war have affected social policy. It is a commonplace among students of the subject that in our recent Western history war has been following war in an ascending order of intensity. In scale, in depth and in time, war has been waged more intensively and ferociously. This crescendo in the organization of war has enveloped a larger proportion of the total population and, as I said earlier, has left its marks on them for a longer period of time. These developments during the past hundred years have affected social policy in a variety of ways. Among these, perhaps the dominating one has been the increasing concern of the State in time of war with the biological characteristics of its people. The growing scale and intensity of war has stimulated a growing concern about the quantity and quality of the population.

[1] Toynbee, A., *War and Civilization*, 1951.

We may mark certain well-defined stages in this progression of biological interests. The first stage of organized interest was with quantity; with the number of men available for battle. This, of course, developed as the scale upon which war was fought increased, and it was no longer safe for the authorities to assume that there were abundant supplies of men available. This growing concern with quantity at different periods and in different societies has been one of the forces which has stimulated the interest of Governments in population trends and in the taking of national censuses. As we know from our own history of vital statistics, opposition was raised in the nineteenth century to census operations because of a fear that they were being carried out for military reasons.

The second stage in this progression is marked by the increasing adoption of qualitative standards applied to military and naval recruits. No doubt a connection can be traced between secular changes in these standards as to what constitutes 'fitness for service' and the increasing mechanization and division of labour in the armed forces. The standards demanded have risen enormously in this country since the day, just over one hundred years ago, when Florence Nightingale discovered that the British Army Medical Service was staffed by a few clerks and an odd messenger boy or two. We now have the most complex system of standards comprising a variety of physical, functional, psychological and social attributes. According to the Editor of the *International Journal of Psycho-Analysis*, 'It was not love but war-time necessity which made American psychiatry turn towards Freud'.[1] He suggests that one of the principal reasons why psychiatry occupies such a commanding position in the American social scene today is because of what he calls the 'unforgettable role' that psychiatrists played in the organization of the war effort.

All this has two important implications for social policy; first, that increasingly higher demands are made upon society for those who are physically and psychologically fit, intellectually

[1]Hoffer, W., *Lancet* (1954), ii, 1234.

bright, and socially acceptable on grounds of personality and character; second, that, as a result, the proportion of men rejected and invalided from the Armed Forces tends to rise rather than fall. Many then become the clients of the social services. This is one example which shows that what is done in the name of 'defence' determines, in substantial measure, some of the roles and functions of the social services. The social costs of the Boer War and the First World War, as measured by expenditure on pensions, widows' benefits, medical care, rehabilitation, sickness claims, rent subsidies, and national assistance, represent a substantial proportion of the social service budget today.

The third stage of interest is reached when public concern about the standard of fitness of men of military age moves out, in a widening circle of policy, to embrace concern about the health and well-being of the whole population and, in particular, of children—the next generation of recruits. This stage was reached in Britain at the beginning of the century, and it is worth inquiring a little more closely into events at that time because of their importance for the subsequent development of public health policies.

It was the South African War, not one of the notable wars in human history to change the affairs of man, that touched off the personal health movement which led eventually to the National Health Service in 1948. Public concern was aroused at the end of the war by the facts that were published about sickness and mortality among the troops, and by a report from the Inspector-General of Recruiting which spoke of 'the gradual deterioration of the physique of the working classes from whom the bulk of the recruits must always be drawn'.[1] At a time when many leaders of opinion still held to the nineteenth-century doctrine of the inevitably of social progress, this report from the Inspector-General came as a shock. Could it be, at the end of a century of unprecedented material progress, that the health and fitness of the bulk of the population was deteriorating? There followed, in rapid succession, one commission of inquiry after another into

[1] See *Report of the Inter-departmental Committee on Physical Deterioration*, Vol. 1, especially App. 1, p. 96, Cd 2175, 1904.

these questions of physical deterioration, systems of medical inspection, the causes of high infant mortality and many other matters affecting the well-being of the population.

As a consequence of this ferment of inquiry we may trace the establishment in 1906 of the school medical service, the school feeding of children in elementary schools, a campaign to reduce infant mortality and many other social measures.

All these elements of social policy stemmed directly from the Boer War and show how, in modern times, our concern for communal fitness has followed closely upon the course of our military fortunes. The story repeats itself in the First World War. In 1917, for example, we may note the introduction of the first instalment of a free national health service when facilities were offered, to civilians and soldiers alike, for the treatment and prevention of venereal disease. At the close of the war a new phrase 'a C3 nation' crept into contemporary journalism after the Report of the Ministry of National Service had told the country that only one man in three of nearly two-and-a-half million examined was completely fit for military service.[1] Most of these men are now in their sixties and account, in substantial measure, for the high proportion who are retiring from work today on grounds of ill-health—a matter to which a recent report from the Ministry of Pensions and National Insurance has drawn attention.[2] It is possible that, among many other reasons, the age of retirement for men in the national insurance scheme has not been raised because of the long-range effects of the First World War.

The ancient Greeks, in attaching some moral significance to the idea of keeping fit, almost as though they had convinced themselves that vigour of body was an absolute good, had, we may now remember, sound reasons for keeping fit. Their civilization involved them in continuous wars; and so, we must admit, has our civilization of the twentieth century.

When we consider the effects of the Second World War, a war in Britain which depended not on the efforts of a fraction of

[1] *Report of the Ministry of National Service 1917–19*, Vol. 1.

[2] *Reasons for Retiring or Continuing at Work*, 1954.

the population but on virtually the efforts of all citizens, we reach a fourth stage in our ascending scale of interest. Not only was it necessary for the State to take positive steps in all spheres of the national economy to safeguard the physical health of the people; it was also an imperative for war strategy for the authorities to concern themselves with that elusive concept 'civilian morale'; with what Professor Cyril Falls called, in his Lees Knowles lectures in 1941, 'demostrategy'.[1] By this he meant, in military terms, that the war could not be won unless millions of ordinary people, in Britain and overseas, were convinced that we had something better to offer than had our enemies—not only during but after the war. This requirement of war strategy was stated, more explicitly, in a memorable leader in *The Times*[2] soon after the last British troops had left the Dunkirk beaches. It was a call for social justice; for the abolition of privilege, for a more equitable distribution of income and wealth; for drastic changes in the economic and social life of the country.

The effect on social policy of these ideas about war strategy was profound. It was increasingly sharpened as the war went on, for not until three years had passed, and victory was at last a rational—rather than an emotional—conception, could the enemy claim that he had killed as many British soldiers as women and children.

Much of the story of the war effort in terms of applied social policies is told in the series of volumes in the Official War History by myself and my colleagues. I shall not attempt to recount the story here, except to draw out of it one or two general conclusions.

The social measures that were developed during the war centred round the primary needs of the whole population irrespective of class, creed or military category. The distinctions and privileges, accorded to those in uniform in previous wars, were greatly diminished. Comprehensive systems of medical care and rehabilitation, for example, had to be organized by the State for those who were injured and disabled. They could not be ex-

[1] Falls, C., *The Nature of Modern Warfare*, 1941, p. 13.
[2] July 1, 1940.

clusively reserved for soldiers and sailors, as in the past, but had to be extended to include civilians as well—to those injured in the factories as well as the victims of bombing. The organization and structure of the Emergency Medical Service, initially designed to cater for a special section of the population, became in the end the prototype of a medical service for the whole population.

In the sphere of food policy, it was no longer thought appropriate for members of the Armed Forces to receive better diets than the civilian population. The scales of rationing—as in many other spheres of need as well—had to be kept in balance between civilian and non-civilian.

This war-time trend towards universalizing public provision for certain basic needs did not come about as a result of the traffic of ideas in one direction only. It also worked the other way; from civilians to non-civilians. Educational facilities in the form of music, drama and the arts, open to civilians in time of war, could not be withheld from men and women in the Forces. No longer could it be said that soldiers 'would get above themselves' if, instead of drinking, they read books and papers, and that army discipline would thereby be endangered—as was said in May 1855 by the War Office to Florence Nightingale when she opened a reading room for injured soldiers in Scutari.[1] By the 1940's the military authorities in Britain had taken to heart—no doubt unwittingly—Aristotle's epitaph on the 'Lycurgean' system of Spartan training for war. This was the way he summed it up:

> 'Peoples ought not to train themselves in the art of war with an eye to subjugating neighbours who do not deserve to be subjugated. . . . The paramount aim of any social system should be to frame military institutions, like all its other institutions, with an eye to the circumstances of peace-time, when the soldier is off duty; and this proposition is borne out by the facts of experience. For militaristic states are apt to survive only so long as they remain at war, while they go to

[1] Woodham-Smith, C., *Florence Nightingale*, 1950, p. 239.

ruin as soon as they have finished making their conquests. Peace causes their metal to lose its temper; and the fault lies with a social system which does not teach its soldiers what to make of their lives when they are off duty.'

To apply this Aristotelian precept to the modern world means, in effect, that a social system must be so organized as to enable all citizens (and not only soldiers) to learn what to make of their lives in peace-time. In this context, the Education Act of 1944 becomes intelligible; so does the Beveridge Report of 1942 and the National Insurance, Family Allowances and National Health Service Acts. All these measures of social policy were in part an expression of the needs of war-time strategy to fuse and unify the conditions of life of civilians and non-civilians alike. In practice, as we have seen, this involved the whole community in accepting an enlargement of obligations—an extension of social discipline—to attend to the primary needs of all citizens.

In no particular sphere of need is the imprint of war on social policy more vividly illustrated than in respect to *dependant* needs—the needs of wives, children and other relatives for income-maintenance allowances when husbands and fathers are serving in the Forces. To trace in detail the system of Service pay and allowances from the Napoleonic Wars to the Second World War is to see how, as war has followed war in an ascending order of intensity, so have the dependant needs of wives and children been increasingly recognized. The more, in fact, that the waging of war has come to require a total effort by the nation the more have the dependant needs of the family been recognized and accepted as a social responsibility.

This trend in the war-time recognition of family dependencies has also profoundly influenced social security policies in general. New systems of Service pay and allowances threw into sharper prominence the fact that in industrial society money rewards take no account of family responsibilities. Nor, until 1939, did many of the payments made under various social services. Thus, one immediate effect was that dependants' allowances were added to Workmen's Compensation and other schemes. Another was that in many respects war pensions and industrial injury pensions had to be brought into line. This was done—as so many other things were done—because it seemed inappropriate to make distinctions between war and peace, civilians and non-civilians.

Looking back over the various points I have made about the relationship between the war effort of a community and its social policies in peace as well as in war one general conclusion may, I think, be ventured. The waging of modern war presupposes and imposes a great increase in social discipline; moreover, this discipline is only tolerable if—and only if—social inequalities are not intolerable. The need for less inequality is expressed, for example, in the changes that take place in what is socially approved behaviour—marked differences in standards of living, in dress, in luxury entertainment and in indulgencies of many kinds are disapproved. They were not only disapproved in war-time Britain but, in fact, there is evidence to show that they were greatly reduced.

It follows that the acceptance of these social disciplines—of obligations as well as rights—made necessary by war, by preparations for war, and by the long-run consequences of war, must influence the aims and content of social policies not only during the war itself but in peace-time as well. 'The discipline of the army,' wrote Max Weber, 'gives birth to all discipline.'[1] In some senses he was not far wrong, but it should be remembered that this thesis rested on an analysis of military organization from the days of Sparta down to the professional European armies at the beginning of the twentieth century. Britain's war effort in 1939 did not rest on a professional military base. Nevertheless, it is, I think, a tenable proposition that military wars demand a military discipline, and that this kind of discipline (or 'warrior communism' as Weber described it) demands certain kinds of perfected conduct from a small section of the population. We have some classic examples of this perfection of discipline in the infantry drill of Spartan soldiers and the exquisite move-

[1] Gerth, H. H., and Wright Mills, C., *From Max Weber: Essays in Sociology*, 1947, p. 261.

ments of Lord Cardigan's cavalry in the Crimean War. Both inevitably required—and this was the point of Weber's analysis—an 'aristocractic' structure in military organization and in society as a whole. Both essays in war came to a bad end. The social disciplines demanded by the civilians' war in Britain of 1939 were very different; they derived their strength from internal sources rather than from external commands, and had to rest on a social system which sought to teach all its soldiers what to make of their lives when off-duty.

The aims and content of social policy, both in peace and in war, are thus determined—at least to a substantial extent—by how far the co-operation of the masses is essential to the successful prosecution of war. If this co-operation is thought to be essential, then inequalities must be reduced and the pyramid of social stratification must be flattened. This, in part, is the thesis advanced by Andrzejewski in a sweeping, untidy but brilliant study recently published under the title 'Military Organization and Society'.[1] In analysing the character of war and its conduct from pastoral and pre-literate societies down to the advent of atomic war, he argues that what he calls the military participation ratio determines the social stratification of a society. Mass war, involving a high proportion of the total population, tends to a levelling in social class differences. On the other hand, professional wars, conducted by military leaders recruited from a social *élite* and depending on support from only a small proportion of the population, tend to heighten existing social inequalities. This study, in my view, effectively answers Herbert Spencer's theory that war conduces to greater social inequalities. It may have been true of some wars in some periods and cultures but not of all wars. However, we must fairly admit that Spencer was writing before the advent of the mass wars of the twentieth century.

The work of these sociologists does, in general, support the arguments I have advanced: that modern war has had—at least in Britain—a profound influence on social policy and that, reci-

[1]Andrzejewski, S., *Military Organization and Society*, 1954.

procally, the direction of social policy has influenced the way in which war is prosecuted. But this, I am confident—more perhaps by faith than by reason—is not the whole of the story in the evolution of social policy. Man does not live by war alone. To explain the social life of a community in terms of aggression and struggle is to explain only part of 'this sorry scheme of things entire'.

CHAPTER 5

The Position of Women

SOME VITAL STATISTICS[1]

IN a period when the possibilities of social progress and the practicability of applied social science are being questioned it is a source of satisfaction to recall some of the achievements of the Women's Suffrage Movement in Britain. The development of the personal, legal and political liberties of half the population of the country within the span of less than eighty years stands as one of the supreme examples of consciously directed social change.

There have been numerous historical and biographical studies of this Movement and of Millicent Fawcett and its other leaders.[2] Many of these studies have analysed the political, legal and vocational consequences, though largely within a middle-class ethos. Few have been concerned with the working-class woman, and particularly with the conditions of life of the working-class mother.[3] Yet, during the present century, far-reaching changes,

[1] The substance of the Millicent Fawcett Lecture given at Bedford College, London, on February 19, 1952. Some additional material of a factual nature has been inserted for publication. Other statistics have been brought up-to-date and references added.

[2] Since this lecture was given Mr O. R. McGregor has published his valuable bibliography on 'The Social Position of Women in England, 1850–1914' (*British Journal of Sociology*, Vol. VI, No. 1, March 1955). Every student of the subject will be grateful to him, as the present writer is, for this extensive, witty and penetrating commentary on the literature.

[3] Even in the field of women's employment nothing has been published for the period since 1850 to rank with Dr Ivy Pinchbeck's scholarly work *Women Workers and the Industrial Revolution, 1750–1850.*

social, economic and technological, have affected her status and role as a wife and mother, as a home-maker, as a contributor to the economy of the family, and in a variety of situations in the cycle of married life. Social historians and sociologists have been curiously neglectful of such studies and have allowed the subject of the position of women in modern society to be dominated by the psychologist, the psychiatrist and the sexologist.[1]

The purpose of this essay is twofold. First, to draw together some of the vital statistics of birth, marriage and death for the light they shed on the changes that have taken place since the beginning of the century in the social position of women. Secondly, to suggest that the accumulated effect of these changes now presents the makers of social policy with some new and fundamental problems.

The fall in the birth rate in Western societies is one of the dominating biological facts of the twentieth century. Commenting on the British statistics, the 1949 Report of the Royal Commission on Population noted the rapidity of the decline in family size after 1900.[2] Viewed within the context of the long period of industrial change since the seventeenth century, it is the rapidity of this fall which is as remarkable as the extent of the fall over the past fifty years. By-and-large, these trends have been shaped by changes in the family building habits of the working-classes during the present century. The first phase of declining family size among non-manual workers, and particularly middle and upper-middle class groups, took place earlier. The absolute difference in the average size of completed families of non-manual and manual workers which was 1·15 for 1900–9 marriages fell by one-third to ·76 for 1925–9 marriages. From a mid-Victorian family size of six or more the average size of completed working-class families of marriages contracted in 1925–9 had fallen to just under two-and-a-half. For all classes, the proportion of

[1] Particularly in the United States. The main index of the New York Central Library, for instance, lists 10,600 separate published volumes under *Woman* and *Women*. By contrast, *Child* and *Children* scores 7,800; *Man* (which includes *Mankind*) 2,200, and *Men* only 446.

[2] *Report of the Royal Commission on Population*, 1949, Cmd 7695, p. 25.

couples having seven or more children during the second half of the nineteenth century was 43 per cent; for marriages contracted in 1925 this proportion had fallen to 2 per cent.[1] It would probably be true to say that at the end of the century about half of all working-class wives over the age of forty had borne between seven and fifteen children.

To speak of a revolutionary change in working-class attitudes to childbearing would hardly be an exaggeration in any attempt to interpret figures of this magnitude. Since the lowest levels in rates of fertility registered before the Second World War there have been minor fluctuations; a short-lived post-war rise and fall; and some indication that family building habits have settled at a little below replacement level. But, as Mr Carrier has observed, this 'apparent stability' provides 'no indication that the future prospects represent full replacement'.[2] The great gains in declining mortality during this century have, so to speak, held population replacement at substantially higher levels than would otherwise have been the case. Little help can be looked for in the future from this source. Moreover, over the past decade or so the indices of replacement have been temporarily inflated by earlier marriages (and earlier births) and true replacement may thus turn out to be appreciably below unity when we are in a position to judge the family building habits of post-war generations.

However, it is not my purpose to speculate about the future. I mention these more recent data simply to point the contrast between now and fifty years ago. This contrast, remarkable as it is in average family size, is even more so in terms of the number of pregnancies—that is, when allowance is made for the losses

[1] See *Report of the Royal Commission*, pp. 24–30; Glass, D. V., and Grebenik, E., *The Trend and Pattern of Fertility in Great Britain: A Report on the Family Census of 1946*, 1954 and Registrar-General, *Census of England and Wales, 1911*, Vol. XIII, Pts 1 and 11.

[2] Carrier, N. H., 'An Examination of Generation Fertility in England and Wales', *Population Studies*, Vol. IX, No. 1, July 1955, p. 19. The average family size at nine completed years of marriage of those marrying in 1945 at ages under twenty-five was lower than that for a corresponding group married in 1930 (*Registrar-General's Statistical Review*, England and Wales, 1954, Pt III, p. 22).

from stillbirths, miscarriages and deaths in infancy experienced at the beginning of the century.

When this is done it would seem that the typical working-class mother of the 1890's, married in her teens or early twenties and experiencing ten pregnancies, spent about fifteen years in a state of pregnancy and in nursing a child for the first year of its life. She was tied, for this period of time, to the wheel of childbearing. Today, for the typical mother, the time so spent would be about four years.[1] A reduction of such magnitude in only two generations in the time devoted to childbearing represents nothing less than a revolutionary enlargement of freedom for women brought about by the power to control their own fertility. This private power, what Bernard Shaw once described as the ultimate freedom, can hardly have been exercised without the consent—if not the approval—of the husband. The amount and rapidity of the change together support such a proposition. We are thus led to interpret this development as a desired change within the working-class family rather than as a revolt by women against the authority of men on the analogy of the campaign for political emancipation.

What do these changes signify in terms of 'the forward view' —the vision that mothers now have and have had about their functions in the family and in the wider society? At the beginning of this century, the expectation of life of a woman aged twenty was forty-six years.[2] Approximately one-third of this life expectancy was to be devoted to the physiological and emotional experiences of childbearing and maternal care in infancy. Today, the expectation of life of a woman aged twenty is fifty-five years.[3] Of this longer expectation only about 7 per

[1] Actual number of years, not consecutive years. If estimated in terms of the distribution of pregnancies over the childbearing period the contrast would probably be greater.

[2] English Life Table, No. 7 for 1901–10, *Supplement to the 75th Annual Report of the Registrar-General*, Pt 1, 1914. It was precisely the same for males in Glasgow in 1950–2. (Glasgow Life Tables, *Supplement to the 99th Annual Report of the Registrar-General for Scotland*, 1954).

[3] England and Wales, 1953–5, *Registrar-General's Quarterly Return*, September 1956, App. B.

cent of the years to be lived will be concerned with childbearing and maternal care in infancy.

That the children of the large working-class families of fifty years ago helped to bring each other up must have been true; no single-handed mother of seven could have hoped to give to each child the standard of care, the quantity of time, the diffusion and concentration of thought that most children receive today. In this context, it is difficult to understand what is meant by those who generalize about the 'lost' functions of parents in the rearing of children. Certainly the children themselves, and especially girls, have lost some of these functions. But despite the help that the mother had from older children she could not expect to finish with the affairs of child care until she was in the middle-fifties. Only then would the youngest child have left school. By that time too her practical help and advice would be increasingly in demand as she presided over, as the embodiment of maternal wisdom, a growing number of grandchildren. In other words, by the time the full cycle of child care had run its course the mother had only a few more years to live—an analogous situation to the biological sequence for many species in the animal world. The typical working-class mother in the industrial towns in 1900 could expect, if she survived to fifty-five, to live not much more than another twelve years by the time she reached the comparative ease, the reproductive grazing field, of the middle fifties.[1]

The situation today is remarkably different. Even though we have extended the number of years that a child spends at school and added to the psychological and social responsibilities of motherhood by raising the cultural norms of child upbringing, most mothers have largely concluded their maternal role by the age of forty. At this age, a woman can now expect to live thirty-six years.[2] And if we accept the verdict of Parsons and

[1] Estimated from the Registrar-General's Occupational Mortality and Life Table Reports, 1891–1900, *Supplement to the 75th Annual Report*, Pts I and II, Cd 2618/9.

[2] England and Wales, 1953–5. *Registrar-General's Quarterly Return*, September 1956, App. B.

Bales, Margaret Mead and others, she has also been largely divested of her role as a grandmother by the professional experts in child care.[1]

What these changes mean is that by the time the typical mother of today has virtually completed the cycle of motherhood she still has practically half her total life expectancy to live. Should she have only had boys, instead of girls or children of both sexes, the necessary adjustments in outlook may seem more obvious; the diminution in role sharper. For the generality of women in most societies of which we have any reliable records this is a new situation. It presents an industrialized society, based on an extensive division of labour, on the early acquisition of occupational skills, on the personal achievement of status through educational and other channels which steadily narrow after the first ten years of adult life, with a host of new social problems. They are problems in the sense that these can be situations in which uncertainty and conflict develop over the individual's future role. What is socially approved behaviour is to recognize the need of the young adolescent for a growing measure of independence. Yet to relinquish the reins of motherhood today is no longer—as it was fifty years ago—a seemingly natural process of life closing in; of adjusting to the disabilities and tiredness of a long cycle of childbearing. Many mothers of today are not worn out by their forties. Nor may it be supposed that they are any more psychologically prepared to become more dependent on their husbands. For that is what the adjustment could spell to some wives as they consciously relinquish the independence-giving and emotionally expressive maternal role. What was in the past an almost unconscious process is now becoming a conscious one. This is to be expected as a natural corollary to the development of self-consciousness, as part of the

[1] This may be true of middle-class white populations in the United States, but there are no systematic studies in Britain to support such a conclusion. On the contrary, Young and Willmott have shown that in Bethnal Green, London, for instance, the mother, whatever her age, rarely ceases to play an important part in the lives of her children and grandchildren. (Young, M., and Willmott, P., *Family and Kinship in East London*, 1957).

intellectualization of child rearing, in the parental role.[1]

These questions are being formed by the conjunction and combination of many forces. Changes in family building habits is one; changes in rates of dying since the nineteenth century is another.

It is common knowledge that there have been great reductions in mortality over the past fifty years, particularly in infancy and childhood where rates of dying have fallen by approximately 75 per cent. What is less well known is that death rates among women have been declining faster than among men. A comparison of the standardized mortality rates (which allow for differences in the age structure of the male and female populations) shows that the rate among men today exceeds that for women by about 50 per cent.[2] This excess has accumulated steadily throughout the century. If rates of mortality are any guide to the general level of health of a population then these trends suggest that, since 1900, the health of women has improved, and is still improving, at a considerably faster rate than that of men.

The relative gains, as measured by death rates, of women over men apply to all age groups, but the really striking changes have taken place over the age of forty-five. This is shown by the percentage male excess at 10-year age groups for two periods:[3]

	25–34	35–44	45–54	55–64	65–74	75–84	85+
	%	%	%	%	%	%	%
1896–1900	15	22	29	24	17	13	9
1951–1955	28	28	62	91	65	37	20

Easily the greatest gains have been registered by women aged forty-five to seventy-four. There is no justification here for a lower pensionable age for women. Their expectation of life

[1] See Parsons, Talcott & Bales, R. F., *Family, Socialization and Interaction Process* (1956), especially Ch. II and III in which the authors discuss marriage as an 'achieved' status.

[2] 1954–5, Table 3, *Registrar-General's Statistical Review, England and Wales*, Pt I, 1955.

[3] Calculated from Table 4, *Registrar-General's Statistical Review, England and Wales*, Pt I, 1955.

at sixty now exceeds that for men by nearly four years, which means that they are covered for national retirement pensions for about nine years longer than are men. Thus, with a pension running for nineteen years from sixty,[1] and if a family allowance and an income tax child allowance runs to age eighteen, there are, in all, a total of thirty-seven years of 'dependency' recognized by the State in social policy.

A large part of these gains in mortality by women has been achieved since 1931. To quote the Government Actuary in reporting on mortality changes between the censuses of 1931 and 1951: 'At ages over forty, however, the experience of the two sexes has diverged. For women, there has been a continued substantial lightening of mortality, extending to age eighty and beyond. For men, on the other hand, the improvement has been much less; at age sixty the 1951 rate is almost the same as that of twenty years earlier. At that age the women's rate of mortality in 1950–2 was about 45 per cent less than that forty years before, while the men's rate was only 22 per cent less.'[2]

These conclusions are more pronounced in the case of married women (and to a somewhat less extent for widows) for all ages up to seventy in contrast with the experience of single women. Not only do married women show much lower rates, but the gains they have made since 1930–2 are more substantial. But even single women show much lower rates than married men after the middle-forties.

Working-class women still show, however, substantially higher rates of mortality than the national average for all women. The expectation of life at age forty-five for Glasgow women was four years lower than that for London women of the same age in 1950–2.[3] But, even so, all the declines registered by women in recent decades (in contrast with the trends for men)

[1] Expectation of life at sixty in 1952–4, *Registrar-General's Statistical Review, England and Wales*, 1954, Pt III, Table XXX).

[2] *Registrar-General's Decennial Supplement*, England and Wales, 1951, Life Tables, p. 11.

[3] *Registrar-General's Decennial Supplement*, England and Wales, 1951, Life Tables, Table V4, and *Registrar-General for Scotland*, Life Tables, 1950–2, App. II, Table 3.

can only be summed up, to use the words of the Registrar-General for Scotland, 'as sensational'.[1]

This phenomenon is not peculiar to Britain. The relative gains by women over men since 1900 appear to be even more sensational in the United States, a fact that has been explained by one medical commentator in these words: 'In this patriarchal American culture males preserve their masculinity complex. Striving to live up to the expectation of maleness, men blow out their coronaries and cerebral arteries, making wealthy widows out of their wives. Men die five years before women in this country, and women possess 83 per cent of the wealth'.[2]

Whatever the reasons may be for the relative—if not the absolute—worsening in mortality rates for men[3] such comments do not explain the dramatic improvements shown by the rates for women. So far as Britain is concerned, a reasonable hypothesis would be that these improvements are in large part attributable to the decline in the size of the family since 1900. This receives support from the remarkable change, after 1930–2, in the relationship between the mortality of single women and that of married women. In Scotland, for instance, while the rates of single women in youth and early middle age fell by something like 25 per cent between 1930–2 (when they were lower than those for married women) and 1950–2, the rates for married women in the same age range fell by about 60 per cent by 1950–2. This fall put the rates for single women about 60 per cent in excess up to the age of forty-two.[4]

Among married women, not only have the hazards of childbirth and the frequency of confinements been greatly diminished, but the number and proportion of mothers worn out by excessive childbearing and dying prematurely from such diseases as tuberculosis, pneumonia and so forth are but a fraction of what they were fifty years ago. Above all, the decline in the size of the

[1] Life Tables 1950–2, p. 12.

[2] Moloney, J. C., in *Symposium on the Healthy Personality*, ed. by M. J. E. Senn, New York, 1950, p. 51.

[3] Some fascinating material on the medical causes of these trends is analysed by J. N. Morris in *Uses of Epidemiology* (1957).

[4] *Registrar-General for Scotland*, Life Tables 1950–2, p. 12.

family has meant, in terms of family economics, a rise in the standard of living of women which has probably been of more importance, by itself, than any change since 1900 in real earnings by manual workers. Nor would it be hard to argue that this factor was far more influential up to the Second World War than any additional benefits derived from the expansion of the social services and improvements in medical care.

Yet when one turns to the history of the Women's Movement in Britain it is odd to find that little attention was given to the problem of continuous childbearing with all its attendant evils of chronic ill-health and premature ageing. The social freedom of working-class women to control their own fertility was not an issue of any importance. Nevertheless, the Victorian myth about the biological inferiority of women was still powerful. For example, the manifesto of 1889, signed by Beatrice Webb, Mrs Humphrey Ward and others, protesting against Women's Suffrage, observed: 'We believe that the emancipating process has now reached the limits fixed by the physical constitution of women.'[1] Such an argument could hardly be brought forward today by those who oppose the principle of equal pay for women.

Before I turn to my last heading of marriage I would make one general point about the long-term consequences of these trends in mortality and fertility. At the beginning of this century, when the total population of England and Wales was 32,500,000, there were 661,000 men aged over sixty-five and 1,337,000 women aged over sixty—a total of 1,998,000 or 6 per cent of the population. Today (1956), we have 2,045,000 men aged over sixty-five and 4,395,000 women aged over sixty—a total of 6,440,000 people of pensionable ages—or 14 per cent of the population. According to the Registrar-General's projections we are likely to have, by 1975, approximately 750,000 more men aged over sixty-five but 1,250,000 more women aged over sixty.[2] About 18 per cent of the population will then be of pensionable ages. While this proportion is not abnormally

[1] Strachey, R., *The Cause*, 1928, p. 285.

[2] *Registrar-General's Quarterly Return for England and Wales*, December 1955, App. B.

high for a more or less stable population is does contain a preponderance of women. The problem of social policies for old age today and tomorrow is thus mainly a problem of elderly women[1]—a fact that is generally overlooked by those who consider that private occupational pension schemes for men will answer all the questions of income maintenance in old age.

When the Women's Movement was in full flood, early this century, most thoughtful observers believed that to release women from the domination of men, exercised through, what John Stuart Mill called, 'the foul means of marriage'[2] would lead to fewer marriages in the future. No student of society would have had the temerity at that time to forecast the remarkable changes which the institution of marriage has undergone since those days. On the subjective plane, it can be said with some degree of truth that the mutual relationships of husband and wife are very different today from the picture of married life which emerges from the literature and social investigations of Edwardian times. The extent to which fertility has come under control by married couples is evidence of this. New patterns in the psychological management of married life have been slowly evolving; the idea of companionship in marriage is being substituted for the more sharply defined roles and codes of behaviour set by the Victorian patriarchal system with (to quote Virginia Woolf) 'its nullity, its immorality, its hypocrisy, its servility'.[3]

It seems that we are at some as yet undefinable stage in the process of 'democratizing' marriage. It follows, therefore, that as the size of the family has declined we have gradually come to expect more and more of our marriages. 'We are more inclined now than we used to be to demand a capacity for response between the partners, to look for intellectual and temperamental compatability, as well as purely material welfare, in addition to the ordinary social and parental satisfactions. The more we

[1] On the basis of mortality in 1953–5, 22 per cent of males and 40 per cent of females born would reach the age of eighty.

[2] Mill, J. S., *The Subjection of Women*, 1869, p. 81.

[3] Woolf, V., *Three Guineas*, 1943, p. 135.

demand in these respects, the more frequently, perhaps, we shall have to count our failures, but also the higher may be our level of achievement.'[1] Perhaps that is why the Royal Commission on Marriage and Divorce saw that its primary task was to seek out 'ways and means of strengthening the resolution of husband and wife to realize the ideal of a partnership for life.'[2]

No doubt the political and legal emancipation of women has contributed to these changes in what is expected from marriage. A more socially equal relationship was foreseen by the leaders of the Women's Movement but what they could hardly have envisaged is the rise in the popularity of marriage since about 1911. Here we turn from the debatable field of value judgments about the quality of married life to the statistics of marriage distinguishing, as we must, between the amount of marriage taking place in a given population and the age at marriage.

As to the first, it is clear that for about forty years before 1911 marriage rates among women were declining. But somewhere around this time a change occurred; the amount of marriage began to increase. It has been increasing ever since, and in a striking fashion since the mid-1930's. An increase of nearly one-third between 1911 and 1954 in the proportion of women aged twenty to forty married represents, as the Registrar-General has said, 'a truly remarkable rise'.[3] Never before, in the history of English vital statistics, has there been such a high proportion of married women in the female population under the age of forty and, even more so, under the age of thirty. Since 1911 the proportion at age fifteen to nineteen has risen nearly fourfold; at age twenty to twenty-four it has more than doubled. Such figures as these hardly support the conclusion of the Royal Commission on Marriage and Divorce that 'matrimony is not so secure as it was fifty years ago'.[4]

[1] Slater, E., and Woodside, M., *Patterns of Marriage*, 1951, p .126.

[2] Report 1951–5, Cmd 9678, p. 7.

[3] *Registrar-General's Statistical Review*, England and Wales, 1940–5, Civil Text, Vol. II. For other recent material on marriage trends see the *Reviews* for 1946–50 (Civil Text), 1951 (Text), 1954 (Pt III), and 1955 (Pt III), and Hajnal, J., *Population Studies*, Vol. I, No. 1, June 1947 and Vol. VII, No. 2, November 1953.

[4] Report 1951–5, Cmd 9678, p. 24.

More marriage has been accompanied by a great increase in the years of married life experienced by married couples. Declining death rates have not only lengthened marriage (and with earlier childbearing very substantially lengthened the years of married life during which there are no children to be cared for), but they have brought about a striking fall in the proportion of marriages broken by widowhood and widowerhood under the age of sixty. It is highly probable that the proportion of broken marriages under the age of sixty, marriages broken by death, desertion and divorce, is, in total, smaller today than at any time this century. It is also relevant to point out that the greater the amount of marriage becomes the greater will be the chances that men and women, with impaired health and handicaps, physical and psychological, and unstable personalities will be exposed to the hazards of married life and child rearing. In other words, a wider range of personality and character variation may now be drawn into the ambit of marriage and parenthood. Formerly, this segment of the population (some part of which could be distinguishable by the incidence of acquired and inherited physical handicaps) might not have entered matrimony.[1] No interpretation of recent divorce statistics or of the facts about 'broken homes' can be satisfactory unless account is taken of this factor. And of the strikingly high rates of remarriage of divorced men and women in recent years. By 1955 this was in the region of three-quarters.[2]

[1] Support for this thesis comes from the trend of mortality rates for married and single women since the 1930's. 'It is to be supposed,' wrote the Government Actuary, 'that those persons who marry are likely, on average, to be in better health than the unmarried; it was, therefore, to be anticipated that, as the number of spinsters became progressively smaller, a higher proportion of them would be of inferior vitality and that their mortality, relative to that of married women, would become heavier.' This expectation is borne out in a striking manner by the comparative mortality rates discussed in these paragraphs (*Registrar-General's Decennial Supplement*, England and Wales, Life Tables, 1951, pp. 14–15).

[2] The 1954 level of incidence of decrees, when related to the number of antecedent marriages from which they arise, indicates that about 7 per cent of marriages are terminated by divorce (*Registrar-General's Statistical Review*, England and Wales, 1955, Pt III, pp. 2–3.) The statistics of divorce petitions and maintenance orders are critically examined by Mr O. R. McGregor in his book *Divorce in England*, 1957, esp. Ch. 11.

Married life has been lengthened not only by declining mortality but by earlier marriage. It is a fact of the greatest social importance that for the past forty years a trend towards more youthful marriage has been in progress. In 1911 24 per cent of all girls aged twenty to twenty-four were married; by 1954 this proportion had risen to 52 per cent.[1] As a result of this trend and rising marriage rates the proportion of women still single at the age of thirty-five has fallen to only about 13 per cent.[2] There are now fewer unmarried women aged fifteen to thirty-five in the country than at any time since 1881 when the total population was only 60 per cent of its present size. Yet 'the last generation in this country to reproduce itself completely was born as long ago as 1876 or thereabouts'.[3]

What broadly emerges from this incursion into the statistics of marriage is, first, a remarkable increase in the amount of marriage in the community, second, more and more youthful marriage—especially among women, third, a concentration of family building habits in the earlier years of married life and, fourth, a substantial extension in the years of exposure to the strains and stresses of married life. All these changes have taken place during a period of increasing emancipation for women. Paradoxically, therefore, fewer social and legal restraints and more equality and freedom for women have been accompanied by an increase in the popularity of the marriage institution.

To survey the changed position of women in English society from the standpoint of the vital statistics of birth, marriage and death raises a great many questions. While it has not been the

[1] According to a survey of 'Britain's six or seven leading marriage bureaux', conducted by *The Economist* in 1955, those who remain single and approach these agencies 'always want to marry a professional man, as do the heroines of women's magazine stories'. But 'it is the civil servants who really go like hot cakes, because of the pension'. (*The Economist*, August 27, 1955, pp. 678–9.)

[2] The rise in the proportion of all marriages which are of minors is another illustration of the trend towards earlier marriage. In 1938 this proportion for females was 16·4 per cent; in 1955 it was 30·3 per cent. For males it rose from 3·4 per cent to 7·8 per cent respectively (*Registrar-General's Statistical Review*, England and Wales, 1955, Pt III, p. 48).

[3] *Registrar-General's Statistical Review*, England and Wales, 1946–50, Civil Text, p. 83.

purpose of this essay to analyse the causes of these changes, or to examine the modern family in sociological terms, it is nevertheless possible to discern from the bare facts the outlines of new social problems which, as yet, we have hardly begun to contemplate while other problems, long recognized, have now to be seen in a different frame of reference. The problem, for instance, of the dual roles of women in modern society; of the apparent conflict between motherhood and wage-earning which now has to be viewed in relation to the earlier and much more compressed span of life during which the responsibilities of motherhood are most intense. With an expectation of another thirty-five to forty years of life at the age of forty, with the responsibilities of child upbringing nearly fulfilled, with so many more alternative ways of spending money, with new opportunities and outlets in the field of leisure, the question of the rights of women to an emotionally satisfying and independent life appears in a new guise.

Yet, at present, practically all forms of educational and vocational training, along with entry to many pensionable occupations, are shut to the woman who has reached the age of forty. Motherhood and date of birth disqualify her, while the unthinking and unknowing may condemn her in moralizing terms for seeking work outside the home. Few subjects are more surrounded with prejudice and moral platitude than this; an approach which perhaps deepens the conflict for the women themselves about their roles as mothers, wives and wage-earners.

Already, it seems, more and more middle-aged mothers are seeking to find some solution to the social, economic and psychological problems which face them or may do so in the future. Dimly they may be perceiving the outline of these problems in the years ahead when the days of child upbringing are over.

Between 1946 and May 1955 the number of married women in gainful employment rose by two-and-a-quarter million to three-and-three-quarter million or 48 per cent of all women at work.[1] The biggest source of recruitment in recent years has

[1] *Report by the Government Actuary on the Provisions of the National Insurance Bill*, 1946, Cmd 6750 and *The Economist*, July 14, 1956, p. 131. These figures include full-time and part-time.

been married women over thirty years of age.[1] Today, the most important group, relatively and absolutely, are those aged forty to fifty. There are now over one million married women of these ages at work, or one in three of all married women in this group.[2] Of all married women under the age of fifty at work in 1951 at least one-fifth had children of school age.[3] The proportion is probably substantially higher now.

Making allowance for seasonal and other work changes, it is probable that the lives of about four million families in Britain are now affected by the paid employment of the wife or mother outside the home.[4] This development has no doubt contributed substantially to the standard of living of a large proportion of working-class families—as it has to that of the nation as a whole. Mothers and wives are likely to be affected first by any rise in unemployment.

In the field of employment opportunities, as in so many other fields, new issues for social policy are taking shape as a consequence of these changes in the position of women in society. The problems for State policy which the woman's movement of fifty years ago brought to the fore were largely political; those raised by the women's movements of today are largely social.

[1] *Ministry of Labour Gazette*, June 1954.
[2] *Ministry of Labour Gazette*, August 1952.
[3] *Ministry of Labour Gazette*, May 1951.
[4] Some aspects of these changes among families in East London are being studied by Miss Pearl Jephcott and her colleagues in a project undertaken by the Social Science Department of the London School of Economics.

CHAPTER 6

Industrialization and The Family[1]

THERE are at least three reasons why industrialization and the family is today an important subject for debate by an international conference of social workers. The first is an obvious one: the opportunities that it offers for discussion and analysis on a comparative basis. The second lies in the fact that the world is increasingly an industrial world and dominated in its values and goals by problems of economic growth. Compared, for example, with the situation only fifty years ago, far more societies—in Asia, Africa, eastern and southern Europe, and Central and South America—are seized with the possibilities and potentialities of economic growth. To these peoples, economic growth spells a higher material standard of life, a release from the age-old passivity of agrarian poverty. Industrialization, as a means of raising the level of living, is thus something to be desired. This, I believe, is one of the most important facts in the contemporary social scene when looked at in international terms: the fact that a substantial part of mankind, compared with only an insignificant fraction at the beginning of this century, is aware or is becoming aware of the benefits of industrialization. In wanting to be industrialized, in thus wanting, as societies, to be radically changed, groups are, in this process of making com-

[1] Paper presented at the International Conference of Social Work, Munich, Germany, August 6, 1956, and published in *Proceedings of the Eighth International Conference*, Frankfurt, 1957, and in *The Social Service Review*, Chicago, Vol. XXXI, No. 1, March 1957.

munity aspirations more explicit, becoming more aware of the gulf between what is and what might be in their conditions of life.

This self-consciousness about material standards is clearly expressed in the United Nations *Preliminary Report on the World Social Situation*[1] and in much of the work of the international organizations. We seem to have passed into an age of more explicit discontents and of more articulate expectations. Inequalities between nations are now being considered in much the same way as inequalities within nations and between social groups. Changes in relative standards are being recognized and measured; the United Nations report points out, for example, that wealthy nations are growing relatively wealthier while poor nations are becoming relatively poorer. The deduction that more people are making from the dissemination of such ideas is that industrial and technological change will provide all the answers to the problems of poverty. What we are thus witnessing on a wider scale than ever before is a demand for change, the motive force for which lies in the idea of progress—material progress—the idea that ruled the life of Britain in the nineteenth century.

The third reason I would give in supporting the choice of this particular subject for discussion is that social work is primarily an activity carried on in industrial, urban societies. The problems of human needs and relationships with which social work has traditionally been associated have had, in scale and concentration, their origin in those societies experiencing the impact of industrialization. The conclusion that some may draw from this historical fact and from the reasons I have adduced in support of the conference theme is that, looking to the future and to an increasingly industrialized world, more social workers will be needed, along with a greater investment in those social resources without which social work cannot effectively fulfil its ethical responsibilities. The call will be for more social workers at all levels of practice but pre-eminently for those intellectually and philosophically equipped to deal with the manifold problems

[1] United Nations document E/CN.5/267/Rev.1, 1952.

of societies undergoing the earlier and more violent stages of industrialization. It must be pointed out, however, that this conclusion rests in part on the assumption that there are lessons to be learned in the twin areas of social work and social policy from those societies which have been highly industrialized over a long period of time. This is the assumption on which much of the debate at this conference will necessarily rest.

Convinced as I am of the reality of 'common human needs', I believe that societies with experience of an industrial environment have something to give, something to communicate if only —and perhaps only—in terms of principles of action. But even here our motives in desiring to fund and pass on the lessons of experience must have that quality of disinterested attachment on which empires, either of a material or an ideological kind, are assuredly not built.

The particular task which has been marked out for me is to discuss the impact of industrialization in countries 'highly industrialized over a long period of time'—in effect, most of Western Europe, Britain, and the United States of America. The subject, both in time and in place, is obviously an immense one; I shall, therefore, be compelled to generalize frequently and to be highly selective.

While I do not intend to discuss the more material and environmental aspects of industrial change in relation to family life, I do wish to comment on two related factors. One concerns the rate (or speed) of industrial change and the intensity of the demand for it; the second concerns the distinction between the long-term as compared with the immediate or short-term effects of industrialization as they have been experienced in Western societies. Both factors are often neglected in the historical treatment of industrial and technological change. Yet both seem to me to be highly relevant in any consideration of the life cycle of the family, particularly in those societies now starting out on the road toward industrialization. Such societies may find themselves confronted with problems markedly different in rate and intensity from those of Western societies. Especially because of modern methods of communication the intensity of demand for change may be much greater, and these societies may have to move with greater rapidity from a peasant, kinship economy into a world of mechanized processes and divided labour in which skill and age, family and work, have little in common.

If these conditions are present, i.e. if the desire for change is widespread and intense and if there are possibilities of rapid industrial development, then it is likely that the family problems arising from change will be obscured by the prospects and promises of a higher standard of living. The social costs of economic advance may thus be pushed out of sight by the strength of the collective motive for an improvement in the material fabric of life. A total awareness of goals, an overriding aspiration for the material objectives of change, can blind people from seeing that change is many-sided and that each factor contributing to economic growth is also a factor contributing to social need. In this context, the present world-wide demand for economic growth is significant, for much of this demand seems to me to overlook the grim experiences of Western societies when they underwent the earlier stages of industrialization.

Much depends also on the pace of change. We are beginning to learn, from advances in knowledge slowly won by the behavioural sciences, that there are limits, particularly in relation to child-rearing practices and family adjustment, to the speed at which social change can take place without causing grave psychological problems. The critical importance to the health of societies of the ways in which new generations of children are socialized within their own families is better understood in the West than it was a hundred years ago. We now know that what is passed on through the family—the central mechanism for the transmission of culture—cannot be rapidly changed. External social changes often involve, however, traumatic changes in the roles played by members of the family, particularly the inner or nuclear family. Different norms of behaviour and different roles that often have to be adopted need to be internalized. People, we should remember, do not 'play' roles like actors. A role is something that a person is. It follows from our understanding of these processes that the capacity of the family to function as a kind of institutional brake cannot be stretched too far without our running the risk, perhaps some generations later, of causing widespread instabilities in family life and much mental ill-health.

If those who are first subjected to industrial change have had stable childhoods within a coherent, meaningful social order, then they may be able psychologically to withstand the pressure of change. Their children and grandchildren may be more likely to show the psychological effects of the long-drawn-out processes of industrialization. They will have been reared in an unstable culture by parents without a sure sense of direction or purpose.[1]

In such ways as these are worked out in the family the long-term and more subtle psychological effects of industrialization. They are part of the price of economic growth, a price that is not paid by those who benefit most in material terms from increased production and a price which is not revealed in all its social and psychological contours until several generations later. It must, therefore, be remembered that most of the long-industrialized countries of the West are still heavily burdened by the as yet uncompensated disservices of the earlier stages of their economic growth. Viewed in terms of the long-drawn cycle of family life, the violent industrial upheavals of the nineteenth century, the poverty, the unemployment, the social indiscipline, the authoritarianism of men and the cruelties to children, are by no means as remote today in their consequences as some economists and historians would have us believe. The reform of housing conditions, to cite one example of a material kind, was both remarkably slow and late in its development, particularly in Britain and France. Much of the reason for this can no doubt be traced to the value which was placed on the ownership of property in the nineteenth century; men desired, as Mill said, 'not to be rich but to be richer than other men';[2] they had also to

[1] For a fuller discussion of these 'generation' effects of change, see Margaret Mead (ed.), *Cultural Patterns and Technical Change* (World Federation for Mental Health, Tensions and Technology Series (Paris: UNESCO, 1953)).

[2] Mill, J. S., 'Posthumous Essay on Social Freedom', *Oxford and Cambridge Review* (June,1907).

own more property in perpetuity than other men. One inheritance, several generations later, is that social workers still spend much of their time coping with the problems of families disabled and deformed by bad housing conditions. The devil in this particular piece seems to have more of the character of Bentham than of Freud.

Against the background of these generalizations about the long-term effects of what we in the West may now call the 'first industrial revolution', I want to consider some of the effects of the 'second industrial revolution'. Both stages overlap; no line of demarcation can be seen. Speaking broadly, however, we can say that the first was marked by the triumph of the steam engine and of coal and iron, and by the shifting of production from the home to the factory. The second has been distinguished by an immense and varied spread of production techniques dominated by the invasion of the factory by electric power. Work has increasingly been split into smaller tasks by the demands of standardized mass production; human labour itself has come to be increasingly ruled by the clock, by the precision of the assembly line, the conveyor belt, and automation. The need for manual strength and long hours of work has been reduced by the development of mechanized processes in which the machine tends to regulate and control the work. This process of technological change, in itself a major factor in raising the standard of living of the worker, has been aptly described by Friedmann as making industrial man an object of rationalized production.[1] The degradation of the worker, bereft of personality and of his roles as husband, father, and citizen, found conscious expression in the idea of 'scientific management'.

To some extent at least, the effects of the first industrial revolution in the West have been recognized and studied. Much has been written about the breakdown of kinship ties and the close social integration of individuals and family groups as a result of the growth of factory towns, industrial movements, migration from the land, and the decay of old crafts and customs. Indus-

[1] Friedmann, Georges, *Industrial Society: The Emergence of the Human Problems of Automation*, trans. Harold L. Sheppard (Glencoe, Ill.: Free Press, 1955).

trialization demanded the breakdown of the mutual relationships of the extended family; paradoxically, the poor law struggled—though ineffectually—to maintain them. Industrialization also demanded in the interests of efficient production the denial of much of the respect that youth had formerly given to age. The machine broke the hierarchy of skill and age in which young men learned to respect older workers and in so doing became, in their turn, self-respecting workers. It also contradicted and denied among manual workers the respect and civility that men had accorded to women as part of the social controls of rural communities. Thus, with the shift from domestic to industrial production women became more dependent on men, not only in economic terms, but in the psychological subtleties of their relationships.[1] Authoritarian patterns of behaviour, sanctioned in the factory, were carried into the home. The survival of the family as a social unit became more dependent on the labour power, the health, and the strength of the husband and father—the one who now 'earned life' for the whole unit. These and other effects of the earlier stages of industrialization can still be traced in the pattern of family life in Western societies.

Much less is known, however, about the more subtle social and psychological effects of—to use again this convenient shorthand term—the second industrial revolution. Yet, in qualitative terms, in their bearing on attitudes, behaviour, and roles in the family, these effects may be as profound in their own way as the more obvious consequences of the shift from domestic to factory production.

The movement of ideas since the 1930's, epitomized in the growing use of the term 'human relations in industry', has led to many studies of the worker within the social system of the factory. One weakness, however, of most of these studies (like the famous Hawthorne inquiry) is that while taking account of the realities of life within the work place they ignore the realities

[1] See in particular Alice Clark, 'How the Rise of Capitalism Affected the Role of the Wife', in *The Family, Past and Present,* ed. Bernard Joseph Stern (New York: Published for the Progressive Education Association by D. Appleton-Century Co, 1938).

outside. The factory or office comes to be seen as a complete, closed, autonomous system, pursuing its own goals and developing its own values and norms of behaviour regardless of the outside world. Seldom are the workers' activities and aspirations outside the factory considered. Rarely, if ever, are his family relationships and his place in the community discussed. In none of the indexes of such studies as I have consulted does 'family' appear. Industrial psychologists and sociologists, in carrying out such studies, seem to be falling into much the same trap as some economists. Hence they observe only a part and a steadily smaller part of man's life in highly industrialized societies. For these reasons, much of what I have to say is conjectural. It is also focused primarily on the manual worker. The effects of industrialization on the white-collar workers and middle classes are no less important, but they do require separate discussion.

In thinking about these various industrial studies, I have been particularly struck by the differences in the norms of behaviour expected of the worker in the factory and of the same worker in his home and in the community. These differences are of many kinds; I shall mention only one or two by way of illustration. Some of them seem to me to be fundamentally in conflict. What society expects of the individual outside the factory in attitudes, behaviour, and social relationships is in many respects markedly different from what is demanded by the culture of the factory. These differences have been accentuated by all the complex industrial developments of recent years.

Stability.—Take, for example, the concept of stability which is so heavily stressed as an expected characteristic of 'healthy' family life. A 'good' parent is one who, by taking deliberate thought for tomorrow, provides a stable background and a regular coherent rhythm in which his children can grow and mature as 'successful' individuals. He is expected to 'plan' for their future, to strive to make them more 'successful' than he has been, and to contrive a stable, economically secure base from which they may climb up the educational ladder into perhaps a successful 'professional' career. For the manual worker in the factory, however, the concept of stability is not an important attribute of the system theoretically or in practice. The dominating characteristics of industrial conditions in the West during the past few decades have been, from the point of view of the worker, irregularity and impermanence. Unemployment, short-time working, the decay of skills as a result of technological change, and the rationalization of production have all spelled, in the worker's psychology, irregularity and uncertainty. Allied to this factor is the increasingly important one of irregularity and uncertainty in status and skill. The development of mechanization —the growing diffusion of automatic or semi-automatic, multi-purpose, and high precision machines—is a continuing and widely distributed process. Old skills—and status positions that go with them—are being down-graded, divided, or made redundant.

Status and rewards.—This constant shifting in the relative economic value—or 'productive status'—of man and machine, accompanied invariably by a continuing process of inflation and deflation of human skills, status, and rewards, must have profound effects on the worker, not only inside, but outside the factory. We must remember that loss of status signifies more than loss of rewards, more than loss of expected respect. It can be a serious injury to the personality. It can lead to less dependable behaviour. It is thus closely linked to what is called a 'sense of responsibility'. In general, the situation of many manual workers is basically a situation of uncertainty about tomorrow, a situation provoking 'immediacy of living' which is much less familiar to most middle-class and professional workers, who can be more assured about their future roles, their status in a known occupational hierarchy, their rewards, their pensions, and the particular tasks they will be doing next year and the year after. Not so the industrial worker. His status is more likely to be an ascribed or assigned one. The middle-class worker's status is more likely to be an achieved or promoted one. The first tends to decline or remain static with advancing age; the second tends to rise, with incremental rewards, to higher levels of accorded respect. Thus, in relative terms, security for the manual worker declines as he grows older (particularly as he can no longer look to a large family for support), whereas for the middle-class worker it increases. Yet both workers, as husbands and fathers, are subject to the same expected norms of behaviour. Both are expected to have the same status relationships and to play the same roles in their own families. There is here a fundamental conflict in values, the dimensions and consequences of which we cannot yet see.

In his studies of the meaning of work and work relationships, Bakke concluded that a man's job was not simply something that brought him money; it was an activity that gave him a place in the social world and in large measure gave meaning to his life. He described the goals of workers in the following general terms: 'To play a socially respected and admired role; to win a degree of economic security customary among one's associates, to gain an increasing amount of control over one's affairs, and to understand the forces which make their impact felt in those affairs, and in all of these to experience satisfying and predictable relations with the members of the groups with which one is most intimately associated'.[1]

In relation to the need of the worker to gain an increasing amount of control over his affairs as age and family responsibilities advance, it can at least be said that the present system of industrial organization falls far short of providing those conditions in which this need may be satisfied.

The definition by Bakke of a worker's goals in highly industrialized societies seems to me a fruitful one. It has the merit of taking account of the worker's life outside the factory. It also helps to explain why 'human relations in industry' has become an important issue in modern societies. And in so doing it should enlarge our understanding of the reasons that lead industrial managements in the United States, in Germany, and in Britain, to offer their workers, often in authoritarian or paternalistic ways, miniature 'welfare states'—complete with pensions, medical care, sickness benefit, subsidized meals, free leisure facilities, and so forth. From another aspect, this formulation of goals throws some light on the reasons for the rapid growth of 'pro-

[1] Bakke, E. Wight, *Citizens without Work: A Study of the Effects of Unemployment upon the Workers' Social Relations and Practices* (New Haven: Published for the Institute of Human Relations by Yale University Press, 1940), p. 247.

fessionalism' among the middle and white-collar classes. This intensive search for professional status is in part a search for a socially respected and admired role and in part an effort to gain an increasing amount of control over one's affairs.

The need for secure status, for continuing respect by others, as one element in the search to achieve personal self-respect, increases as the cruder necessities of material existence are met. Simply to win a bare level of subsistence is no longer, as it probably was in the past, a sufficient reason by itself alone to be accorded—and expect to be accorded—respect by one's fellows and by one's wife and children. In another sense, too, the need for status becomes more of a family need as the idea of 'partnership in marriage' grows and as increasing emphasis is given to the rearing of children as 'successful' personalities. The need for status thus becomes at least as important among manual workers as among the white-collar and professional classes.

Initiative.—Now I want to consider another major characteristic of industrial technology in relation to its effects on family life and to the goals of workers. Stated briefly, it is that the progressive substitution of work regulated from the outside for work more or less freely shaped by the worker himself is, according to Friedmann and other observers, one of the chief characteristics of contemporary industrial evolution.[1] Where the worker is dominated by the machine, by work schedules, by time-study checkers, by pace-setters, and by the clock—by what has been called 'scientific management'—it can all signify submission, dependence, loss of initiative. The individual's will or creative energy is not challenged into action if there is only 'one best way' in which to act; if work, so to speak, 'does itself'. Judgment, selection, and initiative, the ingredients of skill, the basis of self-respect, are not called into being.

One way of looking at the human effects of all these trends in industrial techniques was summed up years ago by Henry Ford in his well-known statement: 'The average worker, I am sorry to say, wants a job in which he does not have to put forth much

[1] Friedmann, *op. cit.*, especially Pt 3, Ch. 1; and William Foote Whyte, ed., *Industry and Society* (New York and London: McGraw-Hill Book Co 1946).

physical exertion—above all, he wants a job in which he does not have to think'.[1] This kind of rationalization about the behaviour of the worker has by no means disappeared either in the United States or in Western Europe.

We need to note especially, in this context as in others, the nature of the conflict between the norms of expected behaviour in the factory and those other norms of conduct which prevail in the wider society and which are expected to influence the worker in his role as a husband and father. In these roles, society tends increasingly to expect him not to submit to 'life as it happens' but to consciously control his affairs, to think about his children's tomorrow, to rationally and not blindly influence their behaviour, and to accord to his wife a greater measure of tolerance, respect, and understanding than many husbands gave to their wives in the nineteenth century.

How does the worker react to these effects of modern industrial techniques and to the apparent conflict in values and norms of behaviour? Even to be provocative about this question one must plunge further into the hazardous sea of speculation, and always one must allow for the infinite ways in which human beings adjust and adapt to a changing pattern of culture.

Nevertheless, I believe we can frame a number of more specific questions. If workers do not respect themselves and do not feel that they are being accorded respect by their fellows in the factory, may they not, therefore, tend to feel that they are not fulfilling satisfactorily, in the eyes of their wives and children, their roles as husbands and fathers? Society expects, for example, that children should admire and respect their fathers for qualities other than the size of their pay packets. In the eyes of the farm worker's child and the child in many middle-class and professional homes, father plays a comprehended and admired role in his work. But what of the child of the industrial worker on the assembly line who has little conception of his place in the scheme of things? Consider also the effects on a wife in a marriage which is attempting to get along on the basis of partnership, on a more

[1] Ford, Henry, *My Life and Work* (New York: Doubleday, Page & Co, 1922), p. 103.

equal sharing of tasks and responsibilities. Will the wife not be affected by her husband's sense of failure, his feelings of frustration, by the irregularities of his rewards and status, and by the fact that he is unlikely to advance in these spheres as they both grow older? In a culture that values efficiency, those who cannot achieve self-respect in their work may come to feel that there is something wrong with them not only as workers but as husbands and fathers. One may be tempted to speculate how far and to what extent these factors are important today in the constellation of motives that are leading more married women in Western societies to go out to work.

In so far, then, as modern industrial techniques lead to feelings of personal dissatisfaction, to a dispossession of personality, the problem thus becomes a family and community problem. If the effects cannot be expressed at work, if relief and compensation cannot be found there, then the worker's home life is likely to be influenced and changed in many subtle ways. In a world of widening choice, as material standards rise, the worker in these situations and subject to these influences may—perhaps must—seek more satisfactions outside the work place and in the home. He may or may not be successful in satisfying in these other spheres his needs for status, for respect, for predictable relations with his fellows, and for a sense of control over his own affairs. In so far as he turns to his home as an outlet, as a source of satisfaction, then it is arguable that two different and opposed patterns of behaviour may develop. One may take the form of submissiveness—of a lack of initiative and a reduced sense of control. The worker will thus be carrying into his family life the conduct expected of him in the culture of the factory. Or he may react, according to his personality, the personality of his wife, and the prevailing characteristics of the community at large, in an authoritarian and punishing way. He may react to the domination of the machine by attempting to dominate others. National characteristics, as they have been called, may determine whether he will or will not behave in this way. Or he may, somewhere along this axis of submission-domination, genuinely find new sources of satisfaction in his own home. He may take a greater share in the running of the home and in the business of family life generally. This, I believe, may be happening in Britain—though not, I believe, in Germany and some other countries. One has only to notice the way in which husbands now do the shopping, take the laundry to the launderette (perhaps because the wife has been out to work), play with the children, and unashamedly push prams, to realize that family life in industrialized Britain is changing. Do husbands now push prams in Germany? Should they?

On this homely note I come to some general conclusions. One is that I do not believe that the problem of 'human relations in industry' can be entirely solved within industry itself. It cannot be solved by tying closer the bonds between employer and employee through the provision of miniature occupational welfare states. Such an approach implies less freedom of choice and, consequently, less rather than more control by the worker over his own affairs. It can also mean, too, more social and psychological pressures toward submissive and conforming behaviour in the work place and thus have disturbing effects in the home when the worker, released from the determinism of the factory, attempts to recover possession of himself. 'To act freely,' as Bergson wrote, 'is to recover possession of one's self.'

Nor can the contemporary problems of family life be entirely solved within the family itself. The family does not function in a social vacuum. How it functions today is, as I have attempted to show, profoundly affected by the forces of industrialization. It is simultaneously benefited and damaged by those forces. The rapidity of change in highly industrialized societies during the last one hundred years has put the family on the defensive. Its responsibilities have grown; it has been placed in more situations of divided loyalties and conflicting values; it has been forced to choose between kinship and economic progress; and it has been constantly subjected to the gales of creative instability.

It is in this context that we need to see the social services in a variety of stabilizing, preventive, and protective roles. Interpreted in this way, and not as the modern equivalent of Bismarckian benevolence, the social services become an ally—not an enemy—of industrial and technological progress. To reformulate the philosophy of social policy, and to rescue it from its present inhibitions derived from a 'welfare state' ideology, is one of the major tasks of the second half of the twentieth century.

CHAPTER 7

The Hospital and Its Patients[1]

IN depth and range of complexity, the hospital as a social institution has few rivals today. In a recent study of the hospital, Dr Edward Churchill, writing from the famous Massachusetts General Hospital, said: 'The hospital is one of the most complex and dynamic instruments of contemporary society'.[2] In Britain, we need to view the hospital in a similar sense operating within the additional complexities of a nationwide Government-financed, centrally regulated system of administration. No community could hope to succeed with such an enterprise without a large fund of intelligence, and what I like to call cultivated commonsense. This country has been conspicuously successful in producing administrators with these talents, but such gifts by themselves are not now sufficient when it comes to controlling and administering a hospital service. Today we must add a wide knowledge of the Health Service as a whole, a thorough grasp of the work and functions of all departments of the hospital, and at least a nodding acquaintance with a variety of technical, medical and professional terms. I do not wish to join with those who would make a mystique of administration, but I must say that in my experience most lay members, newly-appointed, of a hospital board or management committee are pretty useless during their first year of office. Often, their sense of inadequacy

[1] An address given at the Jubilee Conference of the Institute of Hospital Administrators in London on May 10, 1952, and published in *The Hospital*, June 1952.

[2] Churchill, E., in *The Hospital in Contemporary Life*, ed. Faxon, N. W., 1949

and the efforts they feel they must make to justify themselves in their new role encourage behaviour round the committee table which is either sentimental or grandiose, or both. Too much attention is devoted to elaborate development plans for the hospital, irrespective of the needs of the general practitioner and local authority services, and too uncritical a view is taken of welfare and amenity for hospital staffs. If there is no 'ordinary' money available, there is apparently always 'free' money. The existence of this fund is one of the few aspects of hospital management which the new member grasps during his first year of office. In all seriousness, however, I do suggest that it is not until perhaps half the three years have gone by that a new member can play a really useful part in hospital government. The Ministry of Health and the regional boards have, I think, over-estimated their ability at spotting talent for hospital management, and, in setting the term of office at three years, under-estimated the time it now takes to acquire a workmanlike grasp of the complexities of the modern hospital system.

This, however, is but one reflection of the complexities of the hospital world, an instance which I have used for illustration, but which I do not propose to pursue further. The central point I wish to make is that we are here faced with one of the most complex of social institutions, an institution which in recent years has grown immensely in its complexities and to which we have added—and, indeed, are still doing so every day—new complications as a result of the development of the National Health Service. Now, in this situation there are, I suggest, three main dangers.

The first danger is that increasing complexity in structure, functions and administration can lead to increasing economic and social costs without a proportional rise in value rendered to the community. Complex institutions and societies carry within themselves a strong tendency to make and multiply new complexities, and each one in itself represents another possibility of waste, misdirected effort and the growth of organizational fetishes. Clearly, the more complex a situation is, the harder it becomes to put one's finger on sources of inefficiency and the fewer chances there are of self-correction or adjustment from within the institution itself. This points to the need, all too little recognized I regret to say, for externally directed critical studies, research and analysis of the hospital services. No institution, continually in a state of change, constantly subject to the pressure of many vested interests and forces, can hope to remain healthy without criticism. But it is not criticism in quantity that is wanted, or comment of the generalized and often biased type which fills so many of the pages of the now famous Eleventh Report from the Select Committee on Estimates.[1] The need is for informed criticism based on a study of the facts. How necessary the searchlight of investigation and public opinion is to the health of hospitals was first shown by Florence Nightingale who spent so many years of her life in ruthlessly assembling and arranging facts. Even in the last ten years we have had two examples of the working of this principle: an improvement in hospital food for patients, and an improvement in the arrangements for parents to see their sick children in hospitals. The important thing to note here is that both these consequences did not result from any ferment of self-examination in the hospitals themselves or from the professional ranks of nurses and doctors. Broadly speaking, these changes, now accepted as desirable, were the result of pressures from without the hospital. The demand for change came from sources of opinion outside the institution.

The second danger to the hospital and its patients, arising from increasing complexity in the hospital world, is that the ends or aims of hospital work may be obscured by excessive preoccupation with means. Those concerned with policy-making and management are increasingly immersed in the details of administration. Each particular tree, and, indeed, each particular branch of each tree becomes more important than the aims of the hospital as a social institution. Boards of Governors and Management Committees devote more of their time to the conditions of work, questions of rewards, difficulties of status and dissatisfaction among the staff, than they do to the needs of the

[1] Session 1950–1, Regional Hospital Boards and Hospital Management Committees, 1951.

patients. Of course, all these questions are vital to the efficient and harmonious running of a hospital: there must be some system of settling these often difficult issues. But the National Health Service has added greatly to the volume of administrative work of this kind by the introduction of national uniform scales of reward, hours of work, holidays, superannuation, and so forth. The continual need for the ironing-out of innumerable small injustices and anomalies in the working conditions of members of hospital staffs gives rise to a lot of work and partly accounts for the increase in administrative costs since 1948. Do not think here that I am critical of the need for justice and equity among hospital staffs. The improved pay and conditions of work of nurses and other hospital workers has been one of the great benefits of the National Health Service. Indeed, one of the major social consequences of the Service is that it has given not only better conditions but more professional freedom, in the vocational sense of the word, to professional groups working in the hospital. Doctors have no longer to concern themselves with the financial means of the patients; nurses do not have to deal with all the food that patients and their relatives were required to bring into the hospital; almoners no longer have to consider whether this or that patient is a poor law case. An analysis of changes in function among different professional groups would show the extent to which the National Health Service has led to an enlargement of professional freedom. This is an important gain. Nevertheless, it is wise to remember that all social change on this scale, while solving some problems, invariably creates new ones. One of the new problems is the danger that the hospital may tend increasingly to be run in the interests of those working in and for the hospital rather than in the interests of the patients. The fundamental purpose of the hospital must not be dimmed by excessive preoccupation with the means.

The history of social institutions offers us many warnings. We need only remember the fate of the monasteries, or, nearer in time, the shocking conditions of many childrens' homes revealed in the Curtis Report of 1946[1] after the social conscience had been

[1] *Report of the Care of Children Committee* (the Curtis Report), Cmd 6922, 1946.

asleep for too many years. Let me quote again from Dr Edward Churchill's survey of the history of hospitals. Of the changing relationship of the hospital and the medical profession during the twentieth century, he writes: 'This blending of the interest of the doctor with the function of the hospital led to a sense of responsibility and ownership . . . Society, in turn, has been only too ready to relinquish some of its responsibility and relax its efforts. The doctors are supposed to know what they are doing, and comfort is taken in the attitude that it is impossible for a mere layman to judge of such matters.' Dr Churchill continues: 'This situation has created a disturbing undercurrent of thought that only a few observers appear to notice. Is it well for society, or in the long run, for the profession, that this trend continue? Can a not disinterested profession be entrusted with an agency of society that is becoming more vital today than ever before in history? However sincere the efforts of the doctor to provide the best care for his patients, the fact must be faced that these same efforts provide him with the prestige and comfortable living which he claims. It is possible that the profession is unconsciously drifting into a dangerous position not wholly unlike that in which the Church found itself before the Reformation.'[1]

To Dr Churchill's words we may add the rider that the advent of the National Health Service may have arrested this historical trend—or it may not. One thing at least we may be sure of: a social process of this importance, in whatever direction it has been tending since 1948, has not stood still. We have achieved a better or a worse balance of interests; a better or a worse distribution of administrative and executive power.

I come now to the third of my points of danger to the welfare of patients. This is represented by scientific and technological advance. There is no need for me to speak here of the inestimable gains which have accrued in the last decade or so from advances in scientific medicine—diagnosis, treatment and cure; nor do I wish to speak of the possible dangers to patients, inherent in these advances, of their being used perhaps unknowingly as guinea-

[1] Churchill, E., in *The Hospital in Contemporary Life*, ed. Faxon, N. W., 1949.

pigs in the search for increased knowledge. What I have to say relates to the social and psychological welfare of patients in a hospital situation of applied scientific medicine. For a number of reasons, and I shall mention only one or two, these advances of science into the hospital have made it harder to treat the patient as a person. One reason is that more science has meant more division of labour and, inevitably, of course, more professional fragmentation as specialisms have developed and new groups of workers have banded themselves together in professional groups. An increase in the division of labour means that more people with different functions and skills to perform are brought into contact with the patient. Each separate function to be performed, for out-patient as well as in-patient, involves the sick person in a personal contact with more people—more 'experts' (for that is how they often appear to the patient). All this happens at a time when the patient, sick perhaps in mind as well as in body, with fears and anxieties about himself and his family, with more questions and uncertainties in a mind disturbed by illness, is less able to cope with the strain of entering into new personal contacts with many strange individuals endowed with all the authority and mystery which surround the hospital and its gift of survival. As most of us know, to feel ill is to feel unadventurous, to want to retreat from life, to have one's fears removed and one's needs met without effort. Physical illness can play queer tricks with our thoughts and our behaviour. This does not mean, as some all too easily suppose, that we are neurotics. In being querulous and ungrateful, demanding and apathetic in turn, we are in fact behaving as ill people. The demands that people make on society are greater when they are ill than when they are well. Yet the advent of science has made it more difficult, in social and psychological terms, for the hospital as part of society to meet these demands. More science means more division of labour and more experts—more of the mysteries of blood counts, X-rays, test-meals, investigations, case history taking and so forth. These, in turn, mean more departmentalism and, all too often, more departmental thinking. As A. N. Whitehead warned us, the fixed person for the fixed duties in a fixed situation is a social menace. He is particularly a menace to the sick person who is more in need, rather than less, for explanation and understanding. But the departmentalism which stems from a division of labour—from a dividing up of services rendered to a patient—is given more to silence than to communication. Silence from those in authority, from doctor, sister, nurse, administrator, clerk, technician and so on often means a want of imagination: silence consents to fear among those who have great need for explanation and reassurance.

What is it that patients complain of more than anything else in relation to the hospital—'No one told me anything'—'Nobody asked me'—'I don't know'. How often one comes across people who have been discharged from hospital, bewildered, still anxious and afraid; disillusioned because the medical magic has not apparently or not yet yielded results, ignorant of what the investigations have shown, what the doctors think, what the treatment has been or is to be, and what the outlook is in terms of life and health.

If one analyses the recent articles of ex-patients recounting in medical and other journals their hospital experiences, it is interesting how often this theme of the discourtesies of silence recurs. Take, for instance, the story of a mother (published in *The Lancet*), who had to go into hospital for gynaecological treatment.[1] The first house-surgeon to examine her did so in complete silence: no greeting, no smile, no sign that there was anyone in the room but himself and the nurse. In the ward, this patient found that one of the biggest worries of some of the other women was whether or not they were to have abdominal operations. None received direct answers from the nurses, and none dared ask the houseman who also had examined them in silence. It was the ward sister who told the houseman how the patients were feeling; the patients looked on in silence. 'When the morning of the operation came,' writes this patient, 'and there were ten of us to go, I had some difficulty in discovering where I was on the list. It was quite a new idea to the nurses that it

[1] 'The Iron Curtain in Hospital,' *Lancet* (1951), ii, 494.

would be a help to know whether one had to wait all day or whether it was to be got over early.' Again, this patient found it was quite unusual for anything to be said before a local anaesthetic was given. Some women were quite shocked because they were dilated under a local anaesthetic without any warning of what was to be done. Drugs were given without inquiry or explanation; examinations were made in silence; infra-red lamps were set going without explanation; people left hospital without explanation. The barrier of silence seemed impenetrable.

Why should all this be so? Why is it not understood that courtesy and sociability have a therapeutic value? Most of us in our own homes know this instinctively, but somehow or other it gets lost in the hospital. Partly, I suppose, it is the effect on people of working and living in a closed institution with rigid social hierarchies and codes of behaviour. The barrier of silence as one element in a general failure to treat the patient as a person has also been created, as I have already said, because of the division of service to the patient resulting from scientific advances in medicine.

Another important consequence of these scientific advances is the greater need for discipline and accuracy in hospital work. Applied science in medical care means precision and accuracy. This, and the knowledge that lives are at stake, calls for a system of rules and regulations governing the performance of duties and the relationships between different groups in the hospital. If the hospital is to fulfil its function without risk to the patient, it is essential that the requests and orders of the doctors should be carried out by the nursing and other staffs with accuracy and completeness. It follows, therefore, that a certain degree of autocratic behaviour by the professional staff is an inevitable characteristic of hospital life. When the doctors are absent, the nursing staff feels that it is deputizing for them. Nurses possess, or feel themselves to possess, responsibilities which are in fact greater than are covered by their professional authority, or their knowledge and skill. In situations of this kind—and it happens to many people, administrators, professional workers, and others—there is considerable insecurity if the burden of responsibility is felt to be disproportionate to the knowledge and skill possessed. Inevitably, therefore, as Dr A. T. M. Wilson has pointed out,[1] these people tend to deal with their insecurity by attempting to limit responsibility and increase efficiency through the formulation of rigid rules and regulations and by developing an authoritative and protective discipline. The barrier of silence is one device employed to maintain authority. We find it so used in many different settings when we look at other institutions where the relationship between the staff and the inmates is not a happy one. It is not a coincidence that the Curtis Committee Report on the Care of Children drew attention to the fact that in some of the most unsatisfactory voluntary institutions all the children were compelled to eat their meals in silence.[2] This, of course, was not necessary to maintain discipline, any more than many vexatious practices are necessary today in the hospital in order to uphold the authority of the staff in relation to the patients. But certain practices have a habit of lingering on and outliving their usefulness in any type of institutional setting, particularly in institutions like hospitals which are to some extent protected from public criticism partly because they are concerned with people who are peculiarly dependent, helpless and often inarticulate in the face of authority. The practice of talking between doctors and nurses over their patients still goes on although it is now known that hearing is the last conscious function to disappear with anaesthesia. Similarly, hearing may remain acute in severe prostrating illness; when the patient may be too weak to move or to speak and may appear unconscious, the hearing function may nevertheless still be active. Again, patients with nephritis are still nursed in blankets in some hospitals, although it has long been known that those suffering from this disease do not sweat and that blanket-nursing is unnecessary. The continuance of the practice is another nursing relic. Even worse, perhaps, is the survival of that automatic rite known as the ward sister's 'purgative round', where all are sometimes treated alike irrespective of age, condition, previous habits, and so forth. It is

[1] Wilson, A. T. M., *Human Relations*, 1950, III, i, 89.
[2] Cmd 6922, 1946, p. 83.

an example of what I have earlier called an 'organizational fetish'. It has survived from that great age of the purgative habit —the period at the beginning of this century when the medical profession popularized 'inner cleanliness' and social workers were busy teaching 'outer cleanliness'.

In describing some of the forces which have shaped and are still shaping hospital methods and relationships, I do not wish to leave an impression that hospital staffs are deliberately callous to their patients. These things are not consciously and deliberately done to worry and distress patients. They are done unthinkingly by people who are devoted to their calling, working unselfishly and for long hours in the interests of the sick. The fact that they can happen is due to many factors. Advances in applied scientific medicine, the growth of specialism, the fragmentation of services rendered to patients, departmental thinking, administrative preoccupation with detail, the absence of critical self-examination arising within the hospital; all these factors, in total, contribute to making the hospital an increasingly complex institution. To these, I think we must add some failure in education and professional training. The sociology of the patient has been neglected—his attitudes, motives, feelings and basic needs. 'I sometimes think,' said Dr Clark-Kennedy in 1950, 'that the unbalanced scientific training which our universities provide is an inadequate education for a man or woman destined to spend his or her life in the practice of the art of medicine.'[1]

In earlier times, when the hospital was a simpler institution, and when the natural, intuitive sympathies of doctors, nurses and others had not been overridden by long, specialized courses of training, it was not perhaps necessary to emphasize these elementary needs. Then, because so little was known, there was not the same danger of separating the treatment of the disease—the case—from the treatment of the patient as a person. Diseases divorced from patients are abstractions from reality. Today, as standards have risen and as complexities have increased, the

[1] Clark-Kennedy, A. E., *Lancet*, 1950, ii, 661.

dangers of doing harm to the patient—social and psychological harm and not the physical harm of the nineteenth century—have increased. The greatest authority of all time on hospital administration foresaw these dangers nearly a hundred years ago. Florence Nightingale understood that the sick suffer almost as much mental as bodily pain. In her *Notes on Nursing*, published in 1859, she wrote, 'Apprehension, uncertainty, waiting, expectation, fear of surprise, do a patient more harm than any exertion. Remember he is face to face with his enemy all the time, internally wrestling with him, having long imaginary conversations with him'. What remarkable insight for someone who spent most of her life administering and handling facts and figures! 'Do not forget,' she said, 'that patients are shy of asking'—yet how often we forget it today. 'It is commonly supposed,' she said, 'that a nurse is there to save physical exertion. She ought to be there to save (the patient) taking thought.' With all her intense preoccupation with means, the design of hospital wards, the planning of hospital space, sanitation, the proper use of record forms and so forth, Florence Nightingale never lost sight of the fundamental needs of the patient. With these in mind, she spent years searching for factual tools by which she might distinguish the efficient from the inefficient, the good from the bad. It was a great achievement, in those days, to employ the comparative method to measure the relative success of different systems of hospital care. Hospitals varied in the quality of their work as much in those days as they do today, and Florence Nightingale's problem (as it is ours today) was to find out why some were good and some were bad, and what could be done about it. Medical and administrative opinion was against her: she was told, in effect, that because of the number of variables to be taken into account, it was impossible to quantify the work of a hospital; different systems and different conditions could not be compared. Nevertheless, in the field of mortality statistics she succeeded; she proved that it was possible to identify the inefficient hospitals that were doing harm to their patients.

The problem of the hospital in the National Health Service is fundamentally the same today: the need to know how and why some hospitals are relatively more successful, relatively more efficient, in this or that respect and why others are not. Of course, we recognize that the task is much more complex today. More refined tools than mortality data are needed to evaluate the effects of medical care; more precise instruments of enquiry than costs per occupied bed-day are needed to assess differences in financial and administrative costs. Valuable work is going forward in this field under the auspices of the Nuffield Trust, but there is room for much more thought and study in respect to the methodology of investigation—of how we should tackle these problems in the twentieth century. We might, for instance, derive benefit from studying the system of medical audit which has been used for some years by a few leading hospitals in the United States. This is a periodical self-appraisal by the entire medical staff of the work performed in the hospital. On the basis of comprehensive and uniform record-keeping, analyses are compiled which show the morbidity and mortality experience of each service and each individual staff member over a period of time. Initial diagnosis and prognosis are compared with the results of hospital treatment, and the results become the basis for self-education and improvement and for the evaluation of new procedures. This problem of the quality of medical care is one of the crucial problems of social medicine in the twentieth century. Its importance is increased rather than diminished by the advent of the National Health Service, by the growing penetration of medicine by science and technology, by the newer complexities of administration, and by all the risks, of which we are often hardly aware, of losing sight of the individual patient.

This is not just a medical matter. The problem of the quality of medical care is in part an administrative problem; in part a problem of human relations in the hospital; in part a problem of bringing the hospital as a social institution back into society where it properly belongs and from which it has for too long been isolated. Today, all those who work in the hospital need to care much more about how and why the patient comes; what the person experiences as a patient, and what happens to the patient when he returns, as a person, to society. Unless, today, the hospital approaches its task in this way, it cannot claim to uphold the first principle laid down by Florence Nightingale in her *Notes on Hospitals*, published in 1859, when she wrote, 'It may seem a strange principle to enunciate as the very first requirement in a hospital that it should do the sick no harm'. It is necessary to repeat this principle today. Were Florence Nightingale alive now, she would have been shocked to read Dr Goodall's report in *The Lancet* concerning cross-infection in hospital wards, slovenly habits and irresponsible behaviour among medical and nursing staffs, and general inertia towards the prevention of infection.[1] She would have seized on the fact that hardly any of the measures to prevent cross-infection recommended by the Medical Research Council during the last ten years were in operation in the twenty-four wards of eight hospitals studied by Dr Goodall; that too many trained nurses were still counting dirty linen; that most sluice rooms were in a muddle; that refrigerators contained both milk and pathological specimens; that dressing-bowls, by a time-honoured custom, were boiled for twenty minutes when two would have done; that there was an insufficient sense of responsibility among doctors about the wearing of masks; and that many patients had to stay longer in hospital because of an acquired infection, the average increase of stay per infected patient in three surgical wards being twenty-one days.

This catalogue of hospital inertia by Dr Goodall, of primitive customs and habits surviving in an age of scientific medicine, shows once again the need for constant re-examination of hospital activities and administration if the sick are not to be harmed. All these matters to which Dr Goodall draws attention, are, I would remind you, physical matters, potential physical dangers to the welfare of the patient. That these physical dangers can exist in such alarming fashion today suggests that other and more subtle dangers to the patient, social and psychological dangers, may also be as widespread and prevalent if we did but know. It is, I submit, the task of each hospital to examine its

[1] Goodall, J. W. D., 1952, *Lancet*, i, 807.

own heart and to ask itself the kind of questions which Florence Nightingale as a hospital administrator would assuredly have asked had she been alive today—alive to disturb, annoy, worry and help the Ministry of Health and all those concerned with the running of our hospitals.

CHAPTER 8

The National Health Service in England[1]

SOME ASPECTS OF STRUCTURE

I

OVER a hundred years ago, De Tocqueville, opening a chapter on 'The Desire for Wealth' in his famous treatise on *Democracy in America* wrote: 'In America the passion for physical well-being . . . is general.'[2] He saw this passion for bodily comfort, for a sense of individual ease, as an inseparable part of a desire for material well-being. Benjamin McCready, in an essay written for the Medical Society of the State of New York in 1837, said much the same thing: 'the Americans are an anxious, careworn people.'[3]

Today, one might venture to say that Americans want to be healthy, physically and psychologically, because they are constantly aware of a need to be healthy. This consciousness of need, its degree of intensity, and the forms of behaviour in which it finds expression, is in large measure the product of the cultural forces which play on the individual from childhood to old age. What society expects of the individual as a distinctive individual and, reciprocally, what that individual himself feels is expected of him by his fellows, thus represent, in the effects they have in conditioning attitudes to health, important variables in

[1] The Sherrill Foundation Lectures delivered at the Law School, Yale University, USA, in April 1957.

[2] De Tocqueville, A., *Democracy in America*, 'The World's Classics' ed., Oxford University Press, 1946, p. 398.

[3] McCready, B., *Transactions of the Medical Society of the State of New York*, 1836–7, Vol. 3, pp. 91–150.

the demand for medical care. Good health is seen both as a prerequisite for the success of the personality and, simultaneously, as a necessary condition for the enjoyment and exploitation of success. 'The recollections of the brevity of life,' as De Tocqueville also wrote, 'is a constant spur.'[1] Or, as a contemporary observer puts it, '. . . it was the fear of becoming too old to choose which gave old age and death a bad name in this country'.[2]

In general terms, it can thus be argued that the larger the investment by any society in 'individualism' (as a 'way of life') the more may 'health consciousness' spread. Similarly, the limits to what is personally conceived to be tolerable in feelings of bad health or inadequate function may also rise. And as society becomes more health conscious (in the sense of more individuals becoming aware of the higher standards expected of them) the more may each individual become dependent, or at least feel dependent, in an age of scientific medicine, on other individuals—on resources external to himself for the achievement of good health. The high esteem of psychology and science in the American culture both emphasizes and expresses this sense of dependency in the search for good health.[3]

In relative terms, the individual may come to feel more dependent on psychotherapy, on medical science, on the doctors; less on his own inner resources. The high prestige accorded today to the physician—the man who gives service in a professional capacity to others—is not, therefore, in this context surprising. Nor, perhaps, should we be surprised by the particular roles pursued by the collectivity of doctors—the American Medical Association. They are the organized and centralized reflections of ascribed power—the power ascribed by society as

[1] De Tocqueville, *op. cit.*, p. 406.

[2] Erikson, E. H., *Childhood and Society*, 1953, pp. 252–3.

[3] Current discussion in the United States about the immense and mounting use of the so-called tranquillizing drugs is instructive. An editorial in the *American Journal of Psychiatry* has condemned their widespread use as likely to seduce patients into a bogus health and of weakening their adaptive capacities. Other doctors see the excessive use of these drugs as a threat to American society by the effects they may have in 'smothering the incentive to change and progress that derives from fear and anxiety' (*Amer. J. Psychiat*, 1957, *113*, 663 and Dickel, H. A., and Dixon, H. H., *J. Amer. Med. Ass.*, 1957, *163*, 422).

a whole to those who are regarded as professional experts in matters of health and disease, life and death. Within limits, each distinctive culture gets the medical priesthood it wants.

It is, however, one thing for a society to agree on the importance of good health and good medical care; quite another for it to agree on how good health may be achieved and maintained by organizing and distributing its medical resources in alternative ways. I shall, therefore, take as my main theme the organization of medical care, and shall discuss some of the important issues raised by the introduction in 1948 of a national health service in England and Wales.[1]

I hope that I have already given sufficient reason for my choice of this particular theme by presenting you with, at the outset, some brief though controversial observations. These I intend to amplify later on, for there is much to be said about attitudes to health in considering the changing nature of the doctor-patient relationship. Something of what I shall have to say will, I believe, have relevance to the contemporary American scene although I shall not pretend that ways of organizing medical care, found appropriate in England, are necessarily applicable to the United States; the principles may be; the methods may not be. Nor would I make any special claim to knowledge about the present organization of medical care in the United States.

To this warning I would add another. It is, in fact, to testify my belief in the social value of the National Health Service to patients and doctors alike in England and Wales. This belief is based on another belief; that progress in medical science, in psychological theories and in the specialized division of medical skill has converted medicine from an individual, intuitive enterprise into a social service. I would thus make clear at the outset my personal preferences about the principles on which medical care should today be organized and provided.

Just as I know little about the detail of American problems of medical care so, I imagine, you are not familiar with the detail of the National Health Service—despite the interest taken in it by

[1] Because the Health Service is organized somewhat differently in Scotland I confine my discussion to the material for England and Wales.

the American Medical Association.[1] Most of this lecture is, therefore, devoted to a summary account of some features of the organization; the institutional structure through which medical care is now provided for over nine-tenths of the population of England and Wales.[2] My second lecture is focused on the general practitioner and I shall consider how the Health Service has affected his work since 1948. Finally, I shall discuss some of the ways in which science has affected the role of the doctor in the provision of medical care.

II

The legal foundation of the Service is the Act passed by Parliament in 1946.[3] The Service began to operate in July 1948. Subsequent legislative measures and Ministerial regulations issued under the authority of the principal Act have also to be taken into account in considering the present administrative framework.

At the head of the Service is the Minister of Health, advised by the Central Health Services Council and a number of Standing Advisory Committees. These are chiefly composed of professional people, representative of the various interests, who are appointed by the Minister after consultation with the organizations concerned. In practice, the Minister appoints those who are nominated by the professions.

It is the Minister's duty, in the words of the 1946 Act, 'to promote the establishment in England and Wales of a comprehensive health service designed to secure improvement in the physical and mental health of the people of England and Wales and the prevention, diagnosis and treatment of illness, and for

[1] For example, the widespread propaganda campaign against 'socialized medicine' launched in 1950 after the visit to England of a delegation from the AMA (*J. Amer. Med. Ass.*, 1950, *143*, 1420). There is also much valuable information on the role of the Association in 'The American Medical Association: Power, Purpose and Politics in Organized Medicine' (Hyde, D. R., and Wolff, P., with Gross, A., and Hoffman, E. L., *Yale Law Journal*, 1954, Vol. 63, No. 7).

[2] To be more precise, about 95 per cent.

[3] National Health Service Act, 1946, 9 and 10, Geo. 6, Ch. 81.

that purpose to provide or secure the effective provision of services'. It is further laid down that 'The services so provided shall be free of charge, except where any provision of this Act expressly provides for the making and recovery of charges'.

The present position, so far as charges are concerned, is:

1. Those provided with hospital in-patient care and who are in receipt of unemployment, sickness and other social security benefits have these benefits reduced after a specified period of hospital stay.

2. In the public hospitals, those patients desiring privacy and who are provided with (what are called) 'amenity beds' pay a weekly charge which approximates, at the most, to about one-third of the economic cost. The supply of such beds apparently more than meets the demand, for the average occupancy rate of 80 per cent is lower than the average rate for non-amenity beds.[1]

3. A charge of 1*s*. is made for each separate drug prescription supplied by general practitioners and to hospital out-patients. Charges are also imposed for the supply or repair of surgical appliances and equipment, wigs and other items and for hospital treatment following road accidents.[2]

4. As regards the dental service, roughly half the cost of all dentures is now paid by patients. In addition, all those aged over twenty-one (except expectant and nursing mothers) pay all or part of the cost of treatment.

5. Under the ophthalmic service, patients pay the full cost of frames supplied and a proportion of the cost of the lens.

6. Charges are made by local authorities for the provision of home helps in cases of illness and, in some instances, for the prevention of illness, care and after-care services.

7. Although not a charge in the same sense it is important to note that many hospitals set aside private 'pay beds' for the use of patients who prefer to make private arrangements to be treated. These patients pay the doctors providing the treatment and for their maintenance in hospital. This enables consultants

[1] *Report of the Committee of Enquiry into the Cost of the National Health Service*, Cmd 9663, 1956, p. 148 (hereinafter referred to as the Guillebaud Report).

[2] In certain circumstances these charges can be waived.

working part-time in the Health Service to run part of their private practice from Health Service hospitals and gives them and private patients access to specialist and teaching hospitals. The supply of such 'pay beds' amply meets present demand; in 1954, for instance, the average occupancy by paying patients was only 35 per cent.[1]

Any general impression that the Health Service is entirely a 'free' service (in the sense of being free on demand) thus requires correction. In some of its branches (for instance, the dental and ophthalmic services) patients are paying a substantial part of the economic cost, and it has been suggested that the present level of charges is impeding some people from using certain of the services and is discouraging the extension of preventive work.[2]

The principle of free access to medical care, a fundamental principle in the development of the Service in 1948, has to some extent, therefore, been limited in recent years; primarily in respect to dental and ophthalmic care. In another respect, too, some limitation to the effective use of the Service has been brought about as a result of the fall in the relative value of sickness benefits under the National Insurance Scheme. At the end of 1956 these benefits represented only about 34 per cent of average industrial earnings for a man, wife, and two children.[3] Some workers may be unwilling to consult their doctors; others may be compelled to return to work too soon.

An essential element in the principle of free access to medical care is freedom to use or not to use the Service and to choose and change one's doctor. No one is compelled to use the Service. Some 550 to 600 general practitioners limit their work to private, fee-paying patients,[4] and large numbers of other general

[1] *Guillebaud Report*, p. 148.

[2] *Guillebaud Report*, pp. 190–5. Users of the ophthalmic service paid about 38 per cent of the cost to public funds in 1953–4. The corresponding proportion for the dental service was about 22 per cent.

[3] *Ministry of Labour Gazette*, September 1957.

[4] Figures published by the British Medical Association suggest that the number of general practitioners in the UK solely engaged in private practice was 556 in 1951, and between 573 and 615 in 1955. *Brit. Med. J.*, 1951, Supp., May 26 and Supp. October 8, 1955, and March 10, 1956.

practitioners combine Health Service and private patient work. Patients can and do have a Health Service general practitioner, pay privately for a consultant and use the free services of the Health Service hospitals. Or they can pay a general practitioner and have access to free consultant and hospital services. Some have both a private and a National Health Service doctor.[1] And all can vary these combinations of choice as often as they like and for each member of the family. Not a single form has to be filled up except for the need, if one wishes to have general practitioner care under the Service, to be accepted on a doctor's list.

The one limitation to this freedom of choice in the doctor-patient relationship that has been imposed since 1948 was forced on an unwilling Ministry of Health by the profession.[2] In October 1950 restrictions were placed on the ease with which patients could change their doctors.[3] The new arrangements led to some paper work, introduced a waiting period before a change could be effective and, in most cases, required the written consent of the present doctor. Some patients have naturally found this an embarrassing procedure as insured workers did in the 1930's when their liberties were restricted on the grounds that patients changed their doctors too frequently.[4] Similar arguments were used after 1948 but, again, no evidence has been published to support these generalizations about 'excessive' changing of doctors.[5] Among other patients today, with little knowledge about statutory regulations, an impression has gained ground that it is impossible or almost impossible to change one's doctor.[6]

[1] Gray, P. G., and Cartwright, A., Government Social Survey Report, *Lancet*, 1953, ii, 1308.

[2] Minutes of the General Medical Services Committee of the British Medical Association, May 18, 1950, *Brit. Med. J.*, May 27, 1950. See also correspondence in the *Journal*, Supp., October 21, 1950, p. 171.

[3] Ministry of Health circular ECL 98/50, Sept 1950 (see also SI 1951, No. 1695).

[4] Levy, H., *National Health Insurance*, 1944, p. 117.

[5] Nevertheless, the Committee on General Practice set up by the Central Health Services Council thought that the new arrangements struck 'the right balance between freedom and restraint' (*Report*, 1954, p. 13).

[6] Minutes of the General Medical Services Committee of the British Medical Association, March 18, 1954, *Brit. Med. J.*, Supp., April 3, 1954, p. 139. See also correspondence in the *Journal*, Supp., October 21, 1950, p. 171, September 1, 1951, p. 103, and January 19, 1952, p. 19.

One theory held, it would seem, by younger practitioners, is that this restriction on freedom was insisted on by the British Medical Association in the interests of the older, well-established practitioners anxious to safeguard their practices in an era when the demands to enter medicine, including general practice, have been unprecedently high.[1] In 1954, the Government, responding to the anxieties of the profession, set up a committee, mainly composed of doctors, to consider whether Britain is not now training too many doctors.[2]

III

Among all the ideas of the 1930's and 1940's which led to the creation of the Health Service the one which increasingly dominated the mind of the public and the profession alike was the idea of prevention; the prevention of ill-health and incapacity.[3] In the field of medical care, the idea of prevention is largely a product of the twentieth century, not because of any originality in the idea itself but because of its recognized practicability. The impact of scientific advances on medicine enlarged the area and potentialities of preventive action; from the individual to the group, from the group to society. Above all, it raised the level of public expectation. To these matters I shall return in my last lecture. I stress the significance here of the idea of prevention simply because of the important role it played in relation to the two fundamental principles on which the Health Service came to be organized.

The first, in the words of the Coalition Government's White Paper of 1944, was 'to divorce the care of health from questions

[1] *Brit. Med. J.*, 1952, Supp.,ii, 109.

[2] *Lancet*, 1955, i, 439. The Report was published as this book was going through the press (*Report of the Committee to Consider the Future Number of Medical Practitioners*, 1957).

[3] Its development is traced by Professor Mackintosh in *Trends of Opinion about the Public Health 1901–51* (1953). It is significant that the prevention of disease was singled out as the first of the basic principles by the British Medical Association in its scheme for a 'General Medical Service for the Nation', published in 1938 under that title.

of personal means or other factors irrelevant to it'.[1] This principle of free access to medical care services by all who wanted to use them—personal freedom for the patient, professional freedom for the doctor—I have, in part, already mentioned. To those who stood by this principle it meant earlier and easier access to the doctor; thus enlarging the possibilities of preventive action. The corollary of this principle was the further principle of 'comprehensiveness'. The acceptance of this principle meant (to again quote the White Paper) '. . . the creation of a new public responsibility; to make it in future somebody's clear duty to see that all medical facilities are available to all people . . .'.[2]

In terms of physical resources, the method chosen to create this responsibility was to transfer to the new administrative bodies the existing voluntary and municipal hospitals with their clinics and other associated institutions. Some hospitals, nursing homes, institutions run by religious orders and certain facilities organized on a profit-making basis were not taken over. In all, the Minister of Health, with the Government behind him and Parliament in ultimate control, became the nation's trustee for some 2,700 separate hospitals. Or, to put it in terms of the number of hospital beds, most of the remaining one-fifth of beds not then in public ownership were transferred to the Minister.[3] Many of them, and particularly the voluntary teaching hospitals, retained on their boards of governors and management committees a large number of people who had previously served them as voluntary institutions.

One alternative to common ownership was a contractual relationship with the voluntary hospitals. This method was eventually rejected and, briefly, I think for the following reasons. First, because the voluntary hospitals were already heavily financed from public funds.[4] Second, to contract for adequate ser-

[1] *A National Health Service*, HMSO, February 1944, Cmd 6502, p. 47.

[2] Ibid., p. 47.

[3] In July 1948, 1,143 voluntary hospitals with some 90,000 beds and 1,545 municipal hospitals with about 390,000 beds were transferred to the Minister (*Guillebaud Report*, Cmd 9663, p. 51).

[4] The evidence for this statement is to be published by my colleague, Mr B. Abel-Smith.

vices from these hospitals could have meant a substantial amount of interference with and control over the work of the doctor and the hospital.[1] Third, because to pay for services rendered would, in itself, do nothing to solve the need to raise the level of remuneration of many doctors—especially the younger ones—working in voluntary hospitals.[2] The war-time Emergency Hospital Scheme, organized to provide for immense numbers of civilian casualties, had already made attractive the practice of adequate remuneration for hospital work. Fourth, because of the need, in the circumstances of the day, for action to solve the problem of an undermanned and poorly-paid nursing service. Fifth, if the Government limited its responsibilities to a contractual relationship such an arrangement would still leave the majority of doctors as salaried employees of the municipal authorities. Many members of the profession, having had some actual experience of the State-run Emergency Hospital Scheme during the war, decided, according to my interpretation of events, that full-time or part-time service with a centrally controlled organization was preferable to service with the municipal health authorities. Thus, in the political bargain struck between the profession and the Government of the day, the profession made it abundantly clear that it would enter the Service only on condition that all the hospitals, representing four-fifths of the hospital beds in the country, were taken out of the hands of municipal government.[3] The profession's opposition to municipal

[1] Similar to the problems facing health insurance plans in the United States in attempting to control 'excessive services' (see, for example, Davis, M. M., *Medical Care for Tomorrow*, 1955, especially pp. 333–4).

[2] To quote Dr Ffrangcon Roberts in a letter to the *Lancet*: 'In contrast to the registrars the consultants find themselves in clover. Formerly, as everyone knows, the young consultant faced a hard struggle for many years, eking out a livelihood by odd teaching jobs and depriving himself of holidays for fear of missing a patient. Now, from the word "go" he is completely relieved of financial anxiety. He has a permanent appointment at a substantial salary and unaffected by competition, six weeks' holiday with pay, sick-leave and study-leave on generous terms, and a pension at the end of it. He enjoys, too, the exceptional privilege of deciding for himself how much time he gives to the service.' *Lancet*, 1950, ii, 766. See also Douthwaite, A. H., on 'Consulting Medicine', *Brit. Med. J.*, 1951, ii, 433.

[3] See debate in the House of Lords, April 16, 1946, and especially the comments by Lord Moran (President of the Royal College of Physicians) on local government (*Hansard*, H. of L., Vol. 140, Cols. 822–32).

ownership or control of hospitals is as strong today as it was in 1946,[1] and partly explains why the organization and structure of the Health Service takes the particular form it does.

These were all weighty arguments in the debates which shaped the National Health Service in Britain. They took place during a phase of the war effort when the demand for the effective planning and organization of the nation's resources was strong and widely expressed. The 'planning' atmosphere of the times naturally contributed to the making of the Health Service. Perhaps the most important argument in the planning approach was the need for 'territorial justice'—more equality of access to medical care services for people living in different parts of the country. In other words, a geographically comprehensive hospital service could not, it was thought, be provided under the aegis of some 2,000 separate, independent and often competing hospitals. There was no hospital system; this was the striking fact in a country as geographically small, densely populated and homogeneous as Britain. There was instead a collection of individual hospitals, criss-crossed, separated and enclosed by local government boundary barriers, legal, residential and occupational barriers, medical category and financial barriers. There were, indeed, too many barriers to the 'right' kind of hospital, despite the fact that 80 per cent of hospital beds were already provided as a public service. And, withal, the accidents of chance and the idiosyncrasies of history had brought about, by 1939, a situation of gross maldistribution of hospital resources in relation to population needs; a situation which, by the end of the war, was no longer thought to be tolerable on grounds of geography or socially just in relation to the universal rise in the cost of medical care. In the words of the Government's White Paper: 'The anomalies of large waiting lists in one hospital and suitable empty beds at another, and of the hospitals in the same area running duplicated specialist centres which could be better concentrated in one more highly equipped and staffed centre for the area, are largely the result of a situation in which hospital services are many people's

[1] See debate and motion at the 1954 Annual Meeting of the British Medical Association, *Brit. Med. J.*, 1954, ii, Supp. 33.

business but nobody's full responsibility.'[1]

Attempts, during the preceding twenty years, in a few local areas to co-ordinate policy and administration among voluntary and public hospitals had, with one or two exceptions, failed completely.[2] This was no theoretical surmise; it was borne out by the experience gained in the organization of the war-time Emergency Hospital Scheme based on regional hospital areas.[3] These were the lessons of history which led, in 1948, to the creation of new administrative and executive instruments. These new instruments, regional hospital boards and local hospital management committees, represented the one major administrative innovation of the Health Service Act. For the organisation and administration of the rest of the personal health services the Act drew on the past.

IV

Briefly, the present structure of the Health Service takes the form of three main branches:

(i) The hospital, specialist and ancillary services provided through the agency of fourteen regional hospital boards, thirty-six separate boards of governors of teaching hospitals and 388 local hospital management committees. There are thus three administrative tiers (a) the Ministry, (b) the regional boards and (c) the local management committees. Under the general policy guidance of the Ministry, the functions of the regional boards are to plan, co-ordinate and supervise the development of the hospital and specialist services in their regions. To this end, they are responsible for appointing and paying the senior medical and dental staff, and for allocating the regional block grant from the Ministry among the management committees in their regions. The function of these committees is the day-to-day running of the hospitals. In the case of the teaching hospitals, the

[1] *A National Health Service*, HMSO, February 1944, Cmd 6502, p. 56.

[2] *Report of the Voluntary Hospitals Commission* (the Sankey Commission set up by the British Hospitals Association), 1937.

[3] *Problems of Social Policy*, Titmuss, Richard, M., HMSO, 1950.

thirty-six boards of governors are not answerable to the regional authorities but are directly responsible to the Minister for the management and control of the teaching hospitals of the country. The total membership of all these bodies runs to over 10,000 people—unpaid volunteers.[1] It probably represents, in hours of work, a much larger investment of time and energy than that given before 1948 by those serving on voluntary hospital committees. Notwithstanding this, there has been no lack of applicants. The real problem since 1948 has not been to find voluntary members but to strike a fair balance between public and professional representation.

(ii) The second main branch of the Health Service is represented by 'The Family Practitioner Services' (to give them their official generic label). These, which carry the main brunt of medical care, include the general medical service, pharmaceutical service, general dental service and the ophthalmic service. They are under a separate administration, namely, 138 Executive Councils, and are largely controlled in matters of policy by the Ministry of Health in consultation with the professions concerned. Functionally, they are concerned with executing policy, the bulk of their work consisting of keeping records, paying doctors, dentists and members of other professions for services rendered, disciplinary and other professional matters. The nature of the work they do is much the same as that done by their predecessors, the old Insurance Committees which operated under the National Health Insurance Act of 1911.

The areas covered by these Councils are generally co-terminous with those of the local health authorities. There are about 3,500 voluntary members controlling these Councils; they are appointed by the professional associations, by the Ministry and by the local health authority for the area. These Councils, as *ad hoc* appointed bodies, are essentially a political device to avoid placing doctors under a contract of service, whole-time, part-time or sessional, with either a central department or a local government authority. The first was never seriously entertained

[1] National Council of Social Service, *Voluntary Service and the State*, 1952, esp. p. 65.

when the Health Service was planned; the alternative of working to local authorities was, as already indicated, completely rejected by the British Medical Association. General practitioners as well as consultants refused to have anything to do with locally elected bodies.

(iii) The third main branch is represented by the 'Local Health Services'. These comprise maternity and child welfare, domiciliary midwifery, health visiting, home nursing, domestic help, prevention of illness, care and after care services, local mental health services and the administration of the ambulance service. All these services are provided, as a statutory duty, by the 146 major local health authorities. Most of these public health activities were undertaken before the 1948 Act by local authorities, though generally as a permissive power. Now they have to be provided, with the help of a 50 per cent grant from the central Government. Apart from this, the one major change made by the Act which affected local government was the transfer of municipal hospitals to the regional hospital boards.

V

These are the simplest of bare facts about the structure of the Health Service. I thought it essential to give you something of a map to follow, though I have kept descriptive detail to a minimum, partly to allow more time to concentrate on certain issues which I believe to be important. Having, so to speak, reached the stage when discussion can succeed description I suspect that a number of critical questions are already taking shape. Now that the Service has been in operation for about nine years can any conclusions be drawn about this experiment in 'socialized medicine'? How has it worked in practice? Has it led to a deterioration in standards of medical care? What effect has it had on the doctor-patient relationship? Has the removal of the financial barrier unleashed a great demand; led to much abuse of the general practitioner's time; converted him into a signer of certificates, a sorter of minor maladies and a hospital referral agent? What effect has the Service had on the profession itself; on levels of remuneration, career prospects, clinical freedom and the position of doctors in the power structure of administration? Lastly, but by no means exhaustively, is it true that the costs of the Service have risen so steeply that it is in danger of getting out of control?

These are some of the questions which have been asked in Britain. They are, by their nature, the kind of questions which are most easily—if not satisfactorily—answered by either a sentence or a book. The first is obviously not permitted; the second can be consigned to that useful academic file labelled 'Retirement'. I shall, therefore, do what I can in my next two lectures to deal with some of these questions and shall concentrate mainly on those affecting the general practitioner. Problems of administration, financial control, the work of the hospitals and various public health issues will, in general, be ignored, partly because for their understanding a good deal of background information is needed on particular British institutions and systems, and partly because these matters are dealt with at length in a Government Report published last year.

I thus come to a brief summary of this Report which, in many ways, stands as a landmark in the history of the Service. Its publication marked a stage when the initial and, to a large extent, transitory problems had been mainly overcome. The dimensions of the more fundamental and long-term issues in the organization of medical care are now in clearer perspective.

This Report (the Guillebaud Report) was the product of a five-member committee of inquiry set up by the Government in May 1953 under the chairmanship of a distinguished Cambridge economist.[1] Its terms of reference were: 'To review the present and prospective cost of the National Health Service; to suggest means, whether by modifications in organization or otherwise, of ensuring the most effective control and efficient use of such Exchequer funds as may be made available; to advise

[1] Cmd 9663, January 1956. For a detailed analysis of changes in the administration and work of the hospitals, reference should also be made to the series of reports published during 1956–7 by the Acton Society Trust under the title Hospitals and the State'.

how, in view of the burdens on the Exchequer, a rising charge upon it can be avoided while providing for the maintenance of an adequate Service; and to make recommendations.'

The Committee was set up at a time when a powerful body of opinion in the country held the view that this public enterprise was failing. Costs were getting out of control, or, as the *British Medical Journal* put it in a leader: 'The National Health Service is heading for the bankruptcy court . . . and we are facing bankruptcy because of the Utopian finances of the Welfare State.'[1] Another major criticism was that the administrative structure of the Service had too many defects; it was over-centralized, it had curtailed the professional freedom of the doctor, it had given the administrator and the lay member too much power, and that the division of functions under different authorities was having unfortunate effects on both doctor and patient.

Soon after it was set up, the Committee asked the National Institute of Economic and Social Research (a private institute distinguished for its contributions to economic research) to undertake a detailed analysis of the costs of the Service. The task was entrusted to Mr Abel-Smith and myself. The main part of the memorandum on costs we submitted (which was accepted by the Committee) was published in its Report. The whole of our study was simultaneously published as a book.[2]

In preparing these lectures I thought it would be helpful to summarize briefly (a) the main findings of the Guillebaud Report and (b) certain other conclusions from these studies selected because of their relevance to the theme of these lectures.

1. In the words of the Report: 'The rising cost of the Service in real terms during the years 1948–54 was kept within narrow bounds . . . Any charge that there has been widespread extravagance in the Service, whether in respect of the spending of money or the use of manpower, is not borne out by our evidence.' The cost per head of the population at constant prices was, in fact, almost the same in 1953–4 as in 1949–50 (the first full year

[1] *Brit. Med. J.*, Editorial, December 2, 1950.

[2] *The Cost of the National Health Service in England and Wales*, Abel-Smith, B., and Titmuss, R. M., Cambridge University Press, 1956.

of operation). Moreover, the proportion of total national resources (the gross national product) paid for by public authorities fell from $3\frac{3}{4}$ per cent in 1949–50 to $3\frac{1}{4}$ per cent in 1953–4.[1] All the estimates I have seen of the proportion of national resources devoted to medical care in the United States give higher figures,[2] and also show that the cost per head of the population has risen significantly since 1948.[3]

These conclusions about the cost of the Health Service came as a surprise to public opinion. What was expected was a strong recommendation for economy; for restriction; for more charges on patients. Instead, there were recommendations for spending (especially capital expenditure on hospitals[4] and welfare provisions for old people) and for the reduction or removal of certain existing charges. One can only conclude that for nearly seven years public opinion both in England and the United States had been seriously misled, partly because of the inadequate way in which public accounts are presented, partly because of a too simple faith in the validity of official statistics (particularly of estimates made during the war of what the new Service might cost), and partly because powerful sections of medical and lay

[1] Mr Abel-Smith has provided me with more recent provisional estimates. The net cost of the Health Service in England and Wales as a percentage of the gross national product has been: 1949–50, 3·75; 1950–1, 3·71; 1951–2, 3·48; 1952–3, 3·34; 1953–4, 3·24; 1954–5, 3·14; 1955–6, 3·23.

[2] Such estimates are not, of course, strictly comparable because, for one thing, the figures for England and Wales do not include private expenditure on medical care.

[3] United States President's Commission on the Health Needs of the Nation (Magnuson Commission), *Building America's Health*, Vol. 4, Washington, 1953; Goldman, F., *New Engl. J. Med.*, 1950, *243*, 36; *New York Times*, February 6, 1955; *Commission on Financing of Hospital Care* (ed. Becker, H.), Vols. II and III, 1955; Serkein, O. M., *Paying for Medical Care in the United States*, 1953; Seventh Medical Economics Survey, *Med. Econ.*, 1954, *31*, 153; and *Lancet*, 1951, i, 243 (quoting a paper by Professor Seymour Harris to the American Medical Association on medical expenditure in the USA and Great Britain). For recent material on medical costs see *Family Medical Costs and Voluntary Health Insurance: A Nationwide Survey*, by Anderson, O. W., with Feldman, J. J., 1956, and other publications by the Health Information Foundation of New York.

[4] Some 45 per cent of hospitals in England and Wales were originally erected before 1891 and 21 per cent before 1861 (Abel-Smith, B., and Titmuss, R. M., *op. cit.*, p. 54).

opinion were committed too soon to the view that the costs of 'socialized medicine' were bound to be astronomical.

2. In interpreting this conclusion that the cost of the Service has been kept within narrow limits the following summarized facts should be borne in mind: in proportion to the populations at risk over the six years the hospitals did more work both in-patient and out-patient; more doctors (especially consultants), nurses, social workers, administrators, physiotherapists and other professional staffs, later to engage in private practice or other employment at home or abroad, were trained at public expense; more confinements took place in hospital; more road accidents were treated; more provision was made for industrial accidents which would otherwise have called for an expansion of health services organized by employers; a great increase took place in the use of X-rays, pathological and diagnostic services; more of these services were made directly available to general practitioners (in part a switch from the doctor's private practice expenses to the hospital service); the number of voluntary blood donations rose dramatically by over 300,000 to 760,000 in 1955;[1] a larger proportion of those in need were fitted with hearing aids, artificial limbs, spectacles and dentures; more drug prescriptions were issued; more home helps and nursing services were provided for those who were ill at home; more doctors worked as Health Service practitioners; there were fewer single-handed practitioners and more partnerships and group practices; the average number of people on a general practitioner's list fell; a substantial improvement took place in the geographical distribution of general practitioners and consultant services;[2] finally, more medical research was undertaken and completed, as indicated by a striking rise in the flow of articles to scientific and medical journals after 1948.

3. Against this background of quantitative indices of perfor-

[1] *Brit. Med. J.*, 1956, ii, 128.

[2] All these conclusions are based on the facts given in (i) *The Guillebaud Report*, (ii) *The Cost of the National Health Service*, (iii) *Report of the Ministry of Health for* 1954, Pt I, Cmd 9566, September 1955, and *Annual Reports of the Medical Practices Committee*.

mence—of what the Guillebaud Report called 'the Service's record . . . of real achievement'—it is hardly surprising that the Report found nothing basically unsound about its administrative structure. Taking account of the medical opposition to any form of local government control it did not, therefore, propose any major changes in the existing tripartite structure. The Report did, however, recommend, first, that steps should be taken to raise the quality of hospital administration (most of the existing staff were inherited from the old voluntary and municipal hospitals) and, second, that in the power structure of committees controlling the hospitals and general practitioner services the proportion of medical membership should be reduced. For hospital boards and committees a proportion of 25 per cent was recommended;[1] in some instances medical membership had risen to over 40 per cent by 1955. It appears that alarm had been expressed by several witnesses at the high proportion of professional men serving on these bodies to the exclusion of representatives of the consumer interest.

These, in my judgment, are some of the more important findings of this investigation into the National Health Service. They hardly touch on the more subtle, intangible effects of the Service on patient and doctor nor on the critical questions of quality of medical care. They probably shed too comforting a glow on this experiment in public enterprise. In my next two lectures I shall hope to present a more balanced view.

[1] This recommendation was broadly accepted by the Government in 1957. A circular (HM (56) III) to hospital authorities stated that the Minister proposed to follow the recommendations that medical membership of regional boards 'should normally not exceed 25 per cent'. Boards were asked to do the same when making appointments to hospital management committees. Special considerations were said to apply to boards of governors.

CHAPTER 9

The National Health Service in England

SOME FACTS ABOUT GENERAL PRACTICE

I

THERE are a number of reasons which help to explain if they do not justify the conclusion that the record of the Health Service is one of progress and success. Some of the more important ones become explicable only when it is understood how far-reaching were the effects of the Second World War on the British economy. The whole fabric of organized medical care, public and private, suffered particularly. Inevitably, the highest priorities in medicine were reserved for the military and civil defence forces. Even as early as June, 1943, the standard of medical care available for the civilian population was, in the judgment of the War Cabinet, 'dangerously low'.[1] By the end of the war, the ranks of the general practitioners had been depleted by over one-third; of those who remained 10 per cent were over seventy years of age, and in many industrial areas elderly doctors, educated before the First World War when general practice was little more than an empirical bedside art, were struggling with lists of 4,000 to 5,000 patients.[2]

So far as hospital care is concerned I make only two comments. For over fifteen years from 1939 no new hospital was built in Britain. Many of the voluntary hospitals which, by 1939, were virtually bankrupt and were only saved during the war by heavy

[1] Titmuss, Richard M., *Problems of Social Policy*, 1950, p. 531.
[2] Ibid., p. 530.

Government subsidies, faced, at the end of the war, an even more serious threat to their future.[1] Not only were these subsidies being withdrawn but the costs (and the standards expected) of medical care in hospital were rising on an unprecedented scale. The scientific revolution in medicine, beginning in the late 1930's (some of the implications of which I shall discuss later) represented to most of the voluntary hospitals in Britain a sentence of death. Historically regarded, the first wave of applied scientific change has nearly always been economically expensive to established institutions and the voluntary hospitals, with little time in which to put their war-disorganized houses in order, found themselves in a critical situation. Unlike the position in the United States, there were few wealthy foundations to come to their rescue.

In the three years between the end of the war and the introduction of the Health Service, when the air was thick with rumours about what was to happen to the hospitals, both the voluntary and municipal hospital authorities were unwilling to commit themselves to much expenditure. In some respects, therefore, hospital conditions deteriorated further.

When the Service began to operate in 1948 it thus inherited the debts of a decade of sacrifice and neglect, financial poverty and disorganization. Simultaneously, it had to meet, with access to medical care no longer dependent on the means of the patient, an immense pent-up demand for treatment. This back-log of needs, accumulated during the war and its uneasy aftermath, was most vividly depicted by the demand for spectacles, dentures, hearing aids and other postponable adjuncts to better health.[2] To those with little sense of history it was this that gave the Health Service a bad name. Spokesmen of the British Medical Association and the American Medical Association found it all too easy to indulge their fantasies. Superficially interpreted, it was a situation in which any energetic interest group, responsive to the lowest common denominators among its members and well pro-

[1] Titmuss, Richard M., *Problems of Social Policy*, 1950, pp. 450–8.

[2] For an analysis of demand in the early years of the Service see Abel-Smith, B., and Titmuss, R. M., *The Cost of the National Health Service*, 1956.

vided with funds, could hardly fail to exploit.[1] The history of this exploitation will one day be worth recording. And on both sides of the Atlantic.

Against this background it would indeed have been surprising if the Health Service had not been able to show marked improvements in many spheres of activity. Certainly in quantitative terms, the base-line from which it started was a low one. There was so much waiting to be done and, with the removal of the financial barrier to medical care in 1948, needs and the expectation of the standard at which they might now be met, hitherto submerged or inarticulate, came to the surface. And so were crystallized many of the deeper problems concerning the role of medicine and the profession in modern society. All this has to be remembered, if complacency is to be avoided, in interpreting the verdict of the Guillebaud Report on the performance of the Health Service during its first seven years.

Nor, if we push the analysis further back in time, is it easy to make comparisons with the standard of medical care in the 1930's. Critics of the Health Service have rarely made explicit the criteria of value they have in mind in drawing comparisons over time. In failing to do so they have, of course, avoided the question as to whether it is possible to make comparisons in many important respects with conditions in the 1930's. There are now more variables in the equation of medical care; science has penetrated the art of medicine at so many points and changed the relativities of skill, knowledge, and practice. And as functions have changed so have the relativities of status and reward within the profession itself. These difficulties, inherent in comparative studies over time, must be remembered in interpreting the conclusions I shall present later about the work of the general practitioner.

[1] According to a report in the *New York Times*, the cost of the propaganda campaign to 'alert the American people to the danger of socialized medicine' launched by the AMA in 1950 was $19 m. (*New York Times*, September 17, 1950). See also '100 Questions and Answers on the British National Health Service', published by the AMA, in 1949.

II

Has the standard or quality of medical care provided by the general practitioner under the National Health Service deteriorated, as compared with that provided during the 1930's under the mixed system of private practice and National Health Insurance panel practice for insured workers? Has he had to deal with a great increase in demand from patients? Is it true that he no longer functions as a family doctor whereas in the 1930's he did? These are typical of the questions which, as I suggested earlier, are invariably raised whenever the effects of the Service on general practice are discussed. I propose, therefore, to devote the remainder of this lecture to considering some of these questions. The main emphasis thus falls on the general practitioner. He is, so to speak, the pivot of attraction in all the controversy that has surrounded the Health Service since its inception. His future role in the changing field of medical care is the most difficult one to discern.[1] While science has strengthened the prestige and position of the hospital and given it an assured place in the community it has simultaneously disturbed and, to some extent, made uncertain the role of the general practitioner. Yet, in Britain at least, he still remains in the front-line in meeting the need for medical care.

Personally, I believe that the Health Service has made a beginning in the process of establishing a social framework in which the great majority of general practitioners, gradually assimilating the benefits of scientific medicine, may find a more assured and satisfying role than was their lot before 1948. It is, fundamentally, a problem of adjustment: of adjusting to the challenge of scientific medicine; to the changing balance of physical and mental ill-health; to the rising standard of expectations of medical care from a more articulate, health-conscious society. As many are coming to recognize, these adjustments involve the

[1] See Report by the British Medical Association, *General Practice and the Training of the General Practitioner*, 1950. Similar questions are raised in a recent American report 'An Analytical Study of North Carolina General Practice', 1953–4, Peterson, O. L., Andrews, L. P., Spain, R. S., and Greenberg, B. G., *J. Med. Educ.*, 1956, 31 (12), Pt 2.

reform of medical education.

All the time, in statements of this kind, one is making judgments about the past and the present. To give some substance to my conclusions, I therefore found it necessary to assemble in a detailed appendix much of the available information about general practice before and after 1948. In drawing on this material I make no attempt to interpret it in clinical terms.

III

I must preface these conclusions with a brief account of how general practitioners are at present paid under the Health Service. The main source of income is the capitation fee.[1]

Practitioners are paid by Executive Councils with whom they are in contract. They receive an annual payment for each person whom they have accepted as a Health Service patient, with a special 'loading' for every person from the 501st to the 1,500th.[2] This loading was introduced in 1952 to favour the doctor with a medium-sized list and to taper off rewards for the larger practices.[3] There is also a 'built-in' incentive to group practice; doctors in partnership, however they may actually divide their work among themselves, are paid according to a 'notional' division of patients designed to secure them the largest number of 'loaded' fees. Each doctor is at present restricted to a ceiling of 3,500 Health Service patients. He can have as many private patients as he likes. Since the introduction in 1952 of this method of distributing capitation fees there has occurred a substantial increase in partnerships and group practice.[4]

[1] For further details about the structure and rewards of general practice reference should be made to the Annual Reports of the Ministry of Health, the *Guillebaud Report*, the reports of the Medical Practices Committee and, especially, to Vol. 1 of the evidence submitted by the Ministry of Health to the Royal Commission on Doctors' and Dentists' Remuneration (1957).

[2] These loadings were revised somewhat in August 1957, consequent upon the award of an increase in remuneration (Ministry of Health circular ECL 59/57).

[3] National Health Service, *Distribution of Remuneration among General Practitioners*, Report of Working Party, June 1952.

[4] *Annual Report of the Ministry of Health for 1954*, Pt I, Cmd 9566, 1955, p. 51. Also *Report for 1955*, Pt I, Cmd 9857, pp. 52–4.

In addition to these payments, general practitioners receive special fees for maternity services, for treating temporary residents, for the training of assistants (a popular innovation of the Health Service), for drugs and appliances supplied, for local authority clinic sessions, infant welfare, vaccination and immunization services, for part-time school and factory work and for hospital and specialist posts of various kinds.[1] According to a medical survey in 1952, it was estimated that, for the country as a whole, one out of every five or six general practitioners had some kind of hospital post.[2] Doctors in rural areas receive substantial mileage payments,[3] allowances may be paid for a period of up to three years to new entrants in under-doctored areas, there are also initial practice allowances and special hardship payments for elderly doctors with small lists, and general practitioners as a whole, along with most consultants and specialists, are accorded by the income tax authorities something of a privileged position. Compared to the treatment of members of many other professions, general practitioners are allowed to claim as tax reliefs many items of expenditure of a semi-personal character.[4] Telephone charges are also heavily subsidized in the doctor's favour.[5] No assessment of the relative rewards of general practice can properly be made unless account is taken of these factors.

Those doctors taking part in the Health Service are debarred from selling the whole or any part of the goodwill of their practices. Thus, every doctor practising in 1948 was deemed to have

[1] For a comprehensive list of the categories of duties and responsibilities performed by general practitioners see Appendix V, Taylor, S., *Good General Practice*, 1954.

[2] Taylor, S., *Good General Practice*, 1954, p. 343. According to the British Medical Association, the number of general practitioner beds in England and Wales increased by about 25 per cent between 1953 and 1955 (*Brit. Med. J.* (1956), ii, Supp. 38).

[3] As a supplement to capitation fees to compensate doctors for working in rural areas.

[4] Sophian, T. J., *The Practitioner* (1952), No. 1007, Vol. 168, and Thomas, R. C., *Brit. Med. J.*, (1953), i, Supp. 12.

[5] British Medical Association, Report of Annual Representative Meeting, *Brit. Med., J.*,(1956), ii, Supp. 18.

suffered a loss and to be entitled to compensation. The Government set aside £66 m. plus interest to compensate doctors entering the Service for the loss of the right they had previously enjoyed to sell their practices.

Not the least of the attractions of the Service was a generous superannuation scheme devised for all doctors, whole-time and part-time, to take account of their earnings during working life.[1] For example, a general practitioner in an urban area, retiring after forty years, and having had an average of 2,000 patients on his list during these years, will receive an annual pension of close on £1,000 a year plus a tax-free lump sum retiring allowance of £2,800.[2] Towards this he will have contributed about £3,750 (6 per cent of earnings after deduction of practice expenses) all of which will have ranked for full relief from income tax.[3]

Ever since 1948 there has been much dispute about the adequacy of rewards for doctors taking part in the Health Service.[4]

[1] See report of the British Medical Association's Compensation and Superannuation Committee (*Brit. Med. J.* (1957), ii, Supp. 54). This report refers to the fact that 'many practitioners who had opted out of the scheme at the inception by reason of existing insurance commitments now wanted to come into it'. For others, in 1948, it was attractive because of the difficulties they faced before 1939, due to low earnings from private practice, in making provision for their old age. Although comprehensive data are not available the figures for one agency, carrying a large amount of medical business, are indicative. In 1956, the Medical Insurance Agency reported that in 1938 new life business totalled about £500,000; in 1955 the corresponding figure was £5,921,000 despite the introduction in 1948 of the National Health Service Superannuation Scheme (*Lancet* (1956), ii, 260).

[2] In 1956, the average net remuneration per general practitioner from all sources was estimated by the Ministry of Health (and agreed by the BMA) as £2,222, plus an amount equal to the ascertained average practice expenses for that year—in all, about £3,150. (*Brit. Med. J.* (1956), Supp. 70–1). See also Bulletin No. 3 of the Central Consultants and Specialists Committee referred to in a letter to the *Lancet* (1954), i, 1239.

[3] *NHS Superannuation Scheme*, Ministry of Health, Revised edition 1950. The State contribution is 8 per cent. In the example given (estimated in 1956) practice expenses are taken as 35 per cent and remuneration is based on *Distribution of Remuneration among General Practitioners*, Second Report of Working Party, April 1954 (*Brit. Med. J.*, Supp., May 1, 1954, p. 206). Provision is also made for widow's pensions, injury pensions, death and short service gratuities.

[4] Inevitably, this has entailed consideration of the effects of the National Health

To a substantial extent this has been a dispute about differentials; the constant attempts of the consultants to keep well ahead of the general practitioners and the equally constant attempts of general practitioners to narrow the differences. On what basis should society fix these rewards, once they are no longer mainly settled by the play of the market, and how should they be distributed among the different branches of the profession and in relation to services rendered? One thing at least can be said with a fair degree of assurance. The introduction of the Health Service meant the adoption by the Government of a policy of 'levelling-up' for general practitioners. There had been, according to a Government committee of inquiry (the Spens Committee) which surveyed the earnings of doctors in 1936–8, too many general practitioners with low incomes.[1] This proportion, for those at the ages of peak earning

Service on private practice. Receipts from private practice are also one of the factors determining, each year, the amount of the capitation fee. Little is known about the earnings of general practitioners from private practice since 1948, although the BMA and the Ministry of Health have agreed on a global sum of £2 m.—a figure which has remained unaltered since 1948 (*Brit. Med. J.* (1957), i, Supp. 163). This assumes that, ever since 1948, over 98 per cent of the population have been Health Service patients (five consultations per year at 10*s.* per consultation). There is some evidence that private practice has been increasing in recent years, especially among consultants. According to the BMA (in evidence to the Inland Revenue authorities in 1955) 'a very considerable amount of private consultant practice still remained' (*Brit. Med. J.* (1955), Supp. 227). For estimates of the number of general practitioners engaged solely in private practice, see p. 138. A Report by the Government Social Survey in 1952 on General Practice estimated that 22 per cent of the total adult population aged twenty-one and over and earning more than £1,000 a year were not on a National Health Service doctor's list. The proportion for all income groups was 2·3 per cent. In 1954, the President of the Royal College of Physicians, discussing the remuneration of hospital medical staff, implied that any attempt by the Government to investigate earnings from private practice by consultants 'might have unfortunate results' (*Brit. Med. J.* (1954), Supp. i, 229).

[1] *Report of the Inter-Departmental Committee on the Remuneration of General Practitioners* (the Spens Report), Cmd 6810, May 1946. The defects in these statistics (which were collected retrospectively after a lapse of eight years and were not checked with the Inland Revenue authorities) make it difficult to accept them as a cross-section of incomes in 1936–8. Returns were not made by approximately one-third of doctors. If those that did reply included proportionately more of the poorer doctors then the awards subsequently made could have been higher than would otherwise have been the case. However, this is a complex matter which must be pursued elsewhere.

capacity (forty to fifty-five), was put at 40 per cent. An analysis of the figures before this committee suggests that private practice was much less remunerative in the 1930's than most people were aware of then or imagine today. Not only were 'bad debts' probably substantial during the years of heavy unemployment but many people were no doubt reluctant to see a doctor, either because they could not pay or because they already owed the doctor money.[1] Only the existence of National Health Insurance capitation fees saved many general practitioners in industrial areas from poverty. Thus, the Spens Committee 'had no doubt that low incomes have, in fact, been a source of grave worry to many general practitioners and must have prejudiced their efficiency'.

In making their recommendations in 1946 the Committee assumed that there had been an increase of work in National Health Insurance practice and that there would be a further increase when the new Health Service was introduced.[2] As explained later, both these assumptions appear to have been wrong. The adoption of the Committee's Report by the Government, and its full implementation in 1952 after the matter had gone to arbitration,[3] represented at the very least a substantial improvement, compared with pre-war days, in the financial position of the less well-off half of all general practitioners in the country.

The adjudicator's award in 1952 was acclaimed with great satisfaction by the profession. For the first time for over forty years (ever since, in fact, the first intervention of the State in the provision of medical care services) the *British Medical Journal* could write: '. . . the controversy on finance between the BMA and the Ministry of Health has come to an end'.[4] The doctors were satisfied.

[1] This apparently is a common experience today in Canada (Taylor M. G., *The Administration of Health Insurance in Canada*, 1956, p. 13).

[2] *Op. cit.*, p. 11.

[3] Report of the Award by Mr Justice Danckwerts, *Brit. Med. J.* (1952), i, Supp. 113.

[4] Editorial, March 29, 1952, i, 697. In 1954 another important conclusion was reached, this time by the Committee on General Practice set up by the Central Health Services Council. It was agreed that the method of paying general prac-

That was five years ago. Since then, the rise in the cost of living and increased rewards for consultants have led to a new claim being put forward on behalf of general practitioners. I do not wish to enter here on the merits or demerits of this particular claim except to make one comment.[1] Once again we face the question: to what extent should society guarantee the standard of living of one section of its members and insulate them from changes in the value of money irrespective of what happens to other sections? This is one of the fundamental questions which the introduction of the Health Service has brought to the fore. It is one which any society, embarking on an extensive public provision of medical care, must inevitably face. In Great Britain in 1955 approximately 40 per cent of all active physicians were engaged on a full-time salaried basis.[2] In the United States in 1949 the proportion was not greatly different at approximately 35 per cent.[3]

In reviewing the history of these negotiations on pay between the medical profession and the Government, and taking account of the facts assembled in the appendix, I have no doubt that, despite the official attacks on the Health Service by the spokesmen of the profession, it has in practice turned out to be a most attractive proposition among those desirous of following a professional career. Since 1948 all the medical schools in Britain have been flooded with applications. Even within two years of the start of the Service, and before there had been much time to iron out some of the mistakes of the bureaucrats under the Labour Government, Bart's Hospital in London, for instance, was reporting 2,000 applications for 100 places.[4] Since then, many medical schools have been annually confronted with problems of

titioners by capitation fee was the most satisfactory of all the possible methods examined. The signatories of this report included leaders of the British Medical Association and the Royal Colleges of Obstetricians and Gynaecologists, Physicians and Surgeons (*Report of the Committee on General Practice*, 1954, p. 30).

[1] At the time of writing this question is being considered by the Royal Commission on Doctors' and Dentists' Remuneration.

[2] Based on information provided by the Ministry of Health and compiled for the Committee on Medical Manpower, October 1956.

[3] Davis, M., *Medical Care for Tomorrow*, 1955, pp. 53 and 314–15.

[4] *Brit. Med. J.* (1950), i, 506. See also Brinton, D., *Lancet* (1951), ii, 1047.

selection on a similar or even greater scale despite a situation of full employment and the opening up of new professional careers in industry and commerce, science and administration.[1] The Report of the Committee of Vice-Chancellors and Principals into University Admissions has shown that the number of applications per applicant was higher in 1955–6 in medicine than in any other faculty.[2] By all accounts, the competition to enter medicine was far less intense in the 1930's.

Newly trained doctors have been less inclined to emigrate or serve overseas; the pressure to enter general practice in Britain has been very great and, according to the Medical Practices Committee, saturation point will soon be reached;[3] nor is there any evidence that doctors are less anxious for their sons and daughters to follow in their footsteps. In 1944, it was estimated that 80 per cent of the population (the manual, lower clerical and distributive workers) were contributing only about 5 per cent of the nation's doctors.[4] Thus, the vast majority of doctors were drawn from the most favoured 20 per cent of the population among which a high proportion were recruited from the children of the profession itself. There is no evidence that there has been any fundamental change in the picture since 1948. The Report of the Committee of Vice-Chancellors and Principals appears broadly to confirm this. It shows that, in 1955–6, the proportion of students admitted whose fathers were manual workers was lower in medicine than any other faculty;[5] the proportion who had attended local authority schools, primary and secondary,

[1] These demands for training are also reflected in the demands to enter general practice. For example, in Scotland (less popular for medical practice than the South of England), there were in 1955 over thirty applicants for each vacant medical practice (*Health Bulletin*, Edinburgh (1955), *13*, 20). In England and Wales in 1955 there were 5,407 applications for 124 vacant practices—an average of forty-four (*Annual Report of the Ministry of Health for 1955*, Cmd 9857, p. 57).

[2] *Report on an Inquiry into Applications for Admission to Universities*. Kelsall, R. K., 1957, Table B.

[3] *Fifth Report of the Medical Practices Committee for England and Wales for* 1953 (September 1954).

[4] D'Arcy Hart, P., *Brit. Med. J.* (1944), ii, p. 356.

[5] For example, medicine: Oxford, 5 per cent; Cambridge, 6 per cent; London, 13 per cent; all 15 per cent. All (including medicine): Oxford, 13 per cent; Cambridge, 9 per cent; London, 21 per cent; all 25 per cent.

was similarly lower in medicine than any other faculty; conversely, the proportion who had attended boarding schools was highest in medicine (as high as one-third in London, nearly two-thirds in Oxford and Cambridge and one-quarter for all medical students). It also emerges that medicine was the most highly self-recruited profession. Nearly one in five of all the men admitted to medical faculties were the sons of doctors. In other faculties, less than 2 per cent of the men admitted were sons of doctors. Again, these proportions were more striking for Oxford, Cambridge and London. For example, 73 per cent of the men admitted to London University whose fathers were doctors were proposing to become doctors.

The fact that, unlike the past, the State now heavily subsidizes the costs of a much more expensive medical training does not appear to have made a great deal of difference. In 1954 a London medical student paid at most about 19 per cent of the costs of medical training.[1]

By the application of these old-fashioned criteria of supply and demand it would not seem that the profession as a whole is dissatisfied with the prospects and rewards offered to medical men and women under the National Health Service. This was expressed in 1957 by one of the leaders of the British Medical Association in speaking on a debate about remuneration. He warned about the dangers of being compared with other professions; 'some of these other professions had for many years been envious of the doctor . . .'[2] Nevertheless, the doctors in Britain have matters to complain about—some of which I shall discuss in my next lecture—but then I know of no profession

[1] The costs borne by the State amounted roughly to £360 per student per year. Detailed figures are included in a book by my colleague, Mr John Vaizey (*The Costs of Education*), Allen and Unwin, 1958. An opinion survey among Scottish medical graduates undertaken in 1955 by Professor A. Mair found that the cost of medical training 'was not considered a deterrent by the majority of students' (*Brit. Med. J.* (1955), i, 532). The Joint Consultants Committee, in giving evidence to the Royal Commission on Doctors' and Dentists' Remuneration in December 1957, stated that nearly 70 per cent of medical students now received grants from public funds (*Brit. Med. J.*, 1958, Supp., i, p. 6).

[2] Dr S. C. Arthur at a meeting of the General Medical Services Committee of the Association, *Brit. Med. J.*, 1957, i, Supp. 99.

which is not in a perpetual state of discontent, divine or otherwise. It is a role that every profession feels called upon to play to the limits of public credulity. Medicine is no exception.

Whatever else may be said about the National Health Service it can at least be concluded that, under the new regime, doctors have prospered. But this prosperity has brought with it some new problems. Fundamentally, they are social problems. They are, as we have seen, problems of determining the size of the medical profession in the future; of how to select those to be trained as doctors, and of settling their future rewards from public funds. These questions, which cannot be left to the profession alone to solve, were obliquely referred to in picturesque language a few years ago by the Professor of Clinical Pathology in the University of London. Professor Pulvertaft wrote: 'It is not surprising that the opportunity of belonging without expense to the most lucrative profession outside the black market has attracted a flood of applications, far exceeding the vacancies in schools or the requirements of medicine . . . This thirst to succour suffering humanity must make all but the cynic blush with pride; but even the most unsuspicious mind must wonder whether a method of medical recruitment which involves no personal sacrifice, still less hardship, for anyone attracts the right men and women.' Moreover, he went on, 'it is well to remember that the dispensation of national patronage is vested in remarkably few hands. All these candidates come forward with very similar educational qualifications and the eulogies of pedagogues; a handful of deans, with or often without committees, bestows largesse and selects the doctors of tomorrow.'[1]

IV

Financial security is not, however, the only attraction to those who now engage in or hope to enter general practice. To most doctors it is probably of less importance than the conditions under which they work and the kind of relationships they have

[1] Pulvertaft, R. J. V., *Lancet* (1952), ii, 839.

with their patients and their colleagues. We must now consider some of these other aspects of a general practitioner's work.

Fundamental to them all is the question of clinical freedom; the right, as a trusted professional servant, to treat one's patient to the best of one's ability without interference or dictation, and subject only to the ethical code of behaviour laid down by the profession as a whole. There is no doubt that many doctors in Britain saw, in the coming of the National Health Service, a threat to clinical freedom. The State, through its influence over the earnings and financial status of doctors, could reduce them to poverty and thus make them subservient to the will of the politician or administrator. This fear, as I have shown, has not materialized. That is not to say that it should not have been ventilated. Its expression was a symbol of the vital force which goes to the making of our kind of society.

Another fear among general practitioners was that their security as doctors might be jeopardized if their services were dispensed with for some reason or other by the Ministry of Health. Safeguards were written into the Health Service Act, and an independent National Health Service Tribunal was set up with a legal chairman appointed by the Lord Chancellor. This Tribunal is concerned with complaints made by patients against practitioners and thus plays an important role in matters of discipline.[1] It has the power to retain, reinstate and remove the name of a doctor from the list of Service practitioners or to exact some lesser penalty, such as a fine. Though it is not concerned with the redress of patients' grievances the real issues with which it has to deal are clearly related to the efficiency of the Service.

The whole procedure is an exceedingly complex one which has been evolved since 1948 'almost entirely in agreement with the wishes of the professions'.[2] All proceedings of the Tribunal

[1] For a detailed account and discussion of the functions of the Tribunal and the working of the whole procedure see *Report of the Committee on Administrative Tribunals and Enquiries*, Cmnd 218, 1957, esp. Ch. 15 and *Minutes of Evidence*, Day 6, 7, 19, 21 and 24, 1956.

[2] Permanent Secretary to the Ministry of Health, *Minutes of Evidence*, Day 6, 1956, p. 151.

take place in secret and very little is known about the number and types of complaints made by patients in different areas since 1948.[1] The Minister's function is limited either to maintaining the decision taken by the Tribunal or to altering it in favour of the doctor. He cannot alter it against the doctor.

The working of this Tribunal has recently been considered, along with many others, by the Committee on Administrative Tribunals and Enquiries. According to the Chairman, the Committee 'had evidence of a very strong feeling that there is a good deal of dissatisfaction' from the viewpoint of the consumer.[2] It was said that 'justice in secret' prejudiced the public interest; that a ban on legal representation operated to the advantage of practitioners since they were often represented before Service Committees by experienced representatives of their professional organizations; that patients were more handicapped than they had been under the old National Health Insurance procedure;[3] and that the one-sided right of appeal from the Tribunal also weighted the scale in favour of the practitioner.

The British Medical Association, in giving evidence, did not agree with these criticisms of the system. They had not previously heard of anyone who had been complaining that justice had not been done; they believed that 'secrecy was always best'; they did not wish for a right of appeal to the High Court but preferred that the Minister should have the final say;[4] they be-

[1] Dr E. A. Gregg, in giving evidence on behalf of the British Medical Association, said: '. . . I am amazed to hear what I have just heard this morning, because we have not heard it before' (Day 19, 1956, p. 813).

[2] One reason being that, under the Insurance Committee system, when a complainant appeared before the appropriate committee he was usually accompanied by an experienced representative of his approved society who helped him to present his case. Under the present regulations, the professional side may be supported by a member of his profession. The complainant may be assisted by a friend, though not by a legal advocate. Invariably, however, according to the Clerk of the London Executive Council, he is there on his own (Day 21, p. 996). Moreover, according to the British Medical Association, under the old system 'it was found that doctors could not depend upon the decisions of the Department being, in their view, fairly come by' (Day 19, p. 812).

[3] Day 19, p. 813.

[4] 'Our view would be that it would not be to the advantage either of the Service or of the doctor for the appeal to go outside the Ministry' (Day 19, p. 812).

lieved that the right of legal representation should be taken away from the citizen on the grounds that it was for his own good; in short, they were quite satisfied with the existing procedure.[1] Nor did the Ministry of Health suggest any radical changes in any part of the system which, as their representatives said, had been developed in close co-operation with the profession. They clearly thought the public interest was sufficiently guarded, and stressed the importance of the Executive Council as 'a body which represents the consumer'.[2]

The Report of this Committee on Tribunals, while emphasizing the need for the utmost care in any matters which affect professional reputations, did however make a number of recommendations. So far as this particular Tribunal was concerned, the Committee thought that in general it should sit in public; that the right of appeal to the Minister should be abolished, and that at some stages in the procedure complainants should be given official assistance in presenting their cases.

For the professions and the public alike, these and other recommendations of the Committee raise issues of a fundamental nature. Though they cannot be discussed at length here, sufficient has been said to indicate that the fears of the doctors have not been borne out. Their experience, in working on these matters with a Government department, under both Conservative and Labour administrations, has not been unsatisfactory. The Editor of the *Lancet*, Dr T. F. Fox, concisely summed up the lessons of this experience in lecturing on 'professional freedom' when he said: 'I would say, that, in joining the public service, doctors have been given as much security of tenure as is justified in the public interests. They run very little risk of losing their contracts through arbitrary action by the Minister or his servants; their fears of being directed to practice in under-doctored

[1] Day 19, pp. 808–19. Dr A. Barker, a member of the BMA Council with experience of acting as the 'prisoner's friend', speaking at the Annual Representative Meeting in 1957 said that he 'had come to the conclusion that in most cases the domestic, informal atmosphere was favourable to the doctor' (*Brit. Med. J.*, Supp. i, 40).

[2] Day 6, p. 156.

areas have not been realized; and there is still free choice of doctor by patient and of patient by doctor. Another important safeguard of their professional freedom is the declaration that they may speak and write as they think fit.'[1]

Finally, on this question of professional freedom, there was the fear of administrative control or interference in the treatment of patients and other clinical matters. As to this, I cannot do better than to quote the words of Dr Talbot Rogers, one of the influential general practitioners in the counsels of the British Medical Association. At the annual meeting of the Association in 1955 he said: 'Speaking for the general practitioners, he felt that he could say, after seven years' experience of the new service, that they had achieved a remarkable degree of clinical and administrative freedom.'[2] Nor has this freedom, apparently greater than under the old National Insurance system,[3] been purchased at the price of less satisfactory relationships with patients. The Committee on General Practice, set up by the Central Health Services Council, and composed mainly of doctors holding important positions in the British Medical Association, the Royal College of Physicians and other professional bodies, came to this conclusion in its report published in 1954: 'The Committee does not think that in general the advent of the National Health Service has disturbed the relationship between doctors and their patients. The evidence of the British Medical Association, of an enquiry made by the Social Survey for the Committee and of an enquiry made independently, bear out the general impression made by the evidence of individual doctors, that the relationship is good; in some respects indeed, it was found to be better than before, and this was attributed to

[1] Fox, T. F., *Lancet* (1951), ii, 173. See also the testimony of Dr T. Rowland Hill (Chairman of the Consultants and Specialists Committee of the BMA) to the Annual Meeting of the BMA in 1954 (*Brit. Med. J.*, 1954, Supp. ii, 17).

[2] *Brit. Med. J.* (1955), Supp. ii, 119. See also BMA *Memorandum of Evidence to the Central Health Services Council's Committee on General Practice*, 'The doctor has certainly continued to retain complete freedom in clinical judgment and treatment', *Brit. Med. J.* (1953), Supp. i, Appendix B, p. 184.

[3] See *Minutes of Evidence* given by the British Medical Association to the *Committee on Administrative Tribunals*, Day 19, 1956, esp. p. 812.

the absence of the money bar and to increased co-operation among doctors.'[1]

Testimony of this kind from such influential sources of opinion —though admittedly given at a time when no pay dispute was pending—was probably encouraged by the favourable view taken by the profession of its role on the Executive Councils.[2] All the evidence points to the fact that the professional members of these Councils and their sub-committees are in a stronger position as a result of the National Health Service.

Prior to 1948, these bodies (under the name of Insurance Committees) were largely controlled by lay representatives.[3] Today, the lay members may actually be in a minority,[4] despite the view of the Ministry of Health that these bodies represent the consumer.[5] The Guillebaud Committee reporting in 1956 were obviously disturbed by the suggestion made to them that they 'may be popular with the professions because it allows them in effect to run the service in their own way without responsibility to the State or the taxpayer'.[6] Accordingly, recommendations were made to strengthen the lay representation on these bodies. This question, like others raised indirectly from time to time in these lectures, provokes thought about the role of professional interest groups in the fabric of the modern state. It is, however, too large a question for me to venture on here.

V

No discussion of professional freedom in the field of medicine can be concluded without mention of the doctor's freedom to

[1] Of a total membership of twenty-three on this Committee, nineteen were doctors. The Report was published by the Ministry of Health in 1954. The quotation is from p. 13.

[2] Ibid., p. 8.

[3] Levy, H., *National Health Insurance*, 1944, pp. 271–2.

[4] According to one authoritative voice in the British Medical Association (Dr H. Guy Dain) the Executive Councils were a success because 'the professional members outnumbered the lay' (*Brit. Med. J.*, 1953, Supp. i, 277).

[5] *Minutes of Evidence, Committee on Administrative Tribunals*, Day 6, p. 156.

[6] *Report of Committee of Inquiry into the Costs of the National Health Service*, 1956, Cmd 9663, pp. 155–6.

serve his patients according to their medical needs. The Act of 1946 greatly enlarged this freedom—particularly in respect to the treatment of women and children, the old, the disabled and chronically ill, and the middle-income groups in the community. No longer did the doctor have to ask himself whether the patient could afford this or that treatment; whether he should ask the patient to come again; what the patient would think of him as a person and as a doctor if he did so; whether the patient could afford this drug or that special service; how long he could wait before making a definitive diagnosis; whether it would be cheaper for the patient to go to hospital or be treated at home; whether or not it was of financial consequence to the doctor himself and to his patient to call in a consultant, to seek evidence from X-ray and laboratory tests, to advise surgery, or to allow the 'wisdom of the body' to re-assert itself.

All these are important medical gains. The material dialogue, private or public, need not now take place. Its abolition is in the best traditions of medicine. The disappearance of this barrier to clinical freedom has, of course, brought its own troubles and has made us more aware of other problems. But freedom, as we understand it in the West, has never been trouble-free. It has made doctors realize, as Dr Fox put it: 'if we want freedom *for* the profession we must cherish freedom *within* the profession.'[1]

This enlargement of freedom for the British doctor to treat his patients according to their medical needs came at a critical period in the history of medicine. By 1948 the tide of scientific and technological change was in full flood. One of the consequences of change was to push up pharmaceutical and other costs at a rapid rate. Another was to change the relativities of skill and function as between the general practitioner, the consultant and the hospital. A third was to make the older general practitioners feel more insecure and uncertain about the performance of their functions, and thus to fear the coming of the Health Service with more anxiety than perhaps they would have done if scientific change had not been so strong and pervasive at that time.

[1] Fox, T. F., *Lancet* (1951), ii, 118.

To some of these aspects of scientific change I shall return in my last lecture. All I wish to do here is to make the point that within the last ten to fifteen years the potential sphere of work of general practitioners has been extended. They can now treat many diseases which for a time they had lost to the hospital—principally pneumonia, pernicious anaemia, most subcutaneous purulent infections, and most infections of the ears, pharynx, lungs and bowels.[1] As Dr Taylor points out, 'Today the practitioner in the gloomiest slum practice can treat pneumonia more effectively than the most eminent specialist was able to do before the war.'[2]

The total effect of all these changes has, to put it simply, made it possible for general practitioners to do more or to do less for their patients; to be personally responsible for more or less serious illness among their patients; to do more or less preventive work; in short, to be relatively better or relatively worse doctors.[3] We see, in this way, how science, by enlarging the potential field of choice and action, simultaneously enlarges the potential for individual freedom. The National Health Service in Britain could not ensure that doctors, now invested with these greater powers and potentialities, would choose overnight to be 'better' doctors; all it could do was to provide that particular framework of social resources within which potentially 'better' medicine might be more easily chosen and practised.

VI

I now reach a point where it is convenient to return to certain questions I raised earlier on about the quantity and quality of the general practitioner's work. All the published evidence I have

[1] Leader, *Lancet* (1954), i, 659.

[2] Taylor, S., *Good General Practice* (1954), p. 551.

[3] One apparently unanimous conclusion of Dr Hadfield's survey for the BMA of the effects of the National Health Service on general practice was, as the author wrote: '. . . on one point they are clear—that they can do more for their patients.' He went on 'The opinion was expressed to me that, because of the costly new drugs and treatment essential to modern practice, the National Health Service came in the nick of time.' (Hadfield, S. J., *Brit. Med. J.*, 1953, ii, 691.)

been able to collect is assembled in an appendix. I limit myself, therefore, to summarizing, very broadly, the main conclusions of these various studies.

The material I have used relates chiefly to conditions in general practice during the 1930's and after 1948. It should be emphasized, however, that remarkably little is known about the institution of private medical care before 1948. For the first decade of this century there is some information. We know that before the introduction of Lloyd George's Health Insurance Act in 1911 the standard of medical care for the vast majority of the population was abysmally low by present-day standards. Competitive undercutting, fee-splitting, canvassing for patients and other unethical practices were widespread. Most doctors were extremely poorly paid and worked under degrading conditions. The out-patient departments of voluntary hospitals, described by the Webbs as 'mammoth shops, run by underpaid doctors, for the mass treatment of symptoms with free bottles of medicine',[1] (chiefly *Saccharuum Ustum* or brown sugar and water) were regarded by general practitioners as unfair competitors, threatening their main source of income.[2] For these accounts of the past we are indebted to the Webbs and medical writers like Brend, McCleary, Cox and others.[3] But between 1911 and 1948 no detailed field study of general practice was, to my knowledge, undertaken. We know very little about what doctors were paid by private patients, what unpaid bills there were, what services were given, how much work doctors had to do, what the pattern of prescribing was, and so forth.[4] The little that we can deduce

[1] Webb, B. and S., *The State and the Doctor*, 1910, p. 134.

[2] Hardy, H. Nelson, *The State of the Medical Profession in Great Britain and Ireland in 1900*, 1901, esp. pp. 20–1 and 49–55.

[3] Cox, A., *Among the Doctors*, 1950; Brend, W. A., *Health and the State*, 1917; McCleary, G. F., *Fortnightly*, December 1949, p. 409; Webb, B. and S., *The State and the Doctor*, 1910; *Report of the Royal Commission on the Poor Laws*, 1909, Cmd 4499; Special Commissioner of the *Lancet*, *The Battle of the Clubs*, 1896; British Medical Association, 'Contract Medical Practice', *Brit. Med. J.*, July 22 1905.

[4] If information under these heads has ever been collected by the British Medical Association to support their statements about practice in the past it has certainly not been published.

from pulling together many scattered threads of evidence suggests:

1. That the National Health Service has not had the effect of taking away the right of the general practitioner to function as a 'family doctor'. In the past, 'family doctoring' only existed for a small section of the population,[1] chiefly the inhabitants of relatively isolated rural areas and middle- and upper-middle-class patients.[2] Since 1948, with the removal of the financial barriers, it has been more possible for more general practitioners to function as family doctors. Some of the changing of doctors that appears to have gone on in the early years of the Service may simply have reflected the desire of families to get all their members on to the list of one doctor. Unfortunately, and in the absence of any research into the reality of 'family doctoring', this movement seems to have been interpreted by the British Medical Association as 'abuse' (in the sense of competitively playing off one doctor against another). Pressure was, therefore, brought to bear on the Ministry of Health to make it less easy for patients to change their doctors.[3]

2. It has been widely believed, especially among the profession, that the introduction of the Health Service led to a large

[1] Much the same seems to be true of urban areas in the USA. One study in New York in 1939 concluded: 'The family doctor is a vanished ideal among two-thirds of the families and is very imperfectly represented among the remaining third' (Swackhamer, G. V., *Choice and Change of Doctor*, New York, 1939, p. 44. See also Davis, M., *Medical Care for Tomorrow*, New York, 1955, pp. 10–11).

[2] Many factors contributed, before 1948, to discouraging or preventing the general practitioner from functioning as a family doctor. Among the more important were: the restriction, from 1912 to 1948, of medical benefits under National Health Insurance to insured workers; the growth of specialized public health services (divorced from the work of general practitioners) for expectant and nursing mothers, infants, schoolchildren, the tubercular and other separate age and disease categories; the limitations of the poor law medical service; the rejection of 'bad risks' from club and contract practice (disabled people, housewives in poor health, confinement cases, the elderly, the tubercular and so forth); and the particular systems developed by commercial insurance companies and voluntary societies of administering medical and other benefits. Even since 1948 the general practitioner does not seem to have functioned as a family doctor to more than a limited extent (see Taylor, S., *Good General Practice*, 1954, p. 546, and Backett, E. M., and Evans, J. C. G., *Proc. Royal Soc. Med.*, 1953, *46*, 707).

[3] See p. 139.

increase in the average number of items of service required from general practitioners by each patient per year.[1] A detailed examination of all the published reports on the subject, including five large statistical studies on National Health Insurance before 1939 and six or so National Health Service studies after 1948 of varying quality, do not confirm this belief. The most trustworthy data for the latter period show, for 1949–50, a total general practitioner consultation rate for both sexes at all ages over sixteen of 4·62 (attendances 3·00; visits 1·62). For men only aged sixteen to sixty-four (probably a better index to use for comparison with pre-war data) the rate was 3·60 (attendances 2·77; visits 0·83). Two extensive studies of National Health Insurance demand in the 1930's, carried out on behalf of the British Medical Association, give rates of 5·02 and 5·10 (attendances roughly 3·80 and visits roughly 1·25). The only conclusion that can be drawn from these and other statistical materials is that, on average and contrary to public belief, demand has not increased under the National Health Service and may indeed have fallen. Though comparisons are almost impossible with American experience, there is a little evidence that demand may be higher in the United States and that it has been rising in recent years.[2]

What we do not know from these British studies is the level of demand from the private sector in the 1930's. There is some evidence, assembled in the appendix, which suggests that demand from middle-class and professional groups increased after

[1] See, for example, the statements made by Dr S. Wand to the Fourth Annual Meeting of the Executive Councils Association (*Brit. Med. J.*, 1952, Supp. i, 9).

[2] For example: in 1950 the rate of 'physician's visits' per insured person per year was 5·18 in the Health Insurance Plan of New York (*Report of the President's Commission on the Health Needs of the Nation*, 1952, Vol. III, p. 265). See also Baehr, G., *J. Amer. Med. Assn.*, 1950, *143*, 637, and Standish, S., and others, *Why Patients See Doctors*, University of Washington Press, 1955. A more recent study of 'Major Medical Expense Insurance', developed since 1949 by the insurance industry and now covering some eleven million people (March 1957), shows that this form of medical care has led to a serious increase in demand, and particularly to an alarming rise in the cost of medical care. This rise has been described by one insurance leader as 'catastrophic'. (*Major Medical Expense Insurance: An Evaluation*, Pollack, J., paper presented to the American Public Health Association at its Annual Meeting, November 1956).

1948. Only by assuming that demand from these groups was somewhat lower in the 1930's than from insured workers (predominantly men) is it possible to find support for the impression among some general practitioners in some areas of higher total demands after 1948. But there is little evidence to support such an assumption.

It is also relevant to bring into account other evidence which shows in comparing the present situation with that in the 1930's: (a) a decline in the average number of persons per general practitioner in a substantial number of areas; (b) an improvement in the geographical distribution of doctors in relation to needs; (c) a decline in the amount of night-visiting by general practitioners; (d) a remarkable growth in the adoption of voluntary rota systems for evening, week-end and other duty periods and (e) a decrease in the number of statutory certificates issued per 100 patients per year.

3. Finally, I come to the question of quality of care by general practitioners. It is by far the most difficult question, not only because of the theoretical problem of defining what one means by 'quality' but of assessing it in practice.[1] While it is one thing for a medical observer to identify really bad general practitioner work among selected individual doctors at a given point in time[2] it is quite another thing to make comparisons over time between random groups of doctors. No scientific observations were made on these matters in the 1930's. There is some documentary evidence to suggest that for many people receiving treatment under National Health Insurance, Public Assistance and Workmen's Compensation practice the quality of care, by the standards we expect in the 1950's, was very low.[3] Hardly anything is known about private practice except the evidence of such indirect in-

[1] The most serious statistical attempt to measure standards of general practice was recently completed in the USA, namely, 'An Analytical Study of North Carolina General Practice, 1953–4', Peterson, O. L., Andrews, L. P., Spain, R. S., and Greenberg, B. G., *J. Med. Education* (Chicago), 1956, 31 (12), Pt 2.

[2] As Dr Collings and Dr Taylor attempted to do (Collings, J., *Lancet* (1950), i, 555, and Taylor, S., *Good General Practice*, 1954).

[3] See, for example, Levy, H., *National Health Insurance*, 1944 and Wilson, A., and Levy, H., *Workmen's Compensation*, Vols. I and II, 1939 and 1941.

dices as high rates of tonsillectomy, inadequate prenatal care, excessive surgical interference in childbearing, too frequent use of operative procedures in small, general practitioner hospitals and the like.[1] In short, when it is alleged that the quality of care by general practitioners has deteriorated under the National Health Service there is little to support such statements except impressions and memories of past experience.[2]

What evidence there is could in theory point the other way. The supreme requisite of good practitioner care is time; and many general practitioners have, on average, as I have shown, more time to spend with each patient than they had before 1948 if they wish to use it that way, more time for diagnosis, the foundation of all good medical care. Against this consideration has to be set the unknown effects of six other critically important variables: (1) the educational equipment and clinical skill of the doctor; (2) his capacity to understand sick people; (3) the range, content and power of the scientific aids available to the general practitioner; (4) the nature and extent of his contacts with professional colleagues; (5) the facilities available to him for dealing with the social aspects of ill-health; (6) the incidence of ill-health, mental and physical, and the norms of expectation or awareness of what constitutes 'good medical care' among the population as a whole.[3] The role that these and other variables play in the total equation has, without a shadow of doubt,

[1] See, for example, *Reports of the Departmental Committees on Maternal Mortality and Morbidity*, 1930 and 1932; Titmuss, Richard M., *Problems of Social Policy*, 1950, Ch. V, esp. pp. 66–73; and Glover, J. A., *Proc. Roy. Soc. Med.*, 1938, 31, 1219.

[2] For example, in 1955, Dr Hale-White, President of the Metropolitan Counties Branch of the BMA, expressed the view that 'the standard of medical practice in this country was going down and would continue to go down unless far-reaching changes were made' (*Brit. Med. J.*, 1955, i, Supp. 226). As a whole, his address was in much the same vein as one by Wilfred Trotter in 1933: '. . . at a time when it is no longer possible to conceal the unique importance of medicine for the very existence of social life, that profession finds itself of all professions the least in command of social prestige, the least privileged, the most exposed and the hardest worked' (Trotter, W., 1941, *Collected Papers*, p. 3).

[3] For a penetrating analysis of some of the components of medical care and of the changing pattern of disease which now confronts the general practitioner see Morris, J. N., *Uses of Epidemiology*, 1957.

changed in many ways over the past few decades. Time still remains, however, as a factor of supreme importance—indeed, science and the recognition of the mental component in ill-health may perhaps have heightened its value to doctor and patient alike. Nor is this truth in any way dimmed by the fact that the general practitioner today is responsible, as some recent studies have shown, for the treatment of a substantial amount of serious organic and infectious disease.[1] He cannot be dismissed as a specialist in the trivial.

We must, therefore, look for some more searching tool than generalities about 'abuse' and 'deteriorating standards'. If the Health Service did not exist in Britain today, would there be more or less misuse of the antibiotics, the barbiturates and other chemical tranquillisers; more or less unnecessary surgery; earlier or later access to medical care; more or fewer hasty, untested diagnoses; more or fewer unethical practices,[2] and more or fewer income, class, age, sex and geographical differentials in respect of all these and other factors? I suggest that these are the kind of questions which are more likely to stimulate a search for reliable evidence.

I thus end on a hypothetical note, partly because there is no one answer to the questions I have raised, and partly because the nature of the relationship between doctor and patient and patient and doctor, which I discuss in my last lecture, must find a place in any consideration of the changing quality of medical care.

[1] Backett, E. M., and Evans, J. C. G., *Brit. Med. J.* (1954), i, 109; General Register Office, *General Practitioners Records, Studies on Medical and Population Subjects, No. 9* (1956), and Taylor, S., *Good General Practice* (1954), esp. p. 403.

[2] Such as those enumerated in the symposium on 'Ethical Standards and Professional Conduct' (*The Annals of the American Academy of Political and Social Science*, January 1955). There has been little discussion in Britain since 1948 over such unethical practices as ghost surgery, fee-splitting, unnecessary surgery and commission-taking compared with the debate in American medical journals (see, for example, Tipton, G. W., *Bulletin of the American College of Surgeons*, 1954, Vol. 39, p. 159; Hawley, P. R., *Bulletin of the American College of Surgeons*, 1953, Vol. 38, p. 36; Ravdin, J. S., *J. Amer. Med. Asscn.*, 1951, Vol. 147, p. 535; Lembcke, P. A., *American Journal of Public Health*, 1952, p. 276). The absence of publicity does not, however, mean that such practices do not occur in Britain.

CHAPTER 10

The National Health Service in England

SCIENCE AND THE SOCIOLOGY OF MEDICAL CARE

I

IT is in itself an interesting fact that during the past decade there has been an increasing volume of studies and reports on general practice in Britain, the United States and other countries. No doubt much of this interest has been provoked by the growing impact of scientific developments on medicine over the same period. These have raised many questions about the present state of general practice; its historical evolution, and its future place in medical care. From these various studies, official and unofficial, one general conclusion does, I think, emerge.

For many years before 1948 the general practitioner in Britain had been socially and professionally isolated from the broad stream of developments in medicine, public health and social welfare. His education for general practice had been neglected. He was assumed, by consultants, to be something of a mediocrity.[1] In a period when medicine was becoming less of an art and more of a science he was sometimes forced to behave, by

[1] This was frankly expressed by Dr T. Rowland Hill, deputy chairman, Central Consultants and Specialists Committee and vice-chairman, Joint Consultants Committee, in a letter to the *Lancet*, 'It should not be possible for persons of only mediocre attainments to stay permanently in the hospital service simply because they would like to do so' (1957, ii, 291). See also *Report of the Committee on General Practice* (section on training and education) of the Central Health Services Council, 1954.

the rigours of competition, in ways that contradicted the logic of scientific advance. In a period, too, when the potentialities of diagnosis and therapy, in their social as well as their medical components, were rapidly expanding and demanding more team-work, more co-operation, the general practitioner remained, more often than not, a single-handed, professionally isolated, private entrepreneur.[1]

Moreover, the relatively low level of financial rewards for many practitioners before 1939 added to the frustrations of an often unsatisfying professional life. Attitudes to medicine and to their patients which many were, in consequence, led to adopt found their expression in the physical environment in which they chose (or were compelled) to practice medicine. It was an environment which spoke loudly of neglect, voluntary or enforced; of an unrecognized, inert acceptance of low professional standards. This was the situation which the National Health Service inherited and made manifest in 1948 to the first investigators and to the middle-class patients who now began to use the general practitioner's waiting room.

Some reasons have already been given to support the belief that, since 1948, there has been an improvement in the standard of general practice. The long process of social diagnosis, which has been a feature of this period, may in itself have helped towards something of a spontaneous recovery. The Health Service, contrary to widespread opinion, contributed to this recovery, chiefly by providing a social framework in which better medicine could be practised and greater clinical freedom could be deployed. But nine years is a short period set against the accumulated frustrations of many decades. The more isolated the institution the greater the tenacity of custom and tradition.[2] General practice still is, as the *Lancet* said in 1954, in an unsatisfactory state in many areas of Britain.[3] Attitudes to medicine, shaped in

[1] 'The sense of isolation is one of the chief grievances of the general practitioner.' (*Draft Report of the Medical Planning Commission of the British Medical Association*, *Brit. Med. J.*, 1942, Supp. i, 743.)

[2] The importance of tradition in prescribing habits in general practice has been demonstrated in J. P. Martin's study *Social Aspects of Prescribing*, 1957.

[3] Leader, March 27, 1954, p. 659.

the past, still prevail.

One recent example is the rapid development of an impersonal 'emergency call service' or rota system in London and other areas. Within nine months it was claimed that a million patients, whose doctors subscribed, were brought within this scheme which, as a private venture organized on a commercial basis, is outside the National Health Service.[1] This substitution for the freely chosen 'family practitioner' of a corps of anonymous doctors in fast radio cars, unsupported by medical records, not linked to the local health and welfare services, not known to the general practitioners, and operating for evening, week-end and other periods, has been severely criticized by some members of the profession as unethical and in contravention of the terms of service.[2] By April 1957 the General Medical Services Committee of the British Medical Association had come to the conclusion that, to 'check abuse' by doctors, the Ministry of Health should amend the terms of service.[3] The cost to the doctor of belonging to this scheme is allowed in the calculation of practice expenses. This particular development is, I suggest, one symptom of a long-standing professional *malaise* in general practice; more clearly seen today as a result of the penetration of science into medicine and the growing division of labour within medicine itself.

I now turn to discuss the association of these developments with the changing character of demand for medical care and its effects on the doctor-patient relationship. Much of what I shall have to say is not specifically addressed to the more practical problems facing the National Health Service today. I have tried to look at these questions of science and specialism in a broader, historical context. It is necessary to do so if we wish to understand the reality of the present conflicts within the medical profession itself and in the National Health Service. These conflicts

[1] *Picture Post*, September 22, 1956, p. 32.

[2] See correspondence columns of the *Brit. Med. J.*, Supp., June 2, 9 and 16 1956; Annual Report of the Council of the British Medical Association, *Brit Med. J.*, Supp. 166, 1957; and report of the Conference of Local Medical Committees, *Brit. Med. J.*, Supp. 344, 1957.

[3] Annual Report of Council, para. 29, *Brit. Med. J.*, Supp. 166, 1957.

often have a professional base though their presenting symptoms may be superficially diagnosed in economic terms.

II

Although we can, as I have shown earlier, make some quantitative assessment of expressed demand for medical care this tells us, however, very little about the social and psychological, as distinct from the purely medical and biological, factors which cause demand to be made—or not made. We know at the very least that they are extraordinarily complex; that systems of medicine and popular attitudes to health and disease are the products of particular forms of society and cultural patterns. Sigerist has traced for us over the centuries the shifting emphasis in attitudes and practice between magic, religion (wherein all disease came from the gods) and rationality.[1] From the anthropologists we have learnt of the variety of ways in which supernatural sanctions operate to fashion concepts of disease and the behaviour of sick people. 'Health practices and health ideas penetrate deeply into the domains of politics, philosophy, etiquette, religion, cosmology and kinship.'[2] Sociologists have shown how the 'discovery of culture' has changed our ideas about the significance of health and disease to the individual in his various roles.[3] Psychiatrists have broadened our view of the emotional component in sickness and have given us new ways of looking at the growth of personality and the origins of illness. Even the economists have contributed to the discussion by the emphasis they have laid, in the United States, on the 'money-back complex' as a factor in determining demand for medical care and, in Britain, on the 'something-for-nothing-complex' as a factor of demand for medical care under the National Health Service.

[1] Sigerist, H. E., *Civilization and Disease*, 1945.

[2] Paul, B. D., *Health, Culture and Community*, New York, 1955, p. 459.

[3] Simmons, L. W., and Wolff, H. G., *Social Science in Medicine*, 1954, and symposium on 'Sociocultural Approaches to Medical Care', *Journal of Social Issues*, 1952, Vol. VIII, No. 4.

Apart from the central importance of changes in the nature and incidence of disease, we are led to see, therefore, that demand for medical care in modern society depends not only on economic factors, on the distribution of poverty and wealth, but —among other variables—on prevailing concepts of health and disease and on what we think is expected of us in our various roles by our fellows, in the family, at work, and in all our social relations. To the individual, the sensation of pain or stress is in part compounded of his perception of it, and perception depends on a host of factors. Ultimately, many derive from the significance that death holds in a given culture at a particular time.[1] The more that a society as a whole values success in life and fears death the higher may be its demand for medical care in some form or other. The more that the individual personality is sensitive and self-conscious about the roles he thinks he is expected to play in society the more demanding may be his perception of what constitutes 'efficient function' or wholeness for himself and for others. What man himself regards as sickness and as his roles as a sick or well person are the critical factors for, as Charles Lamb observed, 'sickness enlarges the dimensions of a man's self to himself . . . supreme selfishness is inculcated upon him as his only duty'.[2]

These considerations, which I cannot pursue at length in this paper, are of fundamental importance today for any understanding of the role of the doctor and of changes in demand for medical care in modern society. They have to be seen as part of the totality of social change which makes society, in any time dimension, a social process. Two major factors of change (or groups of measurable phenomena) can I think, however, be singled out for closer examination. These, in combination with other factors, have radically changed medical knowledge and its practical application since the beginning of this century, and particularly during the last twenty years.

[1] Few writers have given us such a sensitive picture of an age and of the profound effects of 'the vision of death' on the life of a society as the Dutch historian, J. Huizinga, in *The Waning of the Middle Ages*, 1924.

[2] Lamb, Charles, from 'The Convalescent', *Everybody's Lamb*, 1933 ed., p. 113.

The first major factor can be shortly described as the invasion of medicine by the natural sciences; in other words, the impact of scientific advances on medical knowledge and practice. Specialization, or the division of medical labour, is in itself an important by-product of such advances, generating in its turn far-reaching effects on the practice of medicine.

The second major factor is the social organization of medical skill, techniques and practice; in other words, the accepted and approved channels through which medicine fulfils its purpose and doctor and patient are brought together. So far as Britain is concerned, the main characteristic of change in this sphere is the growth in recent years of State intervention in the provision of medical care services. In the United States and other countries, changes in the social organization of medical care have taken other forms with important, but no doubt in many respects different, effects on the role of the doctor and on demand for medical care.

Though it is possible to visualize these two factors of change as separate, distinctive forces they are, nevertheless, indissolubly linked. Scientific advances have profoundly influenced the social and administrative organization of medical care. This is true of both 'private' and 'public' forms of organization. Conversely, the ways in which medical care services have been organized have influenced the application of science in medical practice. One effect of the interaction of these forces has been to make the doctor more dependent on the natural sciences for the practice of his art and, consequentially, more dependent on society and his fellow doctors for the provision of an organized arrangement of social resources now recognized as essential for the application of modern medicine. These developments were observed by one of the pioneers of the Mayo Clinic many years ago: 'As we men of medicine grow in learning we more justly appreciate our dependence upon each other . . . It has become necessary to develop medicine as a co-operative science . . .'[1]

The public, and to a substantial extent the professional, view

[1] Clapesattle, H., *The Doctors Mayo*, 1941, p. 530.

of medicine and its problems in Britain during the past decade or so has been largely dominated by considerations of social organization and political form (and here I am using political in no narrow parliamentary sense).[1] The introduction of the National Health Service in 1948 heavily emphasised these considerations. As a political animal, the doctor, like the rest of us, saw the effects of the Service on himself and his practice as a more potent and direct influence than the less tangible, accumulative effects of science on medicine. So did the patient. The result has been a strong tendency in recent years to attribute all that is thought of as 'good' or 'bad' in medical care to a particular administrative structure and organization. The preoccupation with such matters of the Government's review of the Health Service in 1956 (the Guillebaud Report) reflects this tendency. Similarly, changes in the role and status of the general practitioner relative to those of the consultant have been ascribed to changes in organization. In consequence, other factors of change, among which the growth of science in medicine is one of the more powerful, have been neglected by those seeking to understand the role of the doctor in modern society.

III

At this point, it seems helpful to give some substance to these generalizations about scientific change. At the risk of being superficial we may consider a few of the more striking advances in recent years. The fact that the so-called basic sciences have, as Ellis remarks, 'swollen, reproduced as it were by binary fission, and swollen again',[2] has greatly accentuated the problem fo medical education. In anatomy a whole new field of living structure has been opened up in barely twenty years by the study of embryology. Physiology has spread so far and wide that it is

[1] A point of view which was clearly illustrated in the Presidential Address by Dr A. Hall at the Annual Meeting of the British Medical Association in 1956. All the problems of work, status and prestige in general practice were attributed directly to the introduction of the National Health Service (*Brit. Med. J.*, 1956, Supp. ii, 58).

[2] Ellis, J. R., 'Changes in Medical Education', *Lancet* (1956), i, 813.

not clear what is left at the centre. Rapid advances in knowledge in the fields of chemistry, biochemistry and physics have contributed greatly to the study of disease. Organic chemistry, for instance, has now reached the stage when it can analyse to some extent most constituents of the body. The detection of disease processes, now of strikingly greater importance in general practice,[1] has benefited from advances on this and other fronts. The science of radiotherapy, which has changed to a remarkable extent in a decade or so, had as its starting point the discovery of X-rays by Röntgen as recently as sixty years ago. Now, with the increasing use of radioactive isotopes and of knowledge gleaned from fundamental research into the structure of the atom, medicine is on the verge of a further significant advance in its understanding of the structure of matter and of living processes. The borderline between living and non-living substances has almost disappeared in the virus laboratory.

From the contribution of workers in various disciplines, biochemistry, haematology and others, we now have the medical knowledge which, if applied, could virtually eliminate nutritional disorders including the nutritionally conditioned deficiencies. All this has happened between Gowland Hopkins's first paper on vitamins in 1912 and the isolation of vitamin B.12 in 1948.

Over an even shorter period of time immense strides have been made in surgical techniques and skills, largely as a result of scientific advances in the prevention of infection, in the tracking down and identification of bacteria, in methods of blood transfusion, and in the prevention and relief of pain. These developments now allow surgery to undertake operations with relative

[1] This point was emphasized by the British Medical Association in its Report in 1950 on *General Practice and the Training of the General Practitioner:* 'One change in general practice as compared with fifty years ago is the increasing importance of the prompt and accurate diagnosis of illness. At the end of the last century, when the resources of medicine were so much more limited than they are today, the failure of early diagnosis was, perhaps, of less significance in treatment. Today, however, the therapeutic arsenal is replete with weapons of immense power for healing, but they are most effective when used early, and this demands early and accurate diagnosis of disease' (p. 33).

safety, to investigate disease and to apply treatments, all of which were hardly thought of a few decades ago.

Next in significance to the relief of pain, without question a far more powerful and effective psychological weapon in the hands of the doctor today than it ever was, are the astonishing advances in chemotherapy which have occurred since the discovery of prontosil in 1935 and the introduction of penicillin in 1940.[1] 'I doubt,' wrote Sir Henry Dale in 1950, 'whether the change in the half-century in any department of medicine has been greater or more fundamental than this.'[2]

The total effect of this irruption of science into medicine is impressive, not only because of the scale on which it is taking place but because of the speed at which advance succeeds and proliferates further advance. 'The pace has accelerated sharply during the past few months,' remarked the *British Medical Journal* in 1957, in noting the discovery of a whole new series of valuable antibiotics.[3] Once the medical significance of new knowledge in the biological and natural sciences has been grasped, the floodgates between theory and practice in medical care burst wide open. Developments in the past few years read like a story of geometrical progression: they include the elaboration of penicillin (about fifty 'dosage forms' now exist), streptomycin, oleandomycin and other antibiotics, the application of nuclear physics, improvements in anaesthesia and thoracic surgery, the treatment of coronary thrombosis with anti-coagulants, knowledge of blood compatibility and the discovery of cortisone and polio vaccines.

Set beside these dazzling achievements in the natural sciences, the advances made in our understanding of the psychology of man since Freud published in 1900 *The Interpretation of Dreams* seem prosaic by comparison. Set, however, in a longer and broader perspective, the work of Freud and his successors has been of revolutionary importance to medicine; it has changed our attitudes to the mentally ill, it has at least helped towards the

[1] See Garrod, L. P., *Brit. Med. J.* (1955), ii, 756

[2] Dale, H. H., *Brit. Med. J.* (1950), i, 1.

[3] Leader, *Brit. Med. J.* (1957), i, 150.

alleviation of mental suffering, it has enlarged the possibilities of preventive therapy, and it has given us new ways of looking at the growth of personality and the origins of illness. For the doctor it has added a new potential of awareness to clinical skill; it has, as John Rickman wrote, 'given a new dimension to the medical interview'.[1] In so doing it has, for doctors and laymen alike, undermined our psychological innocence, sensitized us to an inner world of reality, and made us see all sickness, in whatever guise, as part of a psychological continuum. We are thus changed by knowledge and by our expectations of how new knowledge may change the behaviour of others.

To summarize, even in this cursory manner, some of the more important additions to medical knowledge and skill within a relatively short span of years, leads us to ask questions about their effects on the practitioner of medicine in his social role as a doctor and, in particular, on the nature of his relations with his patient. I address these questions primarily to the situation in Britain as it has developed under the National Health Service.

For convenience, we may consider the effects of these scientific changes in three categories; first, their effects on the division of medical labour, secondly, their effects on the content and practice of particular medical skills and, thirdly, their effects on the relationship between doctor and patient.

IV

Every major advance in tested knowledge in the natural sciences has brought with it, when applied to problems of health and disease, a need for specialization in the acquisition of medical knowledge and skill, in function and in practice. As physics has split from chemistry, and as chemistry itself, for example, splits into so many parts that the specialist in one branch has difficulty in understanding the language of his colleagues, so new problems arise from the division of medical labour. Existing specialisms become too broad for one man to comprehend or to

[1] Rickman, J., *Brit. Med. J.*, (1950), i, 37.

practise as a separate skill; as Robert Platt has pointed out, it is becoming increasingly difficult for one man to understand both cardiology and electrocardiography at the same time.[1] Specialization in theory and knowledge influences the division of labour in both surgical and clinical fields. Surgical specialisms multiply inside the hospital; clinical specialisms grow both inside and outside the hospital. Clinical work divides and sub-divides by disease and its treatment (physical and psychological), by anatomical region, by the age of patients (paediatricians, geriatricians and so forth), and by the social or administrative setting (industrial, educational and so forth).[2]

This increasing division of labour, mainly (though not always) based on a scientific rationale instead of as in the past an accumulation of empirical experience by the individual practitioner, has resulted in great benefits in the reduction and alleviation of suffering and disease. Scientific medicine thus joins hands with humanitarian medicine in being irrevocably wedded to the idea of progress. Irrespective of race, class or age, mortality must be postponed as long as possible.

In combination, these two factors, science and specialization, have had within a few decades a profound influence, not only on the practice of medicine and the extent to which its objectives are realizable, but on the established patterns of relationships and behaviour within the profession itself and between the doctor and the patient. Inevitably, attitudes and expectations adopted by the patient and by society as a whole about the doctor and his work have also been influenced. Some of these effects of change have contributed to the solution of old problems but have simultaneously created new ones. We may briefly consider a few examples as they concern the profession itself and the doctor-patient relationship within the context of the medical care services in Britain.

The rapid growth of specialized skills and functions in medicine has, within recent years, greatly affected medical education.

[1] Platt, R., *Lancet* (1956), i, 61.

[2] It has even been suggested that specialist 'mesiatricians' are now needed to concern themselves with the diseases of the middle-aged (*Lancet*, 1956, ii, 1295).

In the United States, according to some observers, the 'formalization of training programmes for nearly every speciality or subspeciality has created a caste system within medicine'.[1] This gives rise to new group solidarities, as Durkheim put it, based on likenesses in skills, functions and prestige. That these develop early in the medical career is suggested by a comment from the Deputy Chairman of the Central Consultants and Specialists Committee in London when he wrote about an 'unprecedented and indefensible sense of privilege in some younger consultants' today.[2] As these separatisms emerge and receive formal sanction in a variety of ways they tend, of course, to foster their own particular loyalties. These specialized loyalties, by the nature of their internal forces, often emphasize, in an exaggerated form, status differences. Pressures then develop for these status ratings to be reflected in greater differentials in pay.

One of the ultimate consequences, therefore, of these effects of science on medicine is to increase the possibilities of misunderstanding and conflict within the profession. The area of conflict about financial rewards, for instance, expands as one branch of the profession strives to increase its relative advantages while others seek to lessen them. Since 1948, the broad result of this internal professional struggle for status has been that the social distances between different specialists have widened (partly, of course, because of the greater difficulties in the communication of knowledge), while the gulf between the general practitioner and specialists as a body has widened further. These are the 'fissiparous tendencies' deplored by the British Medical Association in 1956 no doubt anxious about the sources of its authority to speak for the profession as a whole.[3]

It is not possible to understand the recent controversies about medical remuneration in Britain without taking account of these factors. They were clearly demonstrated in 1957 when a bitter

[1] Peterson, O. L., Andrews, L. P., Spain, R. S., and Greenberg, B. G., *J. Med. Educ.*, 1956, 31 (12), Pt 2.

[2] Letter Dr T. Rowland Hill, *Lancet*, 1957, ii, 291.

[3] '. . . all sections of the profession must soberly resist any tendency to score off each other or to seek sectional advantages' (Leader, *Brit. Med. J.*, 1956, i, 336).

dispute broke out in public between the consultant and general practitioner branches. The former were accused of negotiating secretly with the Government to further their own interests,[1] one of which was to safeguard the influence it was said that they held over Government policy in restricting the number of consultant posts in the Health Service.[2] 'It would be wrong to disguise the fact,' wrote the *British Medical Journal* at the height of the crisis, 'that the present controversy has revealed a profession divided in itself as it has never been before.'[3] Attractive as it was to use the Health Service as the scapegoat and to threaten strike action, such an attitude obscured the need to recognize the many forces of change which were affecting the structure and cohesion of the profession itself.

Implicit in this growth of separate interests, divided skills and special loyalties is an increasing fragmentation in responsibility for the treatment of the individual patient. The emphasis shifts from the person to some aspect of his disease. Yet while science is pushing medicine, theoretically and structurally, in this direction it is, simultaneously and particularly in respect to the application of scientific medicine, pulling in the reverse direction—towards more co-operation, more dependence on other people, more group practice, more team reliance on special skills and functions. These contrary forces help to explain many of the stresses experienced by the National Health Service today; stresses often wrongly attributed, as we have seen from evidence given earlier, to the administrative organization of the Service itself. They also make explicable the great debate in the United States in recent years on how to divide fees from the patient for divided responsibilities,[4] and what to do about the widespread

[1] See, for example, correspondence and reports of meetings in the *Brit. Med. J.*, 1957, Supp. i, 244, 251, 263, 275 and 298, and leaders in *Lancet*, 1957, ii, 129 and *Brit. Med. J.*, 1957 i, 995, 1106 and 1349.

[2] See, for example, correspondence in *Lancet*, 1957, i, 1352 and ii, 338.

[3] Leader, *Brit. Med. J.*, 1957, i, 1463. See also debate by the General Medical Services Committee of the British Medical Association, *Brit. Med. J.*, 1957, Supp., i, 272-3.

[4] Fitts, W. T. and B., 'Ethical Standards of the Medical Profession', *The Annals of the American Academy of Political and Social Science*, January 1955, p. 21.

practice of fee-splitting.[1] These questions of who should send in bills to the patient, at what stage of medical care, for what amounts and on what criteria of ability to pay both for individual items and for the treatment as a whole, inevitably follow from the increasing division of medical labour. Thus, as Dr Davis observes, in the private sector of medical care in the States, 'the economic relations of doctors, patients, and hospitals become an intricate, and sometimes a tangled, skein'.[2]

We have already noted how these trends in the division of medical labour have been accompanied by changes in status positions within the profession. Professional stratification in medicine, the existence of effective superiority and inferiority relationships, has become more pronounced—more, in a sense, inflexible[3]—partly because these relationships and roles have come to depend more on achieved status through the organized acquisition of specialist skills and techniques at an early stage in the medical career.[4] Moreover, because those who specialize (who aim to fulfil a restricted determinate function) have a higher status in our society the general practitioner becomes more conscious of inferior status. He is the indeterminate man; the one who is more uncertain of his place in the scheme of things; who is uneasy because he has to spread himself so widely and has no special role to perfect; no special skill by which he may himself achieve higher status in his profession.

Formerly, the general practitioner was better able, and what is equally important, felt himself better able on his own initiative to fulfil the role he thought he was expected to play. His 'specialism' lay in his own personality, the use he made of it,

[1] According to Dr P. B. Magnuson (Chairman of the Presidential Commission on the Health Needs of the Nation 1951–2) 'fee-splitting is extremely prevalent' (*US News and World Report*, July 3, 1953, pp. 49–50).

[2] Davis, M. M., *Medical Care for Tomorrow* (1955), pp. 26 and 129.

[3] In the past, according to Sir Heneage Ogilvie, 'every practitioner had a consultant's gold-headed cane in his surgery' (*Lancet*, 1952, ii, 820). This is no longer true; a fact that is not attributable to the National Health Service.

[4] Some of the consequences for medical care of the rise in prestige of the specialist relative to that of the general practitioner are discussed by Todd, J. W., 'Specialization', *Lancet* (1951), i, 462.

and the way he handled his self-conception of role in his day-to-day relations with his patients. He was better able to be himself. Armed as he then was, not much more than forty years ago, with little besides a stethescope, a thermometer and a personal accumulation of bedside observations, he did not have to rely to any great extent on external resources in satisfactorily fulfilling, in his own eyes and in the eyes of his patients, his self-chosen role as a doctor. In this sense, he was a more self-respecting, self-directing, less dependent person. He was an individual, a character; clinical medicine was then more individualistic, personal, and personally competitive. Any conflict between the rendering of professional service and the rendering of professional bills was less obvious; less sharply explicit. What was charged for was predominantly personal service; the intuitive art of an individual and the personal manner in which it was conveyed to the patient. Nor was the general practitioner, in his relationships with the consultant and surgeon, as dependent as he subsequently became. For the nourishment of their practices they depended primarily on him; significantly, it was they who sent him presents at Christmas; he it was who chose which consultant should see his patient when he wanted, not instructions, but a 'second opinion'.

'Scientific' medicine, in adding its own particular objective and subjective uncertainties to situations in which more knowledge and more certainty are now expected by patients, has profoundly changed these roles and altered relationships. The general practitioner has become, for instance, more dependent in some respects on the consultant and the expert and, in a wider sense, more dependent as a whole on resources external to himself. Not only has some part of his diagnostic and therapeutic work passed into the hands of specialists (though, as we have noted earlier, some specialist functions are now within the capacity of the practitioner) but, by and large, his professional relationship with the consultant has been reversed. This change from relative independence to relative dependence, primarily caused by the factors of science and specialization, received its formal and explicit stamp when the National Health Service was introduced.[1] To a large extent, the Service also severed the financial relationship between the general practitioner and the consultant. In part, this can be traced to the fact that the hospital has now become, in place of general practice, a major source of consultant work and the centre of gravity of scientific medicine.

At the same time as these changes have been under way, we have been witnessing a growth in public esteem of the specialist in all walks of life; the generalist is too detached and indeterminate to be in favour in a world of professionalism and expertise. Much, indeed, has happened to change professional roles and relationships since the days when Christopher Wren could experiment with the intravenous injection of fluids and an educated gentleman could comprehend the whole of science.

After the introduction of the National Health Service in 1948 we can trace a steadily rising tide of complaints from general practitioners about their loss in status and their sense of insecurity. Some of the evidence for this has already been cited; other material is in the appendix. But this complaining was not new; it had been growing for many years. A decade before the Health Service was introduced the President of the British Medical Association had said: 'The general practitioner must learn to make his diagnosis without the skilled help which the specialist commands, and to carry out his treatment with makeshift appliances and with amateur nursing'.[2]

The advent of the Health Service converted private complaints into public complaints. It enfranchized complaint, for the doctor as well as the patient. General practitioners, it was said again, had been reduced to acting as sorters, clerks and mere 'disposal

[1] Much material of varying quality on these changes is contained in the *Brit. Med. J.* of September 26, 1953 (General Practice Number) surveying 'General Practice Today and Tomorrow'. It was concluded that the bonds between general practitioner and consultant have weakened; that the latter is less dependent on the former for his living; that the consultant is more aloof, superior and condescending; that social contacts are few or non-existent; and that an intermediate relationship, in the person of the hospital registrar or junior consultant, has come between the general practitioner and the consultant of his choice.

[2] Johnstone, R. J., Presidential Address, British Medical Association Meeting 1937, *Lancet* (1937), ii, 175.

agents'.[1] They had lost status; they had been excluded from hospital work; they were afraid of referring maternity cases to consultants for fear of losing them; they were paid much less than consultant staff; they had no merit awards; they were not knighted or honoured; they were no longer family doctors. The Health Service was held responsible.[2] In one sense it was by sanctioning what had already taken place—and was taking place—and by stimulating further the development of scientific innovation and specialization. These advances were welcomed by consultants; they did not particularly want general practitioners to have access to hospital beds; they were not enthusiastic about allowing them direct access to diagnostic and therapeutic facilities in the hospital; perhaps they were glad to be released from financial dependence on the general practitioner. In their contacts with practitioners a note of patronage crept in; as the *Lancet* wrote in 1953 '. . . it is discouraging to read so much evidence of the frequent failure of consultants—especially among the younger generation—to give the practitioner the help he really needs'.[3]

The similarity between these statements and recent observations about general practice in the United States is striking. In their introduction to a recent study of practice in North Carolina the authors write: 'In the last few decades a new note has been injected into the practice situation in the United States by the growth of specialization . . . The predominance of the specialist organizations has put general practice in a defensive situation and has allocated to it largely negative virtues. The creation of certifying boards in medical specialities has closed many doors to the general physician. The hospital restrictions

[1] The phrase used by the Royal College of Physicians in a memorandum of evidence to the Guillebaud Committee (Cmd 9662, 1956, p. 281).

[2] In addition to references cited elsewhere see Jenkins, J. R. F., *Brit. Med. J.* (1956), Supp. i, 352; Hall, A., *Brit. Med. J.* (1956), ii, 57, and Annual Representative Meeting, *Brit. Med. J.* (1957), ii, 42.

[3] Editorial, September 26, 1953, in reviewing 'A Field Survey of General Practice', by Dr S. J. Hadfield, Assistant Secretary of the British Medical Association (published in *Brit. Med. J.*, 1953, ii, 683). See also 'The General Practitioner and the Laboratory Service', Duncan, M. N. S., *Lancet* (1952), ii, 379.

placed upon general practitioners are well known. In many communities it is easier for a specialist to obtain an appointment in the hospital than it is for a general practitioner. Within the hospital, increasing organization and formalization of responsibility have had a tendency to exclude the general practitioner from more and more fields of medical practice.'[1] Other observers have attributed these developments and a worsening in the relationships between doctors, patients and hospitals to the controls exercised by insurance schemes.[2]

The steady accretion in Britain of all these tangible and intangible changes added to the general practitioners' feelings that they were no longer free agents in medical care; no longer wholly responsible for their patients; in short, they became more conscious of dependent relationships.[3] Yet, at the same time, it was being borne in on them that scientific advances in medicine spelt greater personal responsibilities. The dilemma was most obvious over the choice of drugs. With a phenomenal expansion in the range of choice, the problem of selecting the right drug in the right amount at the right point in the disease process adds to the general practitioner's feelings of insecurity. Some of these drugs are immediately valuable, some are worthless, some harmless, some are extremely dangerous. In these circumstances, the practitioner can walk insecurely with the times, pushed along perhaps by a greater urge actively to intervene in treating patients, and prescribe the latest and most sophisticated of several hundred new preparations. He then runs the risk of surrendering some of his responsibility for the care of patients to the pharmaceutical industry. Or he may spurn all the advances in

[1] Peterson, O. L., Andrews, L. P., Spain, R. S., and Greenberg, B. G., *J. Med. Educ.*, 1956, 31 (12), Pt 2, p. 7.

[2] Leader, *Lancet*, 1957, i, 673.

[3] According to Dr Hadfield 'Many general practitioners feel that consultants regard themselves as superior beings'. One practitioner expressed it in this way: 'The difference is subtle and hard to define, I am still on the very best of terms with our local consultants as before, but somehow there is a difference. In the old days one used to ring them up constantly and discuss cases and people. Now one feels that they are no longer dependent on us, and they seem to be so much taken up with clinics here, there, and everywhere, and somehow one doesn't like to bother them.' (Hadfield, S. J., *Brit. Med. J.*, 1953, ii, esp. pp. 693–4 and 698).

favour of some older remedy which he at least knows something about.[1] Nor does the training which most general practitioners have had help them to adjust to change, for it is primarily based on hospital medicine—a very different experience from the average work of the average general practice.

In all these ways, the work of the general practitioner has been deeply influenced by the consequences of scientific and technological change. Of all workers in the field of medical care, he has been most exposed to the effects of change, primarily because adjustment has had to take place in a situation of virtual isolation. The first impact of the Health Service speeded up these effects and, in consequence, accentuated the general practitioner's sense of isolation. Since this initial phase, however, the Service has, I believe, begun to reverse the secular trends towards isolation and dependence by giving the practitioner greater financial security, more clinical freedom and an increasing measure of institutional support. To the extent that these essential needs are met, it should become easier for general practice to adjust to the changes arising from scientific and technical advances in medicine.

V

Finally, I would make a few comments on the doctor-patient relationship within the context of the changes which I have been discussing. One among the many facets of this relationship which may be singled out is the problem for the doctor of protecting and maintaining his conception of his role as a doctor in face of these changes and the fact—an important and often overlooked one—that he is now seeing a more knowledgeable and articulate body of patients. Though acceptance and submission are still widespread in doctors' surgeries and hospital wards there would appear to be a tendency for more people to adopt a questioning and critical attitude to medical care.[2] The

[1] Some aspects of this problem of prescribing are discussed in J. P. Martin's study *Social Aspects of Prescribing*, 1957.

[2] The increase in recent years, not only in Britain but in the United States and

advertising of drugs, the prestige of science in medicine, the use of television and radio for 'health education', the spread of middle-class attitudes and patterns of behaviour, and a long public health campaign for the early detection and prevention of disease all evoke a more questioning attitude. That is the aim of health education; to make people think about health and disease in a positive way rather than to submit to life 'as it happens'.

Professor Clark-Kennedy, in writing on 'medicine in relation to society', has expressed the view that the attitude of the patient to his doctor has changed considerably in recent years. 'He is aware that his doctor now knows relatively much less about medicine as a whole than he did a few years ago.'[1] Hence his growing faith in specialists. From what evidence exists it would seem that this attitude is more pronounced (so far as demand on the National Health Service is concerned) among middle-class and professional workers.[2] An American study of 'cultural components in responses to pain' has shown that the educational background of the patient plays an important role in his attitude to the symptomatic meaning of pain sensation. 'The more educated patients are more health-conscious and more aware of pain as a possible symptom of a dangerous disease.'[3] In other words, the hypothesis suggested would seem to be that as standards of education and living rise greater significance is attached to sensations of pain as signals of danger to the individual and his sense of self-preservation.

Related to these changes and differences in attitudes and expectations of what the doctor can or should do is the growth in Western society of the idea that pain is avoidable. We are now told, for example, that some 10 per cent of the world's prescrip-

other countries, in actions for alleged negligence may well be an expression of a more critical attitude on the part of patients (Lloyd Hughes, T., *Med.-Legal J.*, 1953, *2*, 17). According to one American observer: 'Malpractice insurance is even more necessary in the United States than in England, as the general public is extremely litigious' (*Brit. Med. J.*, 1956, ii, 596).

[1] Clark-Kennedy, A. E., *Brit. Med. J.*, (1955), i, 619.

[2] See pp. 174-5, and Appendix, pp. 208-9.

[3] Zborowski, M., *Journal of Social Issues* (1952), Vol. VIII, No. 4, p. 27.

tions are for barbiturates;[1] that the American black market in chemical tranquillizers is more important than that in heroin;[2] that the use of these drugs in the treatment of anxiety is a threat to the motive power of American society; and that vast sums are being spent in Britain, publicly and privately, on sedatives and stimulants.[3] Not only, as I said earlier, has psychology given a new dimension to the medical interview but science has also done so. Both the doctor and the patient are more aware of these expanded potentialities in the relationship: more people have grasped the idea that pain can be avoided; that it no longer need be endured without some action being taken; more doctors are aware of the greater powers and responsibilities they now wield in affording relief from pain.

Man is essentially a role-taking being and the role of an ill person has become more formalized, more conscious, more separate and distinctive with the growth of an industrialized, individualistic society. It has, simultaneously, and for many people, made 'good health' a more important and realizable attribute for 'success' in life. The concept of individual responsibility; the toxic and environmental hazards of industrialization; the problem of social isolation in the modern world, the decline in religious beliefs, and the need (as Margaret Mead has put it) 'to make self-consciousness bearable';[4] all these and other social and psychological factors have a bearing on changes in attitudes to health, disease and the doctor.

This heightened awareness of what medicine has to offer, and which has influenced the doctor-patient relationship, has also affected the responsibilities of the family when sickness occurs. The threshold of tolerance of pain among those who are bound by strong ties of affection is lowered by the knowledge that

[1] Davis, H., *Lancet* (1956), ii, 176.

[2] Chapman, K. W., *Lancet* (1956), ii, 176. In 1956 there were over thirty different tranquillizers on the market in the USA, and over thirty billion tablets of one of these preparations alone had been sold to the public (*The Times*, August 9, 1957).

[3] Sargant, W., 'On Chemical Tranquillizers', *Brit. Med. J.* (1956), i, 939, and Brooke, E. M., *Lancet* (1955), i, 150.

[4] Mead, M., in *Creating an Industrial Civilization*, ed. Staley, E., 1952, p. 171.

medical action is possible. Moreover, the more that stress is laid on environmental and psychological factors in child care—on factors that are personally controllable and not predestined—the more may parents be led to feel blameworthy.[1] As the power of medicine increases so does the concept of parental responsibility. The urge to intervene, to do something, to relieve pain in one's child, increases as parents become aware of the potentialities of scientific medicine. What matters here is how situations are perceived and how expectations are formed from different ways of regarding situations. George Mead in his book, *Mind, Self and Society*, stressed the importance in understanding social behaviour of the self-conditioning of the individual derived from past experience and the expectation of future stimuli.[2] Drs Hardy, Wolff and Goodell concluded in their recent book '. . . the culture in which a man finds himself becomes the conditioning influence in the formation of the individual reaction patterns to pain. . . . A knowledge of group attitudes towards pain is extremely important to an understanding of the individual reaction'.[3]

When applied to the present state of medical care in Britain we can, I think, find much in these ideas to illuminate the ways in which the doctor-patient relationship has been affected by science, by specialization and by an increased awareness that pain is avoidable. The general practitioner feels that his authority as an 'expert' is threatened; naturally, he therefore tends to resent what Dr Ffrangcon Roberts and others think are 'the dictatorial powers now possessed by patients' under the National Health Service.[4] He may do so partly because he feels under more pressure to provide explanations (to his patients as well as to himself) for what he does, and partly because of the uncertainties about the outcome of medical action which now prevail over much of his work. Basically, then, the general practitioner's

[1] See the discussion on this question in *Symposium on the Healthy Personality*, ed. Senn, M. J. E., New York, 1950.

[2] Mead, G. H., *Mind, Self and Society*, Chicago, 1934.

[3] Hardy, J. D., Wolff, H. G., and Goodell, H., *Pain Sensations and Reactions*, Baltimore, 1952, p. 23.

[4] Roberts, Ffrangcon, *The Cost of Health*, 1952, p. 115.

situation is, as I have earlier suggested, a situation of insecurity; of a former 'sureness of touch' being undermined by science, by psychology and by specialization; a situation which makes more explicit the conflict between a wish to be independent of external influences (whether emanating from patient, hospital or consultant) and a desire satisfactorily to fulfil the expectations of his patients which, in many instances, confront him with the dilemma of being more rather than less dependent on others.

He may react to these situations of stress by, for example, emphasizing his authoritarian role in the giving and withholding of drugs. Unable to tolerate his own inadequacies he may become intolerant of inadequacies in his patients. He may, for other and similar reasons, attempt to remain on the pedestal on which his patients and society at large have placed him with a lavish supply of prescriptions.[1] To react in this way would be consistent with some of the traditional responses in competitive private practice for it must be difficult, in these days of scientific drugs, to take money from patients and give nothing tangible in return. Thus, we see how science may enlarge the dimensions of the problem for the doctor of giving and withholding.

Authoritarian behaviour was, we should also remember, grounded in the past in medical training whereby a physician went round his ward and, on the basis of empirical experience, issued authoritative orders which none could gainsay. The old compelling empiricisms in medicine, both in the hospital and in general practice, gave to medicine the atmosphere and tradition of an authoritarian art. Nowadays, perhaps, it may be suggested that it matters less what the chief says; the merest houseman can, in theory at any rate, confound his clinical argument with a little sheet of paper from the laboratory.

Scientific medicine has undermined some of these personal, individual authoritarianisms in medicine. It has let into clinical medicine a new spirit of criticism and questioning; it has raised

[1] A public opinion survey in 1957 gave some evidence of the high prestige of the doctor (Brotherston, J. H. F., Cartwright, A., and Martin, F. M., *Lancet*, 1957, i, 981).

more doubts about the value of bedside observations; it has imposed a different set of self-disciplines on the doctor, and while giving a greater potential freedom for independent thought and action it has, simultaneously, made the doctor more dependent on other people. The danger is, however, that in the stage through which we are now passing a new authoritarianism will replace or be superimposed on the old one, partly because of a lack of knowledge of how to use these new scientific instruments, and partly because of the authority that science itself invests in those whose work is scientifically oriented. Society may also be held responsible, for the greater the expectations we place on the doctor the more may we strengthen his need to maintain his role and, while attempting to satisfy others, satisfy himself. In other words, the more that the layman becomes aware of the possibilities of scientific medicine in relation to the threat that his illness represents, and the lower his threshold of tolerance of pain, the more may he induce authoritarian behaviour in the doctor. An attitude of greater trust in scientific medicine and more distrust of the individual practitioner could bring this about.

Such behaviour is also understandable, particularly in the hospital setting, because of the discipline and precision that applied scientific medicine itself demands. The need for accuracy, orderliness and a strict observance of rules increases in proportion as clinical and surgical techniques become more complex, more scientific, more a matter of the co-ordinated and carefully timed activity of a medical and nursing team. Moreover, many of the new therapeutic and diagnostic procedures are, not infrequently, a serious threat to the patient's life. As the risk increases so does the need for accuracy and order. Thus, the system of rules and regulations which governs the performance of duties and the hierarchical relationships between different medical and nursing groups tends to become more complex and rigid. Autocratic behaviour among hospital staffs, with behind them a long tradition deriving from military discipline, didactic teaching and poor law regimentation, is thereby strengthened by the invasion of scientific techniques, by increasing specialization and by the growth of professional solidarities. For many workers in the field of medical care, these developments may spell a greater sense of insecurity if the responsibilities which they think they are expected to carry are felt to be disproportionate to the knowledge and skill possessed. They may defend themselves by a slavish adherence to rule and by cultivating a protective authority. Discipline, required by science for the practice of medicine, may become an end in itself.

Obviously, there are dangers for both doctor and patient alike in this situation transformed by the factors of science and specialization. Not least among the benefits of the National Health Service which I have surveyed in these lectures is the fact that we can now see somewhat more clearly the nature of these dangers. There is a danger of medicine becoming a technology.[1] There is a danger of a new authoritarianism in medicine which, in its turn, might lead to a growth of professional syndicalism. There is the problem of medical power in society; a problem which concerns much more of our national life than simply the organization of medical care. It is, however, beyond my competence to suggest the many checks and balances which might be brought into play to offset these dangers and to correct the unbalance for which science is partly responsible. One at least, I am sure, must be found in the reform of medical education. Another may come in time from the contribution of the sociologist and the social worker to a greater understanding of the dynamics of human relationships. 'Medicine,' as Professor Pulvertaft has said, 'can never become fully scientific unless it becomes completely inhuman.'[2] The task of the future is to make medicine more 'social' in its application without losing in the process the benefits of science and specialized knowledge.

This, to me, is the fundamental justification for Britain's National Health Service. It is the prerequisite for an understanding of the problem; the framework through which medicine may more nearly fulfil its honoured purpose; the means by which the freedom of patient and doctor alike may be enlarged.

[1] This danger is one of the conclusions to be drawn from Dr Charles Newman's valuable study *The Evolution of Medical Education in the Nineteenth Century*, 1957.

[2] Pulvertaft, R. J. V., *Lancet* (1952), ii, 839.

APPENDIX TO LECTURES ON THE NATIONAL HEALTH SERVICE IN ENGLAND

Summary of Evidence and Sources of Reference on the Quantity and Quality of the General Practitioners' Work

PRACTICALLY all the facts and figures given below require detailed qualification in some respect or other.[1] The principal qualifications that are needed relate to: (i) the structure of the population at risk (age, sex, occupation, geographical selection, etc.); (ii) the extent to which these populations are 'live' or 'dead' on doctors' lists; (iii) bias in the selection and sampling of practices; (iv) bias in the movement between the private and public sectors of general practice; (v) the extent to which pre-1948 figures of visits and surgery attendances among private patients were deflated by the fact that the poor law, voluntary dispensaries and various public services carried a disproportionate number of 'bad risks';[2] (vi) the definition of a general practitioner, general practice, medical consultation, surgery attendance, domiciliary visit, patient, prescription and other terms; (vii) seasonal variations in population structure and services rendered; (viii) changes in the pattern of disease and fluctuations in epidemics of infectious disease; (ix) errors in record-keeping by doctors; (x) changes in the use by doctors of ancillary and other services (district nurses, health visitors, general practitioner assistants, hospital facilities, rota systems, locums, secretaries, etc.); (xi) changes in the use made by patients of chemists' shops and self-medication.

Quantity of Work

A general practitioner's work is usually measured in terms of medical consultations per person per year. These are normally broken down into surgery attendances (A) and home visits (V).

[1] A comprehensive survey of the problem of measuring demand has been made by a colleague, Mr Paulding Phelps. It is hoped to publish this analysis in a separate volume on the Health Service.

[2] As they now do in the USA and Canada to a considerable extent (see, for example, Taylor, M. G., *The Administration of Health Insurance in Canada*, 1956, esp. p. 71, and Anderson, O. W., with Feldman, J. J., *Family Medical Costs and Voluntary Health Insurance: A Nationwide Survey*, 1956).

The most comprehensive and relatively reliable post-1948 figures are those provided by the Government's Social Survey from its 'Sickness Survey' of a representative sample of the adult population of England and Wales.[1] This ran from 1945 to March 1952 when it was suspended on grounds of economy. From the mass of information provided the most important figures are those for 1949–50 when the same population base was used. It is possible that this was the period of peak demand under the National Health Service; prescription and other charges were introduced subsequently. The total consultation rate (including those with all doctors at hospitals and clinics) for both sexes at all ages over sixteen was 5·46 per person per year. Excluding consultations at hospitals and clinics the rate was 4·62 (attendances 3·00, visits 1·62). Because, however, of the substantially higher rates for women and persons aged over sixty-five these figures are not comparable with pre-1948 National Health Insurance experience. For men only aged sixteen to sixty-four (probably a better index to use for comparative purposes) the general practitioner rate in 1949–50 was 3·60 (A 2·77, V ·83).

Before comparing these data with material for earlier years we list other figures for the post-1948 period:

1. *Government Social Survey*. Special inquiry in February-March 1952 for the Committee on General Practice of the Central Health Services Council. The result of this study of a national sample aged twenty-one and over was to show a lower weekly medical consultation rate compared with the Social Survey data for 1949–50. In the form in which they were published these weekly rates cannot be converted into yearly rates. The average annual rate (all ages) estimated for a practice of 3,500 was 4·8.

2. *Fry, A.* South London practice (2,500 patients on list in 1948). Annual rate (all ages) between 2·39 and 2·93 during 1948–52. Visits approximately 12 per cent.

3. *British Medical Association* (*Hadfield, S. J.*) 'A Field Survey of General Practice 1951–2.' 188 practitioners. 'Nearly all practitioners told me that, since the NHS began, surgery attendances have increased greatly but visiting lists have, if anything, become smaller.' No facts given.

4. *British Medical Association*. 'A Postal Inquiry among 12,879

[1] During 1945 to 1950, persons aged sixteen and over were interviewed. In 1951 the Survey was limited to persons aged twenty-one and over. (*Annual Report of the Ministry of Health*, 1952, Pt 1, pp. 49–51).

GP Principals, July 1951.' Response 72 per cent. General impression of increased demand but no facts given. Of those replying to specific questions, '53 per cent feel that excessive demands are made upon them to a considerable degree and 41 per cent to a less degree.' 62 per cent said that there had been a 'considerable increase' in the number of services required in the NHS by patients who, before July 1948, had been private patients; 21 per cent said 'slight increase'; 6 per cent 'no increase'; 2 per cent 'slight decrease' and 9 per cent 'not in practice before 1948.'

5. *Taylor, S. Good General Practice* (1954). Survey of fifteen practices in 1951–2. 'Services per patient per year' ranged from 3·5 to 8·7. No analysis by age, sex, or other factors.

6. *Logan, W. P. D.* (*General Register Office*). Survey of ten selected practices in England 1951–4. Medical consultation rates per person per year showing, in most cases, substantial declines over the three years, are given below:

Males		0–14	15–44	45–64	65+	All ages
April to March:						
1951–2	...	3·53	2·68	3·99	4·60	3·36
1952–3	...	3·45	2·57	4·01	5·26	3·36
1953–4	...	3·27	2·39	3·56	4·95	3·10
Females:						
1951–2	...	3·63	3·86	4·68	5·82	4·20
1952–3	...	3·54	3·83	4·25	5·37	4·04
1953–4	...	3·21	3·71	4·12	6·01	3·94

7. *Backett, E. M., and Evans, J. C. G.* Intensive study of one practice in North-west London covering 3,084 persons and 15,788 consultations for the year April 1950–March 1951. Consultation rates:

	0–14	15–44	45–64	65+	
Males ...	5·24	3·31	5·53	8·24	Approximately five per person per year
Females ...	5·56	4·42	5·97	9·50	

Visits represented 36 per cent of total consultations

8. *Report of Committee of Enquiry into the Cost of the National Health Service* (Guillebaud Report), 1956. 'We understand that while general practitioners as a whole are now seeing more patients than before the inception of the National Health Service, they are generally doing more work for each patient. . . . There was some abuse of the service in the early days, but it is now considerably less than it was' (p. 165). No fact given.

9. *Hopkins, P.* London practice (1,370 patients on list 1951–3). Average consultation rate all ages 3·30 for 1951–3. Over 40 per cent of all illness in practice stated to be 'psychoneurosis and stress disorder'. Visits approximately 24 per cent.

10. *Crombie, D. L., and Cross, K. W.* Birmingham practice (4,200 NHS patients on list 1953–4). An analysis of the time spent by one general practitioner during a twelve-month period. 'Slightly more than thirty hours per week were spent in contact with patients, on travelling between them, and on administration. Monthly values ranged from twenty hours per week during August (1953) to thirty-five hours per week during February and March (1954).' No consultation rates given.

There is no evidence here to suggest that demand increased between 1948–54. On the contrary, what evidence there is suggests a decline. We now consider data for various periods before 1939. No figures are given for the war years because of the abnormal experience.

Practically all the inquiries before 1939 relate to National Health Insurance experience; that is to say, to insured workers aged sixteen and over earning less than £250 a year. The great majority of these workers were men aged sixteen to sixty-four. In all, there are five groups of statistics:

British Medical Association ...	1922 and 1930–6
Ministry of Health	1924 and 1936
Bradford Hill (for the BMA) ...	July 1938–June 1939

The main results are given below:

11. *Ministry of Health*, 1924. Sample of National Health Insurance cards (222,006 of which 66 per cent men):

	Men	Women	Total
Attendances per person per year	2·57	2·71	2·62
Visits per person per year	·81	·76	·79
Total per person per year	3·38	3·47	3·41

12. *Ministry of Health*, 1936. Sample of National Health Insurance cards (336,828 of which 67 per cent men).

	Men	Women	Total
Attendances per person per year	2·75	3·19	2·90
Visits per person per year	·73	·83	·76
Total per person per year	3·48	4·02	3·66

13. *British Medical Association*, 1922. Statistics 'supplied by a large number of insurance practitioners' for a total of 665,118 insured persons (no sex or age analysis).

Attendances	... ...	2·76
Visits	... ...	·99
Total	... ...	3·75

14. *British Medical Association*, 1930–6. Statistics supplied each year by approximately 10 per cent of the members of all local Panel Committees for an average insured population of roughly one-and-a-half million persons:

Attendances	... ...	3·71
Visits	... ...	1·31
Total	... ...	5·02

15. *Bradford Hill* (*on behalf of the BMA*) 1938–9. Random selection of 5,418 general practitioners (approximately one-third of total of 17,734 principals in Great Britain) with a total of 6,218,752 insured persons. 'It is concluded that in the year in question the average number of attendances and visits per insured person per annum lay between the following limits, which differ by only 12 per cent':

Attendances	...	3·69–4·13
Visits	...	1·12–1·26
Total ...	...	4·81–5·39 (average 5·10)

It should be noted that the Bradford Hill figures for 1938–9, and those provided by the BMA for 1930–6, are closely in line, giving a total medical consultation rate per person of just over five per year.

In assessing these fifteen pieces of evidence, which constitute all the published data for England and Wales since the First World War, it is probable that the most trustworthy sets of figures are those by Bradford Hill for 1938–9 and by the Social Survey for 1949–50. It must be understood, however, that as indicated earlier all these reports are subject, in varying degree, to criticism on some score or other. They can be accepted only as rough approximations. Comparing the Bradford Hill and Social Survey figures (together with the BMA data for 1930–6) it seems that, on average, the demand from adults has fallen under the National Health Service. While both sets of figures exclude children, those for 1949–50 are much more heavily weighted with old people, married women (who are known to have higher morbidity rates than men and to make substantially higher demands for medical care),[1] the chronically ill, the disabled, the mentally ill and defective,

[1] Sickness benefit claims reflect these differences. The Government Actuary, reporting on the sickness experience of insured persons during 1949–51, has shown how considerable are the excess rates among married women (and also single women) as compared with men (*Fifth Interim Report of the Government Actuary*, 1956).

the blind, war pensioners, and many other 'bad' risks formerly not covered or only partially so by National Health Insurance. Moreover, the average age of the population between sixteen-sixty-four was higher in 1949–50 than in the 1930's.[1] All these factors could well have led, in combination, to a significantly higher average consultation rate after 1948. Indeed, every estimate on future sickness claims made by the Government Actuary from the Beveridge Report in 1942 onwards assumed a substantial increase.[2] Experience since 1948, however, has contradicted these pessimistic estimates. The latest analysis by the Government Actuary shows that, for both sexes, claims during 1949–51 were approximately 15 per cent lower than had been expected.[3]

Against these considerations, which all tend to support the conclusion of a lower average level of demand from adults on general practitioners under the National Health Service, has to be set the unknown factor of demand from private fee-paying patients. If the demand from this group in the 1930's (largely the middle-classes earning more than £250 a year and uninsured married women and children) was lower than National Health Insurance experience,[4] and if their demands rose after 1948 when they became Health Service patients, then *total* demand might have been much the same after 1948 as in the 1930's—or a little higher. General practitioners working in predominantly middle-class areas may thus have experienced some increase in demand.[5]

There is a limited amount of evidence (not only from the BMA—see p. 209) that some sections of middle-class and professional people had, after 1948, higher medical consultation rates than some groups of manual workers—particularly agricultural workers.[6] Analyses of demand for sight-tests and spectacles by the Ministry of Health for 1951

[1] For both sexes, morbidity rates rise sharply with age, especially for serious illnesses of long duration, presumably making heavy demands for medical care (*op. cit.*).

[2] See Ch. 3, p. 58.

[3] *Fifth Interim Report of the Government Actuary*, 1956, p. 20.

[4] This was apparently the opinion of medical witnesses before the Spens Committee in 1946. No evidence was published, however (Cmd 6810, 1946, p. 11).

[5] It is generally known that the British Medical Association sponsored a comprehensive statistical inquiry into the work of general practitioners during 1948–9. As it was completed, it is curious that it has not been published or sent to the Ministry of Health. Had this inquiry shown an increase in demand it would presumably have strengthened the profession's case for more remuneration.

[6] See Table S.S. 10, *Registrar-General's Statistical Review for 1949, Supplement on General Morbidity*, 1953, and *Ministry of Health Report for 1951*, Pt III, 1953, p. 168.

and 1953 showed that, broadly speaking, demand was highest in residential and commercial areas, and lowest in mainly rural areas, with industrial areas holding an intermediate position.[1] This probably expresses the greater need among professional and white-collar workers to write and read well. A fall in demand between 1951 and 1953 was most marked in industrial areas. The proportion of people wearing spectacles is higher among those engaged in clerical, executive and technical occupations than among operatives. Similar analyses of demand for dental treatment in 1951 by age, sex and geographical area showed much the same pattern, the more prosperous residential areas producing higher rates of demand than the industrial areas of the North of England, the Midlands and Wales.[2]

Material of this kind, suggesting as it does a more positive attitude by the professional and middle-classes towards the early use of services,[3] especially of a preventive kind such as dentistry, has a bearing on the work of the general practitioner since 1948. Higher demands for ophthalmic and dental treatment could well mean in the early stages of advice and referral a higher level of medical consultations. Such evidence as this is also supported by a study of hospital in-patient demand in 1949.[4] The conclusion of this study was that 'In comparative terms, men aged twenty-five to sixty-four in social classes I, II and III appear to be making proportionately full use of NHS hospitals whereas semi-skilled and unskilled men of these ages in classes IV and V are making fewer demands than might have been expected from their relatively higher morbidity and mortality rates'.

To summarize, therefore, it may be that there was some increase in demand on the general practitioner after 1948 from patients who formerly paid the doctor privately.[5] As ex-private patients they may have been led to expect a higher standard of medical care.[6] Even so, and

[1] *Ministry of Health Annual Report for* 1953, Pt I, 1954, pp. 90–5 and 250.

[2] *Ministry of Health Annual Report for 1950*, Pt II, 1952, pp. 115–22.

[3] Illustrated in a variety of ways in *Uses of Epidemiology*, Morris, J. N., 1957, especially Ch. III, e.g. the higher take-up of vitamin supplements by middle-class mothers, and the evidence that diabetics in social classes I and II benefited more, or earlier, than classes IV and V from the introduction of insulin.

[4] Abel-Smith, B., and Titmuss, Richard M., *The Cost of the National Health Service*, 1956.

[5] BMA, 'A Review of General Practice, 1951–2', *Brit. Med. J.* (1953), Supp., p. 113.

[6] Hadfield, S. J., *Brit. Med. J.* (1953), pp. 699–700. See also the statement by Dr Charles Hill, MP (formerly secretary of the BMA) that 'one cause of the increased cost of the pharmaceutical services was the pressure of the middle-classes

assuming there is something to be said for this hypothesis, it yet remains true that the level of total demand after 1948 is relatively low; lower than all the figures put forward by or on behalf of the BMA during the 1930's. Taking a longer perspective, what is indeed remarkable about these statistics is their comparative stability. Even more than fifty years ago, the BMA produced a figure of 5·5 medical attendances per patient a year based on a population of over 300,000 persons enrolled under contract practice.[1]

The widespread belief, especially among the medical profession, that the advent of the National Health Service led to an immense increase in work for general practitioners is thus not borne out by the facts—and particularly the published facts by the BMA itself. This conclusion must also take account of certain other important considerations, briefly summarized below:

1. In a broad comparison of work over the two periods (1949–50 and the 1930's) there has been a rise in the number of general practitioners per 1,000 population in a substantial number of areas.[2]

2. There has been a great increase in hospital out-patient facilities.

3. A higher proportion of mothers have been confined in hospital.

4. There has been no substantial change in the quantity of services provided by public health authorities for mothers and babies, schoolchildren and other special groups (for example: in only about one-quarter of 163,164 domiciliary confinement cases in 1954 for which a doctor had been booked under the maternity medical services was he present at the delivery).[3]

5. In some areas since 1948 general practitioners have made extensive use of district nurses who attend at surgeries to give dressings and other nursing attentions and who visit patients to give antibiotic and other injections.[4]

6. There has been an improvement since 1948 in the geographical

for the proprietary medicines to which they were accustomed' (*Hansard*, House of Commons, March 14, 1950).

[1] 'Amount of Remuneration of Medical Practitioners under the National Insurance Act.' *Brit. Med. J.*, Supp., July 6, 1912. See also discussion on the Plender Report in the *Brit. Med. J.*, Supp., August 1912.

[2] Especially since 1948 (see *Ministry of Health, Written Evidence, Vol. 1, Royal Commission on Doctors' and Dentists' Remuneration*, 1957).

[3] Ministry of Health, *Annual Report for 1954*, Pt I, 1955 (p. 88).

[4] Ministry of Health, *Annual Report for 1953*, Pt I, 1954 (pp. 125–6).

distribution of general practitioners in relation to population needs.[1]

7. An important development since 1948 which directly affects both the quantity and the quality of the general practitioners' work is the policy of 'open access' to X-ray and pathological services.[2] By 1955 this method of giving practitioners direct access to diagnostic and X-ray facilities had become quite common in most areas; the least co-operative hospitals, however, have been the teaching hospitals.[3] Contrary to the expectations of some consultants and clinical pathologists, hospitals have not been burdened with excessive demands by practitioners.[4]

8. 'Minor operative surgery is being increasingly given up by the GP. Antibiotics have rendered much of it unnecessary; for the rest, some GP's claim that it is better for their patients to be treated at hospital.'[5]

9. There is a good deal of evidence to suggest that night-visiting (common in the 1930's) is now becoming, in Taylor's words, 'a comparative rarity for most doctors'. A large practice in Manchester, covering over 12,000 people, reported in 1955–6 less than one telephone call a night every two months per 1,000 patients.[6] Other evidence shows that the Saturday evening surgery is a disappearing item in the doctor's week; and, most important of all, that with the development of the National Health Service there has been a rapid growth in voluntary rota systems for evening, week-end and other duty periods.[7] According to Taylor, this represents 'the most important single change which has taken place in general practice, and particularly in industrial general practice, since the coming of the NHS'.[8]

[1] Annual Reports since 1948 of the Ministry of Health and the Medical Practices Committee.

[2] Hadfield, S. J., *Brit. Med. J.* (1953), ii, 697.

[3] Taylor, S., *Good General Practice*, 1954, pp. 322, 327, 329 and 519/20.

[4] Ministry of Health, *Annual Report for 1953*, Pt I, 1954, pp. 85–6, Ministry of Health, *Annual Report for 1954*, Pt I, 1955, pp. 22–3, *Manchester Regional Hospital Board: Abstract of Statistics for 1955*, and *Lancet* (1956), ii, 933.

[5] Taylor, S., *op. cit.*, p. 263.

[6] A total of 12,356 patients and sixty-three telephone calls between 11 p.m. and 8 a.m. during 1955–6. The same report gave only 467 week-end cases during the year (*Darbyshire House Health Centre Report for 1955–6*, p. 3).

[7] See also pp. 180–1, discussing the development of the Emergency Call Service in London and other areas.

[8] Taylor, S., *op. cit.*, pp. 61, 191, 194 and 483–4. For other evidence on these points see Grant, C. P. D., *Brit. Med. J.*, 1955, i, 1049: 'Ex-private patients tend to be somewhat demanding. The fact that they can read a clinical thermometer

10. In 1940 it was reported that 'The panel doctor passes on to the hospital as much of his work as he can. He is not undertaking work if he can avoid it'.[1] Much the same thing was said by the BMA in 1929[2] and by the Ministry of Health in 1937.[3] This, too, is one of the criticisms levelled against the National Health Service: that it has led general practitioners to unload a great deal of work on to hospital out-patient departments. There is no evidence to suggest, however, that in proportion to the populations served and taking account of developments in diagnostic and therapeutic facilities centred on hospitals, that there has been any substantial increase in referrals. Logan's survey of general practice gave a total out-patient referral rate of only 3·1 per 100 consultations in 1952–53.[4] A survey by the College of General Practitioners in 1954–5 of how fifty-five practitioners dealt with some 1,700 cases of acute chest infections showed that referral to hospital was deemed necessary in only 7 per cent of patients, the great majority being managed by the practitioner at home, and that although facilities for special investigations in the pathological and radiological departments of local hospitals were available in only 30 per cent of the patients were blood counts, sputa tests or X-rays considered necessary.[5] In any event, it is very doubtful whether a higher rate of referral to out-patient departments, consultant and diagnostic services necessarily implies any deterioration in the quality of a doctor's work. A fuller use of all the new diagnostic, advisory and therapeutic facilities provided

more readily and have a telephone in their house may sometimes be a nuisance. They are more prone to call one out needlessly on a wet night than those who have to find three pennies and go and brave the storm to find a public call-box.' The author, in making comparisons with the work of general practitioners in the past, went on to say that nights are less frequently disturbed and that off-duty time was much more regular. See also Parry, R. H., and others, reporting on the work of a Health Centre in Bristol in 1953 with a total population at risk of about 30,000 (Parry, R. H., Sluglett, J., and Wofinden, R. C., *Brit. Med. J.*, 1954, i, 388). Before the Centre had opened the doctors had estimated a need to cover ten to twelve calls a night. In fact they averaged during the year one-and-a-half a night for the 30,000 at risk.

[1] Evidence presented by the British Hospitals' Association to the Royal Commission on Workmen's Compensation, April 25, 1940. A. 11,055.

[2] BMA, *Brit. Med. J.* (1929), Appendix XI, p. 130.

[3] Reported in the *Lancet* (1937), i, 932.

[4] Logan, W. P. D., General Register Office, *Studies on Medical and Population Subjects*, No. 9, 1956, Table G.

[5] Research Committee of the College of General Practitioners, *Brit. Med. J.* (1956), i, 1516.

under the National Health Service could well mean a higher standard of medical care—preventive as well as curative.[1]

11. Another widespread criticism of the effects of the National Health Service on the quality of the practitioner's work is that, to put it simply, he has become a clerk and a signer of certificates. Bradford Hill's survey for the BMA in 1938–9 showed that 139 National Health Insurance certificates were issued per 100 insured persons per annum. Logan's survey of ten general practices in 1952–4 gave an annual rate for all National Insurance certificates of forty-eight per 100 National Health Service patients.[2]

12. Finally, it has to be remembered that, in making comparisons with the 1930's, one is comparing the present situation in which 90 to 95 per cent of the total population are using the National Health Service with a situation in which 77 per cent of all men aged fourteen to sixty-four, 39 per cent of all women aged fourteen to sixty-four, and just over 40 per cent of the total population of all ages in the country were insured for medical benefits under National Health Insurance in 1938–9.[3] Thus, account must be taken of the verdict of those who have studied in detail the range and quality of medical care provided by this 'panel system' (as it came to be called).[4] The definition of what was 'medical benefit' or 'adequate treatment' was limited; the constant necessity to balance private against insurance practice often led to two standards of care; restrictive controls by insurance companies and approved societies inhibited a preventive approach to disease and disability; free choice of doctor was more limited; 'family doctoring' was uncommon; there was no definite association of the panel doctor with the consultant at the hospital; many doctors were unable to save for their old age while burdened by heavy debts to insurance companies for the purchase of practices,[5] chiefly because private practice (which,

[1] See discussion on this point by Hopkins, P., *Brit. Med. J.* (1956), ii, 873.

[2] In this connection it should be remembered that before 1948 doctors had a great deal of paper work to do in the rendering and settlement of bills. One doctor recalled his experiences of these accounting tasks in a letter to the *British Medical Journal*, January 26, 1957, Supp. 44.

[3] Calculated from the *Annual Report of the Ministry of Health for 1938–9* (pp. 275–99) and the *Report of the Chief Medical Officer for 1938*.

[4] See, for example, Levy, H., *National Health Insurance*, 1944, esp. pp. 92–5, 108–11, 114–21, 127–32, 136–9 and 302–5; PEP *Report on the British Health Service*, 1937; and British Medical Association, Medical Planning Commission, Draft Interim Report, *Brit. Med. J.* (1942), i, Supp. 743.

[5] As two American observers remarked: 'The young doctor is forced to sign a

according to the Royal Commission on National Health Insurance, had 'in considerable measure disappeared' by 1928),[1] was unremunerative in many areas with heavy unemployment and poverty. As Levy concluded, 'Insurance patients will not get much profit from doctors who think their life intolerable. To raise their standard, mode and outlook of living should be one of the essential tasks of reform'.[2]

The 'discovery' after 1948 by Collings,[3] Taylor[4] and others of the bad conditions of many doctors' surgeries, meanly equipped, inefficiently organized, dilapidated and poverty-stricken in amenity and appearance, was striking and unmistakable evidence of the conditions under which a large proportion of the population had received general practitioner care during the 1930's. Such conditions reflected too the relative poverty and insecurity of many practitioners only a decade or so ago.

contract by which he gradually buys the practice, but on terms that make him a virtual "share-cropper".' (Orr, D. H., and J. W., *Health Insurance with Medical Care*, New York, 1938, p. 147).

[1] *Report of the Royal Commission on National Health Insurance*, Cmd 2596, 1928, p. 184.

[2] Levy, H., *National Health Insurance*, 1944, p. 135.

[3] Collings, S., *Lancet* (1950), i, 555.

[4] Taylor, S., *Good General Practice*, pp. 453 and 501.

APPENDIX REFERENCES

Abel-Smith, B., and Titmuss, Richard, M., *The Cost of the National Health Service*, 1956.

Anderson, O. W., with Feldman, J. J., *Family Medical Costs and Voluntary Health Insurance: A Nationwide Survey*, 1956.

Backett, E. M., and Evans, J. C. G., *Proc. Roy. Soc. Med.* (1953), *46*, 707.

Backett, E. M., and Evans, J. C. G., *Brit. Med. J.* (1954), i, 109.

British Hospitals' Association, *Evidence to Royal Commission on Workmen's Compensation*, April 25, 1940.

British Medical Association, *Report on Contract Practice*, 1904.

British Medical Association, *Brit. Med. J.* (1912) Supp. July and August.

British Medical Association, *Brit. Med. J.* (1929), Appendix XI.

British Medical Association, *Brit. Med. J.* (1937), Special Supplement, May 29.

British Medical Association, *Brit. Med. J.* (1942), Supp. i, 743.

British Medical Association, *Brit. Med. J.* (1953), ii, 683 and Special Supplement.

Central Health Services Council, *Report of the Committee on General Practice*, 1954.

College of General Practitioners, *Brit. Med. J.* (1956), i, 1516.

Collings, J., *Lancet* (1950), i, 555.

Committee of Enquiry into the Cost of the National Health Service (Guillebaud Report), Cmd 9663, 1956.

Crombie, D. L., and Cross, K. W., *Brit. J. Prev. Soc. Med.* (1956), *10*, 141.

Darbyshire House Health Centre Report for 1955–6.

Fry, A., *Lancet* (1953), i, 443. Also *Brit. Med. J.* (1953), ii, 249.

Government Actuary, *Fifth Interim Report on the National Insurance Act*, 1956.

Grant, C. P. D., *Brit. Med. J.* (1955), i, 1049.

Hill, A., Bradford, *Journal of the Royal Statistical Socy* (1951), 114 (1).

Hopkins, P., *Brit. Med. J.* (1956), ii, 873.

Lancet (1956), ii, 933.

Levy, H., *National Health Insurance*, 1944.

Logan, W. P. D., *General Register Office, Studies on Medical and Population Subjects, No. 7*, 1953.

Logan, W. P. D., *General Register Office, Studies on Medical and Population Subjects, No. 9,* 1956.

Mackay, D., *Hospital Morbidity Statistics, General Register Office, Studies on Medical and Population Subjects, No. 4,* 1951.

Manchester Regional Hospital Board: Abstract of Statistics for 1955.

Medical Practices Committee, Annual Reports.

Ministry of Health, *Annual Report for 1938–9.*

Ministry of Health, *Annual Report of the Chief Medical Officer for 1938.*

Ministry of Health, *Annual Report 1950, Part II,* 1952.

Ministry of Health, *Annual Report 1951, Part III,* 1953.

Ministry of Health, *Annual Report 1952, Part I,* 1953.

Ministry of Health, *Annual Report 1953, Part I,* 1954.

Ministry of Health, *Annual Report 1954, Part I,* 1955.

Ministry of Health, *Written Evidence, Vol. I, Royal Commission on Doctors' and Dentists' Remuneration,* 1957.

Morris, J. N., *Uses of Epidemiology,* 1957.

Orr, D. H., and J. W., *Health Insurance with Medical Care,* 1938.

Parry, R. H., Sluglett, J., and Wofinden, R. C., *Brit. Med. J.* (1954), i, 388.

Political and Economic Planning, *Report on the British Health Service,* 1937.

Registrar-General, *Statistical Review for 1949, Supplement on General Morbidity,* 1953.

Registrar-General, *Statistical Review for 1950–1, Supplement on General Morbidity,* 1955.

Report of the Inter-Departmental Committee on Remuneration of General Practitioners, Cmd 6810, May 1946.

Royal Commission on National Health Insurance Report, Cmd 2596, 1928.

Social Survey, *Lancet* (1953), ii, 1308 and *Applied Statistics,* March, 1954.

Taylor, M. G., *The Administration of Health Insurance in Canada,* 1956.

Taylor, S., *Good General Practice,* 1954.

Titmuss, Richard M., *Political Quarterly* (1955), Vol. XXVI, No. 2.

INDEX

Index

Index

Index